Atlantis,
The Dark Continent

Paul Williamson & Linda Braithwaite

www.capallbann.co.uk

Atlantis, The Dark Continent

Cover design by Paul Mason
Internal illustrations by Linda Braithwaite

Published by:

Capall Bann Publishing
Freshfields
Chieveley
Berks
RG20 8TF

Contents

Also by Paul Williamson, published by Capall Bann:

Healing Journeys

Author Contact

Paul Williamson may be contacted at:

P O Box 121
Lancaster
LA1 5GS
England

Please enclose an SAE or two International Reply Coupons

Acknowledgements

Mainly, Linda and I would like to acknowledge and appreciate our two close friends, Lynne and Denise. The four of us became very close as the writing of this book unfolded, especially as we each began to discover how linked we were from our inner reality with various Atlantean experiences that came forward for us. The effect of doing this work, I believe, has contributed to some dramatic and turbulent changes in the lives of all four of us. Our nervous systems have become so much more sensitive and each of us has felt more vulnerable to our emotions. However, I know we all feel it has been worth it. Although the experiences have sometimes been traumatic, overall it has been an exciting inner adventure.

For Denise, I would like to thank you for your patient support and loving heart, when the rest of us hit rocky times.

For Lynne, our permanent secretary, I would like to thank you for your tireless typing and retyping of the manuscript, for the revisions you made and for your loving enthusiasm.

In addition, I would like to thank Jill Robinson for your proofreading and the excellent suggestions you made to improve what we had written.

Part 1 - Introductions

Chapter 1

Opening the Door

From the evidence of modern scientific thought, we cannot be sure that the civilisation of Atlantis ever existed. But our inner minds tell us a different story.

As a therapist, I have been working with past life regression with some of my clients for many years. I do this work either for reasons of self- exploration or as an attempt to help my clients solve their inner problems. When they go through experiences of their past lives, often these experiences can seem very real with a strong emotional and energetic content. Sometimes details of these lives will correlate with other sources about what is known of different periods in history. What can be very interesting is when clients access a past life and give information about times from our past where little is known about this by other means.

Many of my clients have regressed to lifetimes where they felt they were living in the land they identified as Atlantis. By comparing the experiences of one client with another, I have been able to build up a picture of what life on Atlantis may have been like. It is interesting how consistent and coherent this information has been.

Usually, it has been with my clients who have sought long term therapy that I have been able to access with them past lives from Atlantis. With these being such ancient lives, it is logical that my short-term clients needing to do past life work would focus on more recent lives. I have discovered though that often with my long term clients it may be an experience on Atlantis that is fundamental to their healing process and may be an important root of their problems. Past life experiences of being in Atlantis can be very powerful and need a lot of integration.

Sometimes my clients have needed much time and preparation before they were ready for such experiences.

In this book we are going to focus upon the past life regression experiences of Linda Braithwaite and myself. With Linda's regressions we have gone through a large number of lifetimes covering most of the different phases of the history of Atlantis, including different aspects of life and society and how people lived then. Linda's experiences also illustrate the kind of psychological challenges many souls incarnating in Atlantis faced.

Linda has helped me so that I could access some of my own lifetimes from this period. This has been an interesting, illuminating and sometimes difficult process for me. But I hope that by sharing some of my experiences, this will shed additional light upon the nature of Atlantis and its people.

In addition to the experiences of Linda and myself, we will also refer to Atlantis regression experiences from Lynne Williams and Denise Gardner.

Linda, Lynne, and Denise all came to me independently of each other seeking help for different reasons. Eventually all started to access lifetimes from Atlantis and this coincided so that I was seeing each of them for these particular regressions during the same period.

In addition, all four of us are members of the White Dove Healing circle, and we have become friends. I feel quite clear in my own mind that all four of us were guided by some inner purpose and design to do this work together at the time leading to the writing of this book. There are strong indications that we have all known each other in various relationships in a number of different lifetimes that we shared in Atlantis.

As the process has unfolded, there have been various occasions where one of us has helped trigger memories in another. It has been very interesting for me. As I have worked with one of them through a particular Atlantis past lifetime, then without sharing details with each other, sometimes I have been able to work with another of them to go through experiences of the same event from the perspective of a second personality. This has usually coincided very accurately and has helped to build up faith in the reality of these memories. The implication is that these past life memories are not just from one person's isolated imagination, but a collective inner experience.

There has been a challenge for me as a therapist in that sometimes I have been able to recognise myself in the midst of a regression experience of one of the others and this has brought up reactions of thoughts and feelings inside of me. I have had to be strong then to be able to continue to focus upon my client's needs and help her rather than get caught up in my own process. This has been more difficult when the character I identified as myself was an unpleasant one causing some hurt or pain to others. Fortunately, I have received help in being able to deal with these problems and I will discuss details of this later.

Through the recounting of regression experiences to different lifetimes in Atlantis, I hope to show how some of these coincidences have manifested between the four of us. Especially from the more negative lives, our actions have had karmic consequences and the actions of one of us has tended to affect the others through reactions that have taken place. It seems that there has been a need for us to learn by sharing various interactions with each other, learning to love, as well as learning to maintain the integrity of our individual Spiritual paths. Of course, many other souls have been involved. But by sharing our experiences I hope that this will shed some light on some of the possible soul patterns of interactions that exist, and how this occurred during lifetimes from Atlantis.

Chapter 2

The Process of Past Life Regression

There are different ways in which people can access the memories of past lives. For some, this is easier than for others. Once a person has started accessing memories of past lives, it is like a door opening, and further memories may then be forthcoming.

For some people, past life exploration may be a very important and helpful tool for inner growth and self-transformation. There are many people, though, for whom this work may be neither relevant or needed at all. Sometimes I feel that people may need at a certain moment in their lives to access some particular past life memories for a specific purpose in their lives. This is individual and I believe that people are guided when this is needed.

Of course, people may not take up the opportunity for past life exploration even though it may be important for them. Often within past life memories are the roots of our fears and insecurities. It is a natural instinct within people to want to turn away from this. So it does need a certain courage to say `yes' to undergo regression experiences.

The memories of past lives can be accessed in various ways. They can be invoked through hypnosis and guided mediation techniques. They can also come spontaneously through dreams or by resonance when some event in someone's experience has a similar energy to what may be in the subconscious mind as a past life memory.

It is very rare for me to come across people who claim to have past lives as famous people. When this happens I tend to be very cautious. I suppose that some past life `memories' could be instances of wish fulfillment or the subconscious mind coming up with symbols to satisfy some inner need. But mostly for people with whom I work, regression experiences tend to be surprising and quite different from what the person expected.

In accessing the memory of a past life, people will experience themselves as someone else from who they are today living in a different time period from the past and acting out some life situation that is different to now. Sometimes this may be experienced in a more detached way like looking at a scene or it may feel more as if they are actually in it and living it. People will have a sense of identity about the experience, that this is `me', even though it is obviously not them as their present personality.

Guiding people through past life regression experiences, I find it important for them to be as fully involved in experiencing the past life as directly as possible. I feel that the more people are involved in such an experience, the more they will learn. At the same time, I do not want people to go through these experiences at such a deep level of trance that they do not remember anything afterwards and they don't know what is happening to them.

I believe that when people need to access a past life memory, there will be a reason for this. There will be a link from the past life experience with the present life situation and this will need to be integrated consciously.

We all have inner senses through which we can experience past life memories. For some people, one or more of these senses may operate more strongly than another. For example, Linda has a very pronounced visual inner sense. She can see the details of a scene or memory very clearly and she can then draw it. For me, I more know or feel and sense what is happening through a particular memory without always seeing it very well. When I go through a regression experience, I know I can follow this and let the details of the past life unfold.

Going through a past life regression can be a very emotional experience. There may be a release of feelings and bodily sensations. This needs to be encouraged and supported but not forced. Usually, the most important aspect of a past life experience for a person to go through may be where a trauma is involved, even though this may not be very pleasant for the person to experience. However, it is from the release of feelings and thoughts caught up in past life traumas that people can find inner freedom. Because these experiences are from the past, they have no power to hurt the person now.

Following on from an intense past life regression people may continue to experience feelings, thoughts and bodily sensations relating to the past life for some days afterwards. This is part of the integration process. Sometimes several sessions will be needed to clear all the issues of a particular past life. It is good for the client to understand this, and for therapists to be available to support their clients after such experiences where necessary. Usually, these thoughts and feelings related to the past life will pass and then the client will feel much better.

As far as past lives to Atlantis are concerned, people will tend to experience these regression memories like they would any other. They can be very real, involving and sometimes traumatic. Just because these memories appear to come from very ancient times does not make them more remote or distant. Somehow, in the regression process, memories can be tapped that need to come forth. They can come from periods of time a long while ago and still have as much sense of reality as lives that are much more recent, or even present life memories.

In fact, I feel that regression memories from Atlantis can be even stronger than more recent memories. This is, I believe, because people from Atlantis tended to be more sensitive, psychic and Spiritually aware than we are today - though not necessarily wiser. Through their collective mistakes and corruption, I feel that the human race lost much awareness then, which we are only just starting to recover. When people tap into their memory of Atlantean past lives, this can aid them to contact the memory of Spiritual and psychic capacities they had then. In turn, this may help to awaken those capacities in the person again today.

And doing this may be at least part of the inner reason why the person needs to go through these regression experiences.

I feel that this is what has unfolded for Linda, Denise and Lynne. I believe that they have all become more psychic, more Spiritually aware and at peace with themselves as a direct result of integrating their Atlantis past life regressions. When they have been going through these memories, they have been very involved in their process and deeply affected by all that they have experienced.

However, it is the more traumatic and difficult lives that have been the most useful to them and the most liberating. These are the ones where they may have abused knowingly their Spiritual and psychic powers and caused hurt and suffering to others or the land. I am sure that most people who have had lifetimes on Atlantis would have had experiences like that. I know for myself that it can be very frightening to come close to these kinds of memories. But by hiding from these experiences, we keep up barriers within ourselves, which restricts the extent to which we can feel our wholeness as a human being and soul.

Chapter 3

The Roots of Fear

In going through various the Atlantis lifetime regressions of Linda and myself, I have found there to be a mixture of positive and uplifting experiences as well as quite negative ones. I imagine that this is quite similar for most people who have lived lifetimes in Atlantis.

The happy, satisfying and positive lifetimes can be very useful to go through. These can give good feelings inside and a sense of accomplishment. In my own personal regressions when these kind of past lifetimes have had some similarity with my life circumstances now, the fact that I feel I have done this successfully before has been affirming and given me confidence that I am on the right track and I can do it. However, once I have integrated such a regression experience I don't feel that very much has changed inside me. There is not a lot of transformational effect.

With the negative lifetimes though, integrating these experiences can have a substantial impact on people's lives. This is because, in these lifetimes we have to confront our fears.

We all have fears inside us and it is natural that we should want to avoid them, for our fears feel very uncomfortable for us. But they also weaken us. When we put energy into repressing our fears and trying not to be aware of them, then this energy is not available for us to use as positive living impulses for our lives. We become weaker and less whole. By trying to bury our fears we can also be denying ourselves aspects of our nature that are very important and useful.

Therefore, it can be very strengthening to seek support to be able to acknowledge what we fear and let our body experience it. Then we may be able to let it go. This may not be as easy as it sounds. But the more we fear, the more separate we will feel from all that is most essential to us.

In terms of past life regression, it is usually easier for people to go through an experience where they have been a victim of some great suffering at the hands of another than it is to experience a lifetime where they may have caused some significant suffering or abuse to others. But usually if there is one lifetime of one of these then there'll be a linking lifetime of the other type somewhere there too. It seems that we need to learn through experiencing both sides of the coin.

It can be very difficult for us to acknowledge our mistakes. If we do something that hurts someone else, we feel guilt and shame. Deep inside, we do love each other. Therefore, by hurting someone else we are not really being true to ourselves. This can make us feel `bad' about ourselves. Of course we can pretend that we don't love this other person and close the door to this. Then we can cause more hurt and it doesn't seem to affect us. When we feel that someone should be loving towards us and they are not, it is easy for us to ignore our love for them in our actions. And so, suffering and hurt can be self-perpetuating. But the more suffering we cause, the further away we will become from our inner source of love and the more we will fear to approach it.

In Atlantis, the Earth energies were very strong and people could feel a tremendous power and capacity to do whatever they wanted. This power could give people a feeling of self-importance and they could become very selfish. It was a great temptation for people there to only think of their own interests and to forget the needs of the whole. From this base, people could cause great suffering to others and the Earth as some of the past life stories in this book will show.

Going through these more negative experiences can be quite terrifying. As an example, in the case of Linda, she lived much of her present life in fear, not wanting to be hurt, but especially, not wanting to cause hurt to others. As she has been given access to memories of some of her lifetimes on Atlantis, it has been almost unbearable for her to face up to the terrible things she did then. This feels so alien to how she wishes to be now. But she has had to acknowledge that this is part of her, and according to her memories she did do these things so she must accept them. As she has been able to accept these memories, she has become stronger and less needing to be afraid now.

I have noticed that when people have a strong negative reaction to some aspect of life around them, feeling it is wrong, then often those people may have one or more past lives where they were involved exactly in that activity. For example, I have for most of my life felt a strong distaste and wanted to keep my distance from anything connected with military activity. Then, in my own regressions to lifetimes in Atlantis, I discovered two lives, one where I was a military commander and one where I suffered in a war, which have helped to explain to me why I wish not to be associated with this. At first I did not want to have anything to do with these lives - but now I can accept them.

We can learn from our past because what we have experienced in the past has been the building blocks to who we are today. By allowing ourselves to experience past lives where we have generated a lot of fear and negativity, we can bring light and love into the dark areas of our soul. This can help us grow and be happier.

ALBANI

Linda Pope.

13

Chapter 4

Working with Spiritual Guides

For many years, I have been helping people to make contact with their Spiritual Guides. I believe that we all have a guide, like a guardian Angel, watching over us, protecting our soul, and helping us to be true to our chosen path in life. Of course, we make our own choices and we don't have to listen to our guide, or, as it may appear to us, our `conscience'. When we don't listen though, we usually start to get into trouble.

There can be long stretches in our life journey where we may be able to sail along with little effort and enjoy opportunities that come our way. But then, at moments of crisis or challenge, we can really need inner help, if only we can reach out for it. I believe that some of us as souls set ourselves more challenging life tasks than others. However, when we go off the track and start doing things and behaving in ways different to what our soul wants from us, it can be very difficult to get back on track again. When through our actions we are removed from our soul's purpose, we can feel very lost and alone. The more removed we become from living our soul's purpose the stronger these feelings can get, and the more likely we are to make further mistakes. Generally, we are given opportunities to find our way again, but once our personality is separated from its soul's task, then it is hard for us to recognize and accept opportunities that are given to us.

This is why making contact with our Spiritual guide can be so important. Once we are aware of that inner Spiritual connection, we can be closer to our own soul and this can bring a tremendous feeling of joy and peace.

When people who have lost contact with their Spiritual part, are able to find it again, this can be very helpful in the soul's growth. In our present age, I believe we are moving into a time where our perceptions as human beings are opening up, where it is becoming easier again to be in contact with the Spiritual worlds. So, people can learn to be in contact with their Spiritual guides, to feel their love, and accept their help.

In Atlantis, I feel that people were also quite Spiritually and psychically aware, so making contact with their Spiritual Guides was not a problem for people then who wished it.

But this process is not always straightforward. To make good use of our Spiritual Guides we need to be genuinely open to connecting with truth and aspiring to live more humbly and with love. If our will is prominent and if we have strong personal desires, this can influence how much we really contact Spirit. In such cases, we can think we are contacting Spirit, but we are really only confirming the expression of our personal desires. Thus, our contact with Spirit in these instances can be quite delusionary.

At the heart of our soul is love. So, if people have a genuine wish in their hearts to serve, or to help others, then this can help open the Spiritual doorways to contact Spirit truly. However, if a person wants predominantly to use Spiritual powers as a means to fulfill personal ambitions, then this can ultimately become quite destructive and not be serving Spirit at all.

I believe that in Atlantis, people got mixed up between wanting to use psychic powers for personal gain and the wish for genuine Spiritual contact. This happened individually, collectively and on a large scale, causing much confusion and conflict for the souls living then. It was not an easy lesson to learn.

I feel that we need to be careful in our modern age, as our Spiritual capacities are being re-awakened, that we do not make the same mistakes again. Our Spiritual guides have a useful part to play in the process of past life regression. When people go through the experience of death with a past life memory they will usually experience themselves going up to a realm of love and light. It is quite common for them to meet with a Spiritual being that seems like a guide who has been with them during the course of that life. This meeting can be very joyful and happy, and through communication can provide much important reflection about the meaning of that lifetime.

Our guides are aware of our inner needs, so it may be from that we are prompted to undergo a course of past life regressions, when the time is right. When I facilitate a session of past life regression with someone, I ask for help and protection from the person's guide. People's Spiritual guides can help bring forth past life experiences into a person's mind that would be most healing and needed at that time. So, how a particular past life experience unfolds or how a series of lives emerge can be Spiritually guided. When, as a facilitator, I can support and encourage the process to happen like this, then I feel this will be in harmony with the inner needs of the person concerned.

However, people can resist the past life experience that is waiting to be given to them. They may be afraid. Usually, people then need to be nurtured and encouraged gently to allow the experience if they are willing. There is a reason for it. Our Spiritual guides will only allow us to experience what we are ready to face. Our guides will know the kind of inner growth experiences that we need. But it is still up to us whether we say `yes' to this or `no'.

From my experience of working with people's Spiritual guides through channelling, I am aware that guides tend to have specific personality traits and interests. There are usually limits to the amount of knowledge that guides have immediately available to them. Often, they will confirm that they have lived numerous lives on the physical plane and have now evolved beyond that. So as a next step they have become guides to help look after us. They are still learning and their evolution can go on. Some guides have areas of knowledge where they specialise and where they want to teach. This logically, can correspond with the interests of the one they are guiding but is not always so.

Throughout the writing of this book, I have worked closely with Linda's Spiritual guide, Albani, who seems to have specialised knowledge about the history of the human race. She tells us she has studied, from the Spiritual records. Much of what we have learned about the overall patterns of Atlantis has come through her teachings. However, the information she has given us, has come forth gradually, so as not to interfere or preempt our regression experiences. So, with questions arising from particular regression experiences, she has been able to help us gain a larger picture of what was going on.

Linda will tell about her own relationship to Albani. But I have found Albani's influence to be helpful and the knowledge she has imparted fascinating. For me, her input has complemented the regression sessions and helped give more meaning to them. Later in the book we will include some passages of channelled teachings from Albani about the overall civilisation of Atlantis.

Chapter 5

Karmic Responsibility

By studying the patterns of how various past lifetime experiences weave together for my long term clients, as well as listening to channelled teaching from members of our Healing group, and my own intuition, I have tried to understand how the process of `Karma' operates for souls.

I feel, that as souls living on the physical plane, we need to learn about the consequences of our actions. So, whatever we give out with our thoughts, words and deeds, we need to experience what it is like to receive what we have projected outwards and to become aware on different levels of what we have done.

This is not necessarily easy. Because we have free will, we can do really what we want. There are many temptations, and influences that can prompt us to be more preoccupied with our own personal needs and less sensitive to the needs of others. So, most of us make lots of mistakes.

Our task, it seems, is to be as truthful as we can in our actions, with what we know deep inside and to act for the best, not only for ourselves but for all beings.

Such a task does not seem possible for the average human being to learn in just one lifetime. It feels as though, to cover all the various aspects of this task, that many, many lifetimes are needed, to grow strong and secure in the ability to be true and loving as a human being whatever the circumstances. As a soul, we want to experience life in all its various aspects.

When souls first come to Earth, I suppose that they first need to learn how to survive, how to manage thoughts, emotions and desires, and how to establish an individual identity without being swept away by influences that are around. As a soul learns different skills and abilities while living on the physical plane, I believe that this learning will remain in the soul and cannot be taken away. So then, when the soul grows in its learning it may become ready for more challenging tasks, and put itself into more difficult situations as a human being, to learn how to cope and achieve its goals.

It is possible that a soul may set for itself a particular learning task for one lifetime and then for some reason or other, not fulfill that. Then it is very likely that this soul may need to go through another lifetime with perhaps slightly altered conditions to try again with that same task, until that lesson is learnt.

I feel that the development of the soul has many layers and aspects to it and I do not pretend to understand it all. But when a soul needs to repeat a lesson it has not learnt, it may not be given that task again in the next lifetime, but maybe only several lifetimes on. In the meantime, the soul may develop in other ways.

When we make mistakes, this may be very painful, but then it may provide some powerful learning opportunities for us.

In my own case, I know that as a soul, I am interested in the path of Healing, and this is something which I feel has been developing through many lifetimes. However, I sense that I have had to learn what it is like when I use healing gifts to hurt people instead of helping them. I know that there are a couple of lifetimes on Atlantis where I have done this. So then, because deep inside, healing is so precious to me, as an expression of love and of Spiritual help, these experiences have been very painful to me. Having used my healing gifts to hurt people in these lifetimes I have had to experience other lifetimes where people were using their healing gifts to hurt me. Then I could feel what it was like from the other side. And that is how it is balanced out. Such experiences make me feel very strongly that I don't want to use healing wrongfully. I hope I have learnt my lesson, whatever the temptation or provocation.

I can feel though, that having gone through these difficult experiences has made me stronger. I could make terrible mistakes and I have done so and I don't want to do so again. Experience is a great teacher for us.

By going through the memories of these experiences in my present lifetime now, it can help me to understand the learning that my soul has gone through. It also helps me to feel a greater compassion for those who suffer - because I know I have suffered through my own wrong doing. This kind of process can work in a similar way for anyone seeking self- knowledge and personal growth through past life regression experiences.

Sometimes souls will go through a lifetime, lose their way, and end up destructively causing a lot of hurt and distress to others. That soul will then need to go through another lifetime experiencing what it is like to be on the receiving end of that kind of hurt and distress. As much as the soul can accept this, then it may afterwards be ready again to move on further. However, sooner or later the soul will want to go through a lifetime similar to the one where they lost their way, to discover if they can manage such an experience successfully. Because the tendency to lose the way was established the first time round, getting through this may not be easy. Souls can easily make the same mistake again and then perpetuate a cycle of negativity. Once such a cycle is operating, it can be very difficult to escape from this. Each time some hurt is caused, this creates a situation where that kind of hurt will need to be experienced from the other side. Psychologically, this can result in a personality building up huge inner barriers to try to protect itself from pain. This in turn prevents the personality from access to its soul. Ultimately, this can result in several lifetimes of intense suffering.

Once a soul is going through such a cycle of negativity, opportunities will be given to try to turn this around. Guides will try to help. But this help may be refused.

Perhaps, the richest and most rewarding life for a soul is when a negative cycle of experiences can be ended and turned around.

From my experiences of past lives in Atlantis, the lifetime as a Military Commander was very significant in this respect. It seems I was going through a cycle of quite negative lives and this one could have continued in a very similar vein. But my compassion was awakened and I ended up following the path of my heart and trying to do some good. At the end of that regression experience I remember a sense of tremendous relief.

Throughout most of its history, Atlantis seems to have had rather a free and permissive society. There were Healing Sanctuaries, Temples and places of power where people could connect with Spirit, with `the One', and the Spirit of the Earth. But people could easily ignore or neglect these places. There was much beauty and power in the natural energies of the land. People were able to develop their psychic powers and use these powers to help others or for manipulation. Much of the time though, there was no strong moral fabric to the society. So, all of this in the melting pot provided a very fertile ground for all kinds of corruption and suffering. The possibilities for corruption were a trap for souls living at that time, so were hard to avoid.

Chapter 6
Processing Atlantis Past Lives

The experience of working through Atlantis past lives can ultimately be very satisfying, but can also be very difficult. I have found not just with my friends Linda, Denise and Lynne, but also with many other clients with whom I have done these regressions, that Atlantis past lives tend to need more processing and support than other regressions, especially the negative ones. Whereas with most past lives, I can work through these with my clients within one or two sessions, with the more challenging Atlantis past lives, this can typically take several sessions.

Perhaps it is the psychic sensitivity that people had then, or just the kinds of things that people would do, without due consideration for the consequences. However, it would not surprise me if there are many people on the Earth today who are still recovering psychically from mistakes that they made while living as souls in Atlantis.

As people start to relive Atlantis past lives through regression, this can bring with it deep, powerful and strong reactions. I feel that the negative experiences from these lives tend to embed themselves firmly within the subconscious mind as strongly held core limiting beliefs and emotional expectation. So as people start to relive these experiences with regression, it releases much energy, feelings, thoughts and physical sensations. This can uncoil itself gradually or in a rush sometimes. But certainly a person needs to be quite strong and courageous to face up to this.

With these regressions, it is not something where I have been able to confine the effects of it to the actual session where I was working with my client. Often the releases have continued to spill out afterwards. I'll give some examples relating to the experiences of my friends.

From one particular Atlantis past life, Lynne suffered from many unpleasant symptoms that lasted intermittently for weeks, as we worked through the different layers to this past life character and how he lived this life. These effects were very physical and emotional. She had chest pains. On some days, for no apparent reason, she had a very short temper. There were times when she felt acutely depressed, even though she knew she was not depressed from her normal everyday life. On a couple of days, she contracted a high fever and had to take time off from her work. All this seemed to relate to the past life. She noticed that sometimes during the sessions or afterwards, she would suffer from severe headaches. We realised that this was her mind resisting and not wanting to acknowledge aspects of the imagery and memory of the lifetime wanting to come through. As she dropped her resistance and allowed the imagery, her headache would go. But it wasn't easy, because she was afraid, and did not want to experience herself as this character. Once though, the door to this experience had been opened, she had to go through it and complete the experience.

Thankfully we were able to do this successfully, and in the weeks following on from this regression Lynne felt very happy and joyful.

There was one Atlantis past life for Denise which was particularly upsetting. It was one where she had abused the power of crystals. However, in this life, Denise found that there were stark parallels between the events of that lifetime and her present lifetime. She even felt that there were many people who she knows now whose souls were characters in that lifetime then. So, as well as dealing with energies and emotions emerging from the past life itself, this experience triggered repressed memories, grief and emotions from her present life.

Denise was someone who did not cry easily and had not done so since she was little. But through this regression sequence, bucket loads of tears were released. Fortunately, Denise had the time and space to allow this to happen. So this experience had a lot to do with her coming to terms with her present life child self and this was triggered at a very deep level.

Linda too, has had some very strange body sensations and upsets as a result of regression sessions, some of which will be mentioned later in chapters about the specific lives. Sometimes though, Linda has had imagery from a particular past life stay in her mind and she has not been able to shift it. This has generally been a sign that there is something in this image which has not been fully processed, where there were thoughts, emotions and fears still needing to come to the surface. Because Linda is so visual, the state of visual imagery in her mind has tended to be a reliable clue as to how her inner work was progressing.

For me, it has been a good experience also to process difficult Atlantis past lives where I would have headaches, feel awful and be shivering afterwards. It has helped me to be able to appreciate more what my clients are going through with their own experiences, even though this has not been at all pleasant for me to experience.

It is quite common, as I work through these lives with people, that they will skip important moments from the past life experience and not acknowledge them. Linda, Lynne, Denise and myself have all done this many times in Atlantean past lives. This usually takes place in such a way that the person undergoing the regression is not even aware of it having happened. As a therapist, it is often not obvious to me either. I will be asking my client to go on to the next most important moment in the past life story, and sometimes some vital slice of the drama will be missed and without trace.

But usually, it is not possible for my clients to get away with these kinds of omissions so easily. Afterwards, they may be left with some uneasy feelings in connection with some aspect of the regression. When this does not settle, for me it is an almost sure sign that something is likely to have been omitted and not processed fully. Generally, when a lifetime has been fully processed the person will feel peace. But until that happens, there may be either a need to recover further aspects of the regression lifetime or a need to explore particular events within deeper psychological layers of the experience. Sometimes a particular event will need to be processed a number of times. If there is a lot of fear involved and it is a traumatic event, the person may initially feel numb about it. So with each occasion that this event is touched upon, more of the energy that is trapped there may be freed, and deeper layers of thoughts, feelings and physical sensations can emerge.

It is normal that people may be afraid of acknowledging traumatic moments from a past life regression. There is a natural childlike tendency to want to hide from it. So people do have a choice whether or not to proceed further into one of these experiences and they may choose not to do so, or wait some time before they feel strong enough.

Linda took many months to process fully her Atlantis past life as Sofira. Initially, there were many parts of this lifetime that she had missed out. And then as we started to recover those missing parts, we discovered that those overlooked experiences were progressively more awful as we came to deal with them. She needed as enormous amount of trust both in me and herself to acknowledge the worst moments in this lifetime - for the experience felt so alien to her as she is now, even though as she became open to it, she had to incorporate this experience as part of herself.

Another challenge in processing past lives from Atlantis or past lives generally concerns the identification of souls from a past life as people whom you may know now. I have become increasingly aware through regression work that most of us have a group of souls around us whom we tend to meet over and over again. As souls, we may be part of a group who love each other very dearly and want to help each other evolve. Then, there may be another soul with whom we get entangled, say through some trauma, and this soul may not really belong with us. It may take many lifetimes to sort out things with this soul to become free from each other.

Then perhaps, through love the two souls may choose to continue to associate with each other, or part from each other depending on what feels right.

However, some caution and care needs to be given when it comes to identification of souls. There may be an element of wishful thinking in this, if we want somebody to have been associated with us in a particular situation from the past. These expectations could colour and affect our perceptions. On the other side, our perception may be correct, but the person we identified may not want to know about it and may deny that anything like that is true for them. So we need to be careful what we do when we gain knowledge of this kind.

Once, Linda, in a workshop, was allowing me to demonstrate with her to a group, the process of past life regression. Linda entered into one of her Atlantis past lives. It was one we had not explored before and it had quite a traumatic death sequence. Gill, one of our Healing group, was witnessing Linda's experience and throughout the regression, Gill continued to feel strange and sick inside and very uneasy. Afterwards Gill told me that she wondered if she might have been one of the characters featuring in Linda's regression. Independently of Gill, Linda later told me that she felt Gill's energy very strongly as one of the characters involved in the death sequence. She had not wanted to speak it aloud during the demonstration.

Usually, I feel, when we sense these connections through our body and our emotions our perception about these matters will tend to be quite accurate.

Another problem can come up when the energy of a past life relationship is released into the present. While a regression experience is still being processed this can be quite confusing. The relationship from the past life may be very different from the relationship enjoyed now and feelings may come up that don't seem appropriate to be expressed in the present life as they once may have done in the past. However, I feel that generally, when a past life soul identification is made, there will be a reason for this. I feel that mostly it will be wise not to try to close down feelings that are evoked but to allow them. Then it may be useful for people to seek help from deep inside from their guide to know what to do with them.

For instance, from her lifetime as Sofira, Linda identified me as the character Sheeran who was her lover in that lifetime. Near the end of that life, Sofira killed Sheeran. After she went through this experience, Linda felt great guilt and uneasiness towards me for a long time. It was not easy to console her. However, we have learnt since that there are other lives in which my character has killed her, and the roles have been reversed. Experiencing that has made both of us consider the need for forgiveness, and I think that both Linda and I are quite determined not to bring suffering like that into each other's life this time around.

Often people need help and support to process Atlantis past lives. I encourage my clients to write down their experiences. But it is usually good if there is friend or someone with whom they can share these experiences - someone who will listen openly and not judge critically. Because these experiences come from a very sensitive and vulnerable place within, it can be very damaging if the friend or confidant is not receptive to what is told to them. So care needs to be taken with this.

Ultimately, the best help may come from within. When people have made contact with their Spiritual guides, it can benefit the person greatly to ask for help from this source. Otherwise, prayers asking for help from `God' or `Spirit' can do just as well. The act of asking inwardly for help can bring positive responses to enable past life experiences to be processed more fully. Responses may come in the way of helpful thoughts and insights or sometimes calming and healing energy.

Spiritual Healing is another form of help that can aid greatly in the integration of past life experiences. This can help settle a person's energy system and bring calm and peace.

It is on deep levels of our inner consciousness that Atlantis past lives need to be processed. I feel that we need to be loving and gentle with ourselves to enable this to happen successfully.

But the rewards can be tremendous, bringing peace and fuller understanding of ourselves and life itself.

Chapter 7
Linda's Story

My Background

I was brought up in a small market town in the Lake District. As an only child I was lonely, and made few friends. I spent many long hours on my own, exploring the beautiful countryside all around me. I loved to be in the woods, watching the changing seasons and the cycle of life as it unfolded. The trees were my friends and I knew them all. They had an energy I could feel and I used to curl up at the bottom of their huge trunks and sense the life force all around me. I found this a great comfort in my loneliness.

Being an unhappy child, as I grew older, I withdrew into myself and my own world more and more. I hated school, and frequently played truant, going to watch the trains on the local railway. In summer, I would sit for hours in the flower-filled grass of the embankments. I loved the railway and I used to go behind the station, to a fence, observing the activity around the steam engines as they took on water and used the turntable. It particularly pleased me if I got a friendly wave from the engine crews.

Although I thought nothing of it at the time, on some of my solo wanderings in the woods and along the lakeside, I was `met' and accompanied by an American Indian. He just seemed to `appear' and I accepted his presence without being afraid of him. His name was `Red Eagle'. He became my secret friend and was gentle and kind. He told me wonderful stories about the animals, and taught me about the plants and trees, the Earth and the stars. Everything seemed so magical with him.

I never told anyone about him, not even my parents; I sensed they would not understand, anyway. One year, our school organised a painting competition, so I did a portrait of my friend, and won first prize. Everyone commented on the unusual subject and how life-like he was.

As I grew older he appeared to me less and less, and eventually went away. When I came to leave school I had nothing in the way of exam qualifications, so, at fifteen, had to seek work. There were few prospects in our small town, so it was decided by my family to move away. I found it heartbreaking parting from the mountains and woods I loved so much. Eventually, we came to Morecambe and settled. We had only been there a short time when my father left. One day he just went out and never came back. By then, I was working in a local Chemists and Mum had started to take in sewing so we could make ends meet. We were living in a small, dreary flat and life was difficult. At school I had learned to sing, and colleagues at work persuaded me to join a local operatic society. Quickly, I made lots of new friends and at last began enjoying life. When I was nineteen I met Michael and we started going out together. Two years later, we married, I started nursing and life was looking up.

Soon after that though, Michael became seriously ill and lost his robust health; he became unable to work. We moved away to Devon to make a `new start', but things did not work out for us. After a few traumatic and unhappy years, we returned to Morecambe.

Although, my parents were Church of England, they never practiced as such, rarely gong to church. They didn't push me one way or the other, even though I did attend Sunday school for a while. I found institutionalised religion boring and irrelevant.

Slowly, I began to realise, deep inside, I needed to understand and try to explain all of the traumatic events that seemed to beset me. I was deeply unhappy with my life. There had to be more to things than what I perceived.

My experiences at work, over the years, with seriously ill and dying patients set my mind thinking. Gradually, this helped to awaken my interest in Spiritual matters. I began to look for answers, scouring libraries and bookshops. In the seventies, there wasn't much literature on such subjects available. Then, a book was published which changed all that - Raymond Moody's best selling `Life After-Life'. Devouring this book, I realised that it made sense. Somewhere it struck a familiar chord and I was fired with enthusiasm to know more. Most of the books I could find were American; they seemed way ahead of Britain on this subject. I read everything I could lay my hands on. Eventually, the subjects of reincarnation, past lives and Spirit guides came to my attention. I discovered that most of the writers mentioned the existence of personal `guides' or `guardian angels', Spiritual beings who were with us throughout our life, loving and protecting us, assisting us through life's ups and downs. Intuitively, I had always felt that everyone had someone like this with them, and was not alone. However, I had had no conscious contact with my guide and had no idea who he or she was. How I longed to know. Really, I hadn't any idea how to get in touch. I tried the suggestions in the books, even just asking, but nothing seemed to work at the time. Obviously, I was doing something wrong.

Also, by now, I had come to accept the principles of reincarnation and past lives. It all seemed to make such perfect sense. Then, of course, the most pressing questions for me were: `Who was I? Where was I? What did I do?' I searched and searched and produced nothing. This was incredibly frustrating. After many years of hoping for some `happening' or 'déjá vu' experience, I resigned myself to the fact that I may never know.

In time, I became ill and required an operation. This done, I developed a Bell's Facial Palsy which did not resolve. Although in the nursing profession, and confident with modern medicine, I found that no one could help me, and began to seek alternative answers. Through a friend I went to a local clinic and met Sonya, a naturopathic healer. At that time, she was learning what was considered then a new therapy, called the Bowen Technique. I was invited to a private session with some of her friends, as they were looking for `guinea pigs'. Agreeing to participate, this proved to be the turning point for which I had been waiting for so long. After the session, I was drinking a welcome cup of tea when I started to get spontaneous images of a past life. The details and clarity astonished me. No wonder I had always loved trains. I had been a Russian engine driver called `Yuri'.

This event opened the floodgates of my `memories'. In my dreams I began to see vivid details of my life as Yuri, and more imagery came to me quite unexpectedly. I knew I should record all of this information, and started keeping a journal, with each entry dated. Also I drew sketches of the clear pictures that I was seeing. With friends, I discussed these exciting developments, and they suggested that I should go to a professional therapist and be regressed. However, at that time it didn't feel right.

For four years, I meticulously recorded all the details of my inner experiences concerning this Russian past life and did much research. Then one night, after a particularly vivid dream, a voice in my head said "This is the last communication about Yuri, the rest is up to you". It was December 1997.

The following February, as a birthday treat, I visited a local crystal therapist for some healing and energy balancing, to discover what this form of treatment felt like. We had never met, and she knew little about me. During the treatment she suddenly spoke - "Within four weeks you will meet a man who will change your life". I laughed and made the usual lighthearted comments, feeling this was just a little too far-fetched. Soon after this, my close friend Denise came to me and explained that she had decided to go and have a past life regression, to deal with some issues that had come up for her. She told me she had found a local therapist and I ought to go too. All at once, I `knew' that the time was now right, I had put this off long enough. Organising an appointment with Paul, I quite unwittingly fulfilled the crystal therapist's prediction. It was just four weeks later.

Albaní

After several sessions with Paul, he suggested that I join a healing development class he was running. So, on the due date, I went along.

I began to learn much more with his teaching and was both surprised and delighted that I could actually channel healing energy. This I found immensely satisfying. We also began to learn about our Spirit guides.

It was about halfway through the eight week course that Paul invited me to join his Healing Circle group. This was something I had wanted for so long. Immediately, I felt at home with the various members of the group and my learning continued apace. A whole new experience was opening up for me.

One evening, at the class, a regular member of the group came to speak to us, and to demonstrate channelling. Her Spirit guide would `come through' her, speak to us, and answer questions. I had never seen this before and was fascinated. While in trance, our friend's guide began to speak. It was her voice, but obviously not her talking, I sat in amazement, quite unable to ask any questions, although afterwards, I could think of lots. I was impressed with the absolute trust that must be required by the channel. To allow a Spirit being to `take you over' and speak through your body seemed such a brave thing to do. I felt frightened by the prospect that I would ever do that.

Soon though, things started happening. I had been to Penrith one particular day and was driving back down the M6. It is a trip I do regularly and I know the route well. The motorway was relatively quiet and I was enjoying the drive through the mountains on a sunny spring day. The scenery was glorious and I was in a relaxed mood. We had just come over Shap summit when I heard a really clear voice in my head, so clear, it was as if someone in the car had spoken. "Leave the motorway at the next exit". I was about halfway from home, and, as it was such a beautiful day, decided to do as instructed, and take the back road through the Lune gorge to Kendal. I left the M6 at Tebay. A short way along, the road re-crosses the motorway. I looked over the bridge and saw, to my astonishment, the southbound carriageway was at a complete standstill. A trailer had broken loose and was lying smashed to pieces right across the road.

I thought about this all the way home, thinking about the `voice', and how incredibly clear it had been. I resolved to ask about this when our group next met, but before our next meeting another incident occurred which saved my life.

Again, I was driving on a regular route. In front of me was a heavy lorry, moving slowly, and another car. I knew there was a straight stretch of road ahead, where, if safe to do so, I could overtake. When we reached this section, the road was clear. The car in front of me overtook and I planned to follow. In the split second between the decision and the action of putting my foot on the accelerator, the voice spoke again. "Don't overtake!" My foot froze, and the lorry in front indicated to turn right, and moved into the middle of the road. He was going down a farm track, which I would never have expected. I released a pent up breath and allowed the car to slow. Again, the voice had been sharp, clear and insistent, and had saved me from a terrible accident.

At our next group meeting, I was keen to share my experiences. That evening, when one of the group was channelling her guide for questions, I asked about what had happened to me. The answer surprised me. "That is your guide speaking to you. If you are hearing so clearly, you are obviously in good contact and should be able to channel". The reaction on my face must have looked somewhat comical. Me a channel? I felt shocked and excited. For the rest of the evening I was suitably quiet and thoughtful. My mind was in a whirl when I went home. Then suddenly, I realised somewhere deep inside, that I did want to channel. Something within me had changed. I felt I was ready to do it now.

One night during the following week, I awoke from a deep sleep, `sensing' someone close by. I couldn't see anyone, but felt a distinct presence. My husband was fast asleep and all was quiet. Then I heard the voice again, female, gentle but clear. "Hello, my name is Albani". That was all. Her presence was gone, like someone had left the room. I sat up, staring into the darkness, feeling elated, excited; it was difficult to get back to sleep.

Paul offered to teach me to channel. Reassuring me, Paul put me through a relaxation process, then asked me to allow Albani to come close. The feeling that followed was extraordinary, and difficult to describe. I could sense her close to my right side, almost touching me. Then I felt a definite sensation as she merged herself with me. It was deliciously warm, tingly, and very pleasant. I felt myself beginning to `drift'. Next, I became aware of my voice speaking, but it wasn't me! After that, I just seemed to go into a deep state, from which some time later, Paul brought me back. I had done it and I was thrilled and delighted. The feeling in my body was physically wonderful. The session had been recorded on tape, and it was the oddest of feelings hearing my voice, speaking so differently, answering questions and talking so knowledgeably about the world of Spirit, past lives and personal matters.

Thus started my relationship with Albani. Soon, I began to get images of her in my inner vision. I could `see' her clearly. Her appearance is tall and slender, fair skinned, with beautiful deep blue eyes. She has long white blonde hair, which she wears plaited and usually wears a long turquoise or lemon gown. Sometimes she wears loose trousers. She seems to like a change, just like we do.

I cannot now imagine what life would be like without her by my side. Knowing she is there is a great comfort. At times in the past, when I had to face a really difficult family crisis or other seemingly unresolvable problems, something just made me sit down and cry out "please help me". On one occasion, I was certain I `felt' an arm around my shoulders, giving me comfort. I thought at the time it was my imagination but I know differently now. The sense of her presence is wise and loving. She is my friend, my guide, and my close companion. There is a bond of love between us that is very deep and beautiful. I know now she was there all the time, waiting for me to take that first step..... and the longest of journeys starts with a single step......

My interest in Atlantis

When I started working with Paul, I realised, through conversation, that we had a mutual interest in the ancient civilisations, the history of the Earth, and in particular in the legendary lost continent of Atlantis.

I had always, as long as I could remember, been fascinated by the stories of lost and ancient civilisations - Lyonesse, Lemuria, Mu, etc. Somehow they sparked something inside me. The very fact that there was little known about them added to the mystery. Most books on the subject were speculative and sceptical, as little in the way of proof had ever been found. I loved the `fantastic' element in the tales, the `magic'. The idea that these people, who lived before recorded history, seemed to possess knowledge and abilities beyond our own, intrigued me.

There were many things `mysterious' in which, I was interested. Throughout my life I had visited ancient sites, stone circles and the like. I could `feel' their energy, sense an ancient connection to the Earth. The fact that these places too, were little understood, made them much more attractive.

Over time, I visited many of these sites in Britain. One year, I made a trip to the Isles of Scilly, a really magical place. I realised, as I stood on a rocky headland, I may actually be standing on the ancient land of Lyonesse, of Arthurian Legend. Then, as I looked out across to the west, over miles and miles of ocean, my thoughts turned to Atlantis.....Somewhere out there, beneath the waves, I felt, lay what remained of that legendary continent.

I first learned of Atlantis as a child, in old, musty library books. The place fascinated me. There was nothing much written, just a few lines, and old theoretical maps, drawn hundreds of years ago, which showed a large land mass, roughly mid-Atlantic. I drew pictures of places and people, seeing it as a green and fertile land, with great buildings, cities and temples, and a proud people, tall and dark haired, who ultimately brought about their own destruction. From my inner vision, I could `see' them, fleeing the sinking land in small boats, fire and chaos behind them.

My friends and parents dismissed the sketches as a product of an over-active imagination, but I knew they were real......I had lived there.

Eventually, I decided to explore this part of my past. Paul and I discussed this and I was taken back, back to a place that was real and beautiful, with snow-capped mountains, green valleys, large cities of white stone and the dark haired people I had seen in my imagination.

The one thing I did not expect were some of the darker aspects of life I was about to uncover. In a seemingly idyllic physical setting the people were corrupt, cruel and arrogant. It was a society that thrived on corruption, ambition and greed. Some of the things I discovered took my breath away with horror. To see some of these events was very difficult. To realise that I had directly particip-ated was almost impossible to accept.

Over time, I have learnt that inside me I have the memory of many lives on Atlantis, throughout it's 15,000 year history. Some, I'm happy to say, I've experienced as positive and healing, but many were not.

In a substantial number of the experiences described in this book, I was responsible for some terribly dark deeds indeed. For a long time I have struggled to come to terms with some of these events. However, as I have done so, I have felt cleansed and renewed, and have been able to start a process of forgiving myself, deep within, for the terrible things I did, all those thousands of years ago.

It has been very difficult for me to begin to see the shortcomings of my own soul's path. But I have begun to `see' with a new vision, a way forward now. I sincerely hope that all the bad things are behind me. I am striving hard to accept this life's trials and tribulations gracefully, knowing that they are a pattern I have both chosen and had to redress to balance myself.

Chapter 8

The Regression Experiences In This Book

It was soon obvious to me after I started working with Linda, that she had a whole range of past life experiences that she wanted to explore. Some of these extended to times and places that were not very familiar to me from my previous work with clients, but which nevertheless I found very interesting and sometimes compelling in their contents. Linda had a very rich and involved inner life with an active awareness of her soul's history that seemed to stretch back for aeons. My work with her using hypnosis and guided meditations had the effect of opening her awareness much further and deeper. I found that Linda was a person who could quite spontaneously enter into an altered state of consciousness in her everyday life. She may get flashes of past life memory or other psychic impulses coming to her. Within her dreams also, this was another means for her to gain further access to her inner life. Of course, all this increased through her work with me. But I was struck by the authenticity of her experience. When she shared with me, I felt she was telling me the truth as she knew it. She trusted me and it was very important for her for me to accept her experiences. I could do that, even though some of her experiences challenged my own concepts and belief systems.

Linda was facing some quite severe problems in her life and I wanted to help her with this. But as I began to delve with her into her past life memories, what seemed most helpful was that these experiences could be like a gateway to her Spiritual self. With her emotional sensitivity, the regressions could give her deep self-understanding and release.

It was not long before we started to access Atlantean past lives. At first, it appeared that there were indications of only two or three lives from Atlantis that may be relevant. But the number just kept on growing, and the involvement needed and complexity of these lives grew too. After a while, regressions to other places seemed to lose their significance and tracing the threads of Linda's Atlantean experiences became predominant in our work.

The seed thought of writing a book about Atlantis gradually developed, especially once Denise and Lynne also embarked on their own Atlantean past life inner journeys. Linda's guide Albani was instrumental in encouraging this idea. But Linda recognised that for her, the most important aspect of the work was the help that it was giving her to her own inner development.

As time went on, there were many of Linda's Atlantean experiences where she felt that she recognised me as one of the other characters in the experience. Sometimes I could even sense this before she spoke it. At other times it was less immediately clear to me. But this helped to awaken in me a curiosity and interest to know what had been my own experience of these lives and others in Atlantis. I wondered how I could do it?

Then gradually came the idea which seemed like a unique experiment to help me access my own past lives from Atlantis. I had been very impressed with Albani's guidance and help with Linda around her experiences. Albani had much knowledge relating to Atlantis and she also displayed much therapeutic sensitivity regarding Linda's inner needs at times when I could not help. So I thought that I would ask Albani if she could be my therapist and help me access my Atlantean past lives. I did not feel that I could ask Linda because she had had no training as a therapist, but her Spiritual guide Albani appeared to be quite competent. When I spoke to Albani about this, she seemed to be quite excited by the prospect, but she also explained to me that she had not done anything like this before.

Finally, we conducted our first experiment doing this. I guided Linda into a trance so that she could channel Albani. Then Albani guided me into regression.

I found that I felt very safe with Albani's guidance. I had been feeling quite nervous and insecure about how well I would be able to accomplish my aims. But Albani's voice was firm and sure. She lead me with an induction that I had never used with clients before. However, it was simple and effective and I found myself entering into an experience of an Atlantean past life, experiencing it much more fully with more detail than I had expected.

Following on from the regression, when it had ended, I could talk with Albani about my thoughts, feelings and doubts and she was able to reassure me and help me to process the experience. Altogether it was a very satisfying and successful experiment and formed the beginning of many further regression experiences which I have had. When I had come out of my regression and finished talking with Albani, I could then bring Linda out of the trance and the session would be over. I have been very grateful for Linda's help with this. We taped the sessions so a record of it would remain for afterwards.

As we have built up our 'bank' of Atlantean past life experiences, we have found that we could only include a small selection of these for the purposes of this book. This is really only because we did not want the book to be too voluminous, for many of the experiences we have not included are very interesting and we will devote a brief chapter later in the book to mentioning some of these.

We have tried to choose lives which would help present some of the main contours of the history of Atlantis, some of the main aspects of its culture, the way people lived, and the mistakes which people could make. Then we also wanted to give some insights about the personal soul journeys which Linda and I have each made through our Atlantean sojourns and lifetimes that were very significant in this. So then, there could be an inner and outer component to the regression experiences, which we hope will be interesting to the reader.

The regression experiences have been arranged for the purposes of the book in historical order, from the foundation times first, through to experiences connected to the final destruction of

Atlantis at the end. This does not reflect how these lives unfolded in our therapy sessions, for the progress from one regression lifetime to another rarely follows an historical pattern, but tends much more to unfold through a kind of resonance linking similar experiences. But in the way we have set out the experiences, we hope that this will be simple and coherent to read.

We realise that the history of Atlantis is a vast subject, but we hope that the thoughts of this book and the regression experiences will add to that knowledge. We have not attempted to study what others have written on the subject, but to rely solely upon the experiences that have come to us. With that, we have tried to be truthful and honest to what our inner experiences and intuition have told us to be so.

Chapter 9

Channelling Albani's Commentaries

Throughout the writing of this book, I have had many engrossing conversations with Albani, Linda's Spiritual guide. To do this, it has been a simple matter to guide Linda into a trance state and to ask for Albani to come forth and speak. She does this very easily. Sometimes Albani has begun to channel spontaneously with Linda drifting into trance of her own accord. Linda's consciousness would willingly move aside to let Albani speak, and then Linda would have no memory of the conversation afterwards. Usually we would tape these sessions so Linda would have the opportunity to study what Albani said.

The amount of detailed knowledge concerning various aspects of Atlantean life that Albani has been able to share has been impressive. However, as with all channelled teachings, I have found it very important to challenge within myself what has been said, and really use my own intuition to test what feels `true' from the information that has been given.

I have noticed that Albani has tended to be selective about what she has told us. For instance, if one of us was about to undergo a regression to a particular period in Atlantean history, we would be told very little about this in advance. Then, the experience of the regression would come purely through our own minds and not be coloured by Albani's thoughts or by expectations we had set up within ourselves by what she had said to us. For me it has been essential that we proceed in this way. I have not wanted to know what might happen in one of my regressions beforehand. Otherwise it could be argued that the regressions in this book are projections from Albani's thoughts rather than genuine individual experiences. And I know that this is not true.

Throughout the rest of the book there are a number of commentaries by Albani about various phases of the history of Atlantis. These sections have taken a question and answer form and are largely unedited transcripts from channelled sessions that have been recorded on tape. As I have implied, these commentaries were compiled after the relevant regression experiences related to these periods, had been accessed.

We are going to start with Albani's commentary about the beginnings of Atlantis. From there we will move on to regression experiences related to the first settlements on Atlantis, and then go further

Part 2 - The Regressions and Commentaries

Chapter 10

The Foundations of Atlantis

Commentary by Albani

Paul: How did the continent of Atlantis form physically, and how did people first start coming there?

Albani: *The formation of the continent was as with all other land, and came through Earth movement and a general change in the structure of the Earth's surface. This is an ongoing process. But in the earlier times, the Earth was more unstable and change occurred at a much faster rate than it does now. As you know, down what is now the central Atlantic, is a major fault and a major movement point on the Earth's surface. This is how the continent came into being. It came from this area. Land mass was formed as it always is by a thrusting upwards of the general surface from beneath the water. This occurred, in modern terms quite quickly, but it took a long, long time in reality. At the same time other Earth movements were occurring. It is a reciprocal thing. If one thing moves, then something else has to move to allow for it. There has to be a give and take within the surface. It is like, if you imagine ice flows moving. One moves and then another moves and they release the pressure together on themselves. This is a reasonable picture to us, because as you know, beneath the crust of the Earth is a molten material. It is upon this that the actual crust and surface structures move, albeit, slowly by your standards. This is roughly what happened.*

Along the central line, there was the most activity. As the land forming material came through in the form of volcanic activity the actual surface of the land flowed outwards from this central point, to the east and to the west, and formed a longitudinal continent which eventually settled as the Earth movements settled. Along the central spine of the land where there was most activity were the high mountains. For these were pushed up in the last activity which settled down when the continent settled down. Towards east and west were lower mountains, lower hills, and the flat plains leading to the sea.

When this eventually settled down, a lot of the land was barren. But immediately upon the land cooling and becoming ready for life, then life appeared. It happened in many ways. At that stage the land was very fertile, much more fertile than you could possibly imagine, I feel. Anything that landed, seeds or anything like that, would grow very quickly.

What also happened, which is not unique to Atlantis, but something for which it is well known for, is the crystal formation. As you know, these minerals are formed under great pressure. And that is exactly what happened when the mountains were forming. The formation of these huge crystal beds tended to be roughly down the centre of the continent, where the highest mountains were situated. They were numerous, and very, very large. These exerted a tremendous energy. It is this energy which the crystals exerted that drew life and eventually drew people to the continent. For this energy went out into the general energy field of the Earth and was a tremendously powerful influence.

There are other lines of crystals in longitudinal sections down the Earth still. They are very much an essential part of the Earth's magnetic field. But most people do not know of their existence. They tend to be in mountain chains and places of very ancient volcanic activity.

Paul: Can you say something about the size and shape of Atlantis?

Albani: *It was essentially on a longitudinal axis - north to south-much longer than its lateral axis, east to west. The equatorial belt roughly came across about two thirds of the way down. The bulk of the continent was in the northern hemisphere. Again bearing in mind that these are slightly different measurements now, that is roughly where it was. The overall size covered a vast area. Its northern point - now I need to transpose the old geography onto the modern geography - the northern most point was approximately in a latitude level with what is now, I think, Portugal. The southern most tip would go down to about the tropic of Capricorn. It was much, much bigger than what you call modern Europe. One of the easiest ways to describe it is, if you imagined the mass of land of what you call North America turned on its side and moved across to the Atlantic, then that would be slightly larger than the Atlantean continent. In other words, if you took the American continent from Newfoundland down to California , turned it diagonally, and moved it across to the place I have described, leaving out all the various protrusions which are around, and try to imagine it as almost an ovoid, I think that is about right. It is not an easy thing to describe, as you can appreciate.*

The climatic conditions varied from the north to the south. The north was more temperate, the south more tropical. But the Earth was warmer then, so you would have to allow for that. It was also more rich with vegetation. For as you are probably aware, the area that is now the Sahara desert was lush vegetation and forest. The change in that was again caused by people's neglect, which is entirely another story.

But, the continent of Atlantis had a very equable climate and it was a very pleasant place to be. A lot of people would think it was like the Greek Elysian fields, or the various idyllic places that have been described over the years by your poets and artists. The mountain chains were high and were snow capped, even on the equator, as is Mount Kilimanjaro.

The range of vegetation reflected the climatic differences. What was there were plants and biological diversity, which in many ways does not exist now. Certain things were unique to that land and were lost when the land submerged. Certain things were

46

brought with the people escaping the land. For some of the more enlightened people leaving realised that here were very precious things. They took with them seeds and plants and various things like that to take to their new place. But these have changed biologically and evolved. So there are many things in that form which existed on the Atlantean continent, that are no longer with us.

This is not a particularly bad thing as you may think, for nature has changed, the biology has changed and it has simply been an ongoing process of change.

But there were plants, that were used then that are around now and in the very southern area, it tended to be more lush and perhaps what you may describe as rain forest. But it wasn't quite like that. It wasn't quite as dense as the rain forest you know now.

The animal life was much the same. There were mammals, small mammals, but a tremendous variety of birds. Atlantis was rich with bird life. Again some were unique, and were lost with the continent. Birds, could fly away, be transported by people, and this did happen.

Up in the mountains, you had snowfields, the land above the tree line, where different plants grew and where different biological patterns existed. Of course, people with their skills would inhabit all these places.

But the essence of Atlantis was its energy. It was tremendously energetic because of the amount of crystals which were there within the land.

Paul: How did the animal and human life come to Atlantis and from where did it come?

Albani: *Originally there were very temporary land bridges and they were due to the instability of what was then the ocean floor. The main land bridge was from the Iberian peninsula. A lot of animal life crossed from there. There were also very brief connections with what is now the African continent. These were very tenuous links and were soon broken by the movement of the Earth's crust. But in the very short time they existed, animal life*

*moved across and from that evolved into their own unique patterns
on the continent of Atlantis.*

*When people arrived they brought with them domestic animals
and this added to the physical diversity of the fauna on the land.
Birds flew there. But some birds were brought by people, because,
as you know, some of them cannot fly that far.*
*Insect life and plant life travels in a different way, very often
together. Insect life came with the animals, in a parasitic form, or
simply by being carried as eggs or various forms of pupa or things
like that. Quite inadvertently, things even actually float upon the
sea, and survive a long sea journey and land on beaches upon a
land, and become alive again. Some things can stay in a form of
dormancy until the conditions are right. So you have various and
many different ways of populating a new land.*

*All that time ago, the people, the population of the Earth and the
general energies of the Earth, were much, much stronger. The
people were more psychically aware. They were more aware of
these energies and what they meant. As you have probably
realised, the migration of animals is purely to do with them
sensing the lines of energy, and knowing which way to go by this
road map that is in their heads. They work with these lines of
energy. They follow this within themselves, quite automatically.*

*People at this time also had a great deal of this ability. Some
people still have. It is part of the psychological make up of the
human form that you should be able to tune into lines of energy.
But most people nowadays have lost this ability as with their
psychic sense.*

*But then, some of the people on other continents, sensitive people,
for there were always some people more sensitive than others,
sensed this new land. They knew that out there across this ocean
was something strong and wonderful. It was drawing them. The
crystal energy was drawing them into the grid. They sensed along
their own grid-lines. They sensed that out there, was something
very important, and a new land. They could feel its energy. They
could feel its magnetic attraction, for this is what the Earth
wanted. It wanted the human population to spread. It had created*

this beautiful new land and essentially it was there for people to use. For the Earth looks after her children. She made this beautiful place for them. As one place was becoming less energetic and losing its power, then another was created to replace it. It is an ongoing process.

As Lemuria was failing, and becoming worn out and tired, then Atlantis was created, as well as other land movements.

Paul: So you're suggesting that there were much more dramatic land movements then, than what most scientists in our present age would acknowledge?
Albani: *Yes, indeed. That is because the Earth in its younger years was more dynamic.*

Paul: But we are looking at only 25,000 years ago?
Albani: *Yes they were the last major changes. The last major change was probably the sinking of Atlantis, for that was when the depths of the Atlantic ocean was formed, and I think, things settled down more after that.*

But there were periods of what you would call, great instability, and a lot of movement, and periods of great settlement when things did not happen. This is again a cyclical thing over a long period of time. But yes the movements were much more dramatic - which I think, fortunately for the Earth's population today, seems to have settled down.

There are movements today, but they are purely adjustments of pressure in many ways, and very often associated with the activities of people.

Paul: Most scientists would tend to view early settlements of human beings, especially around that time of about 25000 BC as being primitive, more hunter/gatherer societies. You seem to have a different view of that?
Albani: *Yes. For you are looking at a different history. You are looking at something which people have not yet perceived, although now more is coming forward that there were civilisations at that time, which were more advanced than has been previously*

49

thought. It is simply that they have not had the proof of this, and as you know, scientists must always have proof. It will come - it is coming now. They have the proof there, but they do not understand what it is. There is much speculation in some areas as to what is being found. Eventually, they will realise, but at the moment it is challenging their scientific thought.

Having said that, you have to accept. You have to accept initially that Atlantis existed. You also have to accept that Lemuria, Mu and the Siberian civilisations also existed. That is the first step. So, if they existed then therefore the civilisations must have been more socially advanced than is thought. They were not purely hunter gathers as would be assumed. Yes, primitive society did exist in certain places. But there was also a great deal of civilisation too and you simply have to accept this, for these continents were there. These people did exist. It is still within the memory of many, many people who are in existence today.

This is why there is a much broader acceptance today, certainly of Atlantis. But Atlantis is the last in a long line of lost continents. Therefore, perhaps the rational mind can accept Atlantis a little better, for it is, shall we say, more recent. But going back beyond that, pushes the modern mind a little into thinking that perhaps this is all fantasy. However, this is not so.

Paul: From which places did the people come mainly to settle Atlantis?
Albani: *Mainly they came from places immediately bordering it. The biggest source of migration came from Lemuria, which was at the top end of what is now South America - from the southwest towards Atlantis.*

Paul: As I understand it, Lemuria was going through a lot of instability at that time, and most of the people were leaving?
Albani: *Yes, for as the events leading to the formation of Atlantis settled down, and the continent settled into being, then on the other side, or further across the Earth's plates, the opposite was happening. Again, it is a reaction of one Earth movement to another. Lemuria as a continent was becoming more unstable.*

The continent of Lemuria had been in existence a long time. Again, it had a central fault line. That was on the fault line that is now on the western side of South America, and runs right up the American plate. This line went down roughly the centre of Lemuria. As you can probably imagine, as the other fault line moved, then so did that one, and caused a great deal of change. Eventually, part of Lemuria, the western part went into what is now the Pacific Ocean. There are simply small remains, as in the small islands that are a long way off the west coast of South America. The main one which most people find interesting is Easter Island.

Paul: So Easter Island was once part of Lemuria?
Albani: *It was, but only a tiny, tiny part.*

Paul: What were the other main places from where the population came?
Albani: *There was what is now known as the European area, which is to the north east. People came from that direction. Yhey did not essentially use the land bridges, that was mainly for animals. People could sail across, use the boats, and they could approach by sea.*

Also, there were crossings from what is now the African land. So they were the main points.

Strangely, the area that is now North America was not well populated at the time. The main bulk of immigrants came from Lumeria to the south west of Atlantis. However, there was considerable settlement in the north east also. It was like an opposite, at either end, and smaller groups came across from the African area, for the African continent was less populated too.

Paul: Were each of these civilisations quite advanced? What was the cultural influence of each of these groupings?
Albani: *The most advanced were the people who came from Lemuria for they came from the most ancient of the lands. The ones from the north east were not quite so far advanced culturally, but they all came from a tradition that honoured the Earth energy. For this was quite natural at that time. As I have said, the whole*

of the Earth's population was much more sensitive and much more aware of this. Therefore, no matter what part they came from, the people were very much aware of the honouring of the Earth energy. So the cultures that had grown up were somewhat similar. For they all were based on roughly the same principles. They approached from a slightly different manner. But the essence of their belief and culture were much the same.

Climatic variations made a difference with these people. But essentially they were coming from almost the same direction belief-wise. They felt part of the land, felt a kinship with the Earth mother, for this sensitivity was strong.

The people from Lemuria came from a very ancient tradition, for they were originally populated from Mu. Therefore, the tradition was carried forward. The ones from the African continent were also reasonably well advanced. The ones with the least cultural advancement were the ones from the northeast, from the colder climates of the north.

Paul: Were there any primitive type people settling in Atlantis?

Albani: *No. For essentially they did not move much, for it was the more advanced who were more aware of what was happening. For these people had priests, or psychic leaders within their societies. In order to have that, they needed to have a reasonable advancement within the social structure. The primitive peoples, although very aware of the Earth energies, were quite stationary. Some were nomadic, but they tended to stay within their own climatic area. They did not feel the need to move, and felt very attracted to their own land. The more advanced civilisations had the ability to build ships. They had the knowledge, need and urge to move on, the need for advancement. This comes with advancement in the intellect sense.*

Paul: What about language? What kind of language was brought to Atlantis?

Albani: *This was as varied as the people. It is hard to describe in modern terms, but eventually, as in many continents which have come from a diversity in languages, a common tongue developed, for the need to communicate was strong. Within that, as with the modern situation, there was a common tongue, but also regional* *variations. I am not necessarily speaking of dialect, but of language. Atlantis was a very large continent, and it took some time for various groups of people to actually come across each other. When they did, they managed to communicate, and over time this developed into a common tongue.*

The language in modern terms is extremely difficult to describe. I think the nearest that modern people would have any conception of, for it was a different form of tongue, would be the ancient Mayan language. That is as near to Atlantean as you are likely to get.

Paul: So when we come up with the names of characters from these different past lives, then the sound of the names we sense, is perhaps a near approximation to what those people may have been called then?

Albani: *Most definitely. It is a phonetic approximation, and if the names appear modern as in modern English, this is purely and simply the only way you can express it. The language itself would be difficult for say, someone who speaks English, to intonate. It was a very guttural and throaty language with a lot of syballant sounds. You would use the letter 'x' from your alphabet a lot. To learn the Atlantean language now, you would need to learn it phonetically, and you would also have to learn a very different system of writing and written work, which they had, as all of the ancient civilisations did.*

Paul: How did they write?

Albani: *It depended a lot initially on where the area was, for they used what was around at the time. In the southern part, where the weather was warmer, they used a form - the nearest you have to it would be the Egyptian papyrus. But it was made from plant substances. It was essentially, I suppose, a thick form of paper, and was not too dissimilar to modern paper. The method of making the marks came from forms of paint and ink.*

Ink and paint have existed for as long as people have inhabited the planet. It has always been realised that these could be used to make a mark upon something. Pigments of the Earth have always been used by people for self-expression.

ALLANYA AND JANYA

LINDA POPE

54

Paul: How did people in those times express their sexuality?

Albani: *The answer to that is very liberally. There were no real rules that were put on the population. They did not feel that there were any barriers. They were open minded. In most of the population areas, this was not considered a problem. There was little in the way of barriers between the sexes and initially there was a great deal of equality.*

People who you now refer to as 'gay' or homosexual, were accepted quite normally. There were no inhibitions. It was a very sexually free society. But this could lead to a great deal of problems, as some of the regressions have shown you!

Chapter 11

The First Settlements

Introduction

We are going to begin our regressions with Linda's incarnation as Allanya. In this life, Allanya was one of a group of healers travelling in ships from Lemuria to form a settlement in the `new land' of Atlantis.

Her story is a very personal one but also very tragic. Because of all the trauma involved, Linda found it very difficult to access all the details of this lifetime. It took several sessions for us to complete this, and during the course of the therapy, Linda felt very vulnerable. Consequently, with the feelings that it brought up, it was rather an ordeal for her to write it out. However, from inside herself, she knew she had to do it. I believe that her account is a faithful record of what she experienced in regression, and we hope that it will be of interest.

This particular experience is one of many shared lifetimes that I have had with Linda from Atlantis. I have discovered that I was one of the other healers in that group, and my name was Janya. Subsequently, I have been through my own regressions to this incarnation as Janya and I will be including some information about this following Linda's account of Allanya.

Even though, for much of that lifetime, Janya and Allanya were close, their experiences were very different. Therefore, I hope by sharing some aspects of Janya's life that this will give some additional perspective of the forces at work in the creation of this new settlement in Atlantis - and what went wrong!

Whenever Linda has had a past life regression session, she has made detailed notes afterwards of the contents of the regression. Her memory is very good and accurate and these notes could easily stimulate further thoughts, feelings and imagery related to the experience. Linda has been able to use these notes as a base for the regression accounts which are included in this book.

For me, my regression sessions were recorded upon tape. I have used the transcripts of the tapes as a foundation for my regression accounts.

We have tried to check and crosscheck details we have written to ensure that as much as possible, what we have written is a true representation of what we have experienced.

Linda's Regression - Allanya

I can see land - long golden beaches with thick vegetation behind, and beyond those, low hills. The energy is amazing and it makes my whole being tingle. Everyone comes on deck to look and I see the other ships keeping pace with us. The wind blows my hair, and I can smell the sweetness of the land, so much fresher than the salty tang from the sea.

I leap over the side as our keel hits the sand, and splash through the shallow water. The vibrations tingle up my legs as soon as I touch it. They flow up and through me. My whole self is vibrating with this incredibly strong energy. Everyone is coming ashore. There is dancing, singing and shouting. All the people are so excited. I dance and skip around too. This energy is so amazing and I have never felt anything like it before. It makes me realise how depleted our old home felt. That seems so far away now.

Slowly I climb to the top of the beach. I am looking for my friends in the general throng. There as so many people, it is hard to make them out. Then I see Janya coming towards me, with Saranne and Salash close behind. Janya has a broad happy grin. They too are thrilled with this new place. We hug each other delightedly. Gradually, a semblance of order establishes itself, and the ten of us gather at the top of the beach, to give thanks for the safe journey, and the new land. We sit in a circle, join hands, and invoke the Earth spirit. Everyone is quiet and people have gathered near us, kneeling, silently joining us in prayer.

My name is Allanya and I am one of ten healers sent to help establish a settlement in the new land.

It is later and we have been here a year or so now. Our community is well established and thriving. More people have joined us and our numbers are growing. We have just completed our new temple and Sanctuary. It is built inland from the sea, a short way along a river. The temple itself is built on an Earth energy point. It is a large and continually expanding complex of buildings, courtyards, gardens and rooms for healing and prayer. Basically it is circular in design, with all the various buildings radiating out from a central open courtyard. To the east of this is the main structure, a large mound. This comprises of seven terraces, set in an artificial lake and is fed by a natural spring with water that has healing properties. The mound itself is on the main energy point, and central to our ceremonies. Many people have helped with this enormous project. The buildings are constructed of the local white stone which sparkles in the sunlight. It looks really beautiful. The seven levels of the mound correspond to the seven levels within the human auric body. On each level, are plants of the correct colour, to match the colours of the energy centres within us. The mound is hollow, with a circular chamber at the bottom. From this rises a vertical shaft, open to the sky at the top. This channels the Earth energy.

We live and work in the surrounding buildings. Outside the temple complex, a short distance away, is a large and thriving town. It is built alongside a river, and is between us and the sea. There is a very pleasant walkway through the forest that connects us to the community. The town is cared for by a `Council of Elders'. They have though, as time has progressed, become a little separate from us and feel that we are `different'.

Janya and I are partners now. We had our pairing ceremony shortly after we arrived. I suppose I always knew this would happen. For a long time I have liked him. He is strong, and I find great comfort and support in his strength. We also complement each other with our healing skills and energies, which are different, thus making a good balanced pair.

Sometimes, we go into the town to treat people who cannot come to us, the infirm and the immobile. Often, I am called to attend to women in childbirth. With this, I seem to have special skills, which I enjoy. Also I have a special talent for using my voice to stop bleeding. I create a vibration and harmonic that soothes and eventually will stimulate regeneration in damaged tissue. I have a healing sphere, an amethyst, which accelerates the vibrations and healing energies I use. All of us of the original ten were presented with these spheres in our old home, as an honour, and a symbol of our healing skills. They are all both rare and beautiful, pulsating with life and they are very precious. Each one is a different mineral. Janya's is a very strong banded obsidian. They are kept in a special room in the temple.

It is now the summer solstice and we are performing one of our major ceremonies. This is to honour and replenish the Earth energies that sustain us and our planet. We use the elemental `rods' which represent Earth, Fire, Air and Water. Four of us are chosen for this ritual. The two men carry Earth and Water. In this particular ceremony, I am working with my friend Saranne, and her partner Salash is working with Janya. We set off separately, from the four directions, and cross the water to the mound. This is representative of crossing from normal everyday consciousness to a more sacred inner world. There are four stairways up each side of the mound. Slowly we each climb upwards, bearing our elemental rod. When we reach the top, we hold them high and allow the ends to touch. We are standing around the top of the open shaft, which is about six feet across. The power then starts to `flow' and it is amazingly strong. It is difficult to remain standing. The energy flows upwards in a glorious fountain of light, which connects with the Earth's energy grid, feeding it and bringing us balance and light. We perform this ceremony four times a year on the Solstices and Equinoxes. Crowds of people come to watch and pray, and later there is much celebration, singing and dancing.

It is evening, some time afterwards. I am sitting in the main courtyard. Usually, this is a peaceful place and I enjoy coming here, but tonight I can hear raised and angry voices coming from one of the rooms nearby. I recognise Salash's voice, Saranne and Doran. Doran is one of the other healers, but I don't like him. He is shouting, but I can't make out what's being said. I have just returned to the temple as I have been in the town seeing a woman client of mine. Janya is also out, and I am expecting him back soon. The argument upsets me and I go back to our quarters, somewhat disturbed.

It is a little later. Janya has returned and Salash and Saranne have come in. They are angry. It seems that Doran wants to change our rituals and ceremonial practices to include some form of sacrifice. He says he feels the Earth energies here are so strong that they need new procedures and the strength of a blood ritual. Vehemently, we are all opposed to this, but Salash says there are a surprising number in agreement with him. This is a very disturbing development. We have been here about seven years and, up to now, things have gone really smoothly. Doran and his close friend Danash have always been rebels, going their own way to some degree, but this is awful. It frightens me.

It is some months later. I am going to prepare a room in one of the annexes to treat a woman needing help. It is a quiet place, just slightly off the main complex. For some time I haven't used this particular room. When I enter, I see a large wooden chest in the corner behind the door. I'm sure that's new - I don't like the `feel' I'm getting from it. By curiosity I am drawn to open it. It is not locked, only held shut by a loose clasp. Plucking up courage I lift the lid. Inside are numerous small canvas bags. I pick one up. It is squashy, full of a powder of some sort. Suddenly I realise with horror that someone has come in. Doran!

I throw the bag back and slam the lid. He looks angry. Closing the door behind him he comes towards me. I back away feeling really scared. The room is small and I can go no further than the far wall. I am trapped. He comes close to me. His eyes are so full of anger. Squirming I try to edge further away. He starts to undo my dress. He has a knife and he threatens me with it, holding it against me. Next, he touches my breasts - I feel shudders of revulsion - I can't stop him - I'm totally helpless. He orders me to lie down and he rapes me. The feelings flowing through me are horrible and out of control. I try to allow my mind to detach. This isn't happening. But my body reacts. I can't help it. He is violent and rough deliberately. He wants to hurt and humiliate me. At last it is over and he stands up. I feel sick - revolted, dirty. He has hidden the knife away in his robes. Glaring at me, he grabs my upper arms and his fingers dig into my flesh, hurting me. Threateningly, he tells me if I speak to anyone of this he will kill me. When he leaves the room relief floods over me. I start to cry, but realise with horror that I must not allow anyone to see me like that. It takes me a long time to calm down and when I have composed myself I leave. I am shaking and feel dirty inside. What can I do? I cannot tell Janya for he would immediately go to Doran and confront him. He would put himself in danger and likely get killed. I can't let that happen. Therefore, I must say nothing.

It is some months later. Life has settled down and I have tried to come to terms with what happened. It has, however, affected my intimate relationship with Janya. I'm sure he senses a difference in me. Sometimes I feel distinctly `cool' towards him. The memory of the hurt is still there and I feel as if Janya will `know' somehow. During the daytime I go about my normal duties, and whenever possible, avoid coming into contact with Doran. He still frightens me and he knows it. I feel he has `control' over me, in some way.

One day, I am late for my meal in the dining area. I am alone when Doran comes in. Looking down at my meal, I try to ignore him. However, he comes across anyway, takes hold of my chin and lifts my face, staring directly into my eyes. It is awful and I can't get away. He tells me I must attend a meeting of his new group at a house in the town tonight saying that if I do not, he will `let people know' how I betrayed Janya by being with him. I panic. What can I do? I can't allow that to happen - I will have to go. Somehow, I will need to keep in the background and involve myself as little as possible.

Going into the town as instructed I walk to this house, near the river. When I enter I am welcomed and shown into a large meeting room. I am surprised by the number of people there, about 20 or so. With shock, I realise there are several from the Sanctuary itself. Doran is leading this meeting with Danash and Ellya assisting him. It seems from what they are saying that some sacrificial rituals have already taken place. During the proceedings, a tray of drinks is passed around. We all have to take this, like a sacred thing. It is strange stuff, sweet and rather sticky, but very pleasant. It makes me feel very relaxed and much more at ease. Perhaps this isn't too bad after all. I'll go along with them, and stay in the background. Doran is saying that everyone present must attend the ritual in a few days time, including me. Suddenly I feel the need to get out, but I cannot. I can't leave now. I'm stuck and he would blackmail me. I don't like the idea of sacrifice, even an animal but he says it is a gift of blood to the Earth and that blood feeds the Earth. Even so, I'm not entirely happy. I'm going to have to go but I will shut my eyes and stay at the back.

It is the night of the ritual. I am walking through the forest with a large group of others. There are about 30 of us. It is all the ones from the meeting plus some other townspeople. Some are from the ruling council. The lady walking next to me is the wife of one of the elders and she is helping me. She knows it is my first time and that I am nervous. However, she seems nice and genuine. Inside I feel worried about killing a creature. The only way I feel I can escape is by shutting my eyes.

We have arrived at the place, which is a natural hollow about 50 feet across, deep in dense woodland. It is getting dark and there are torches around to give us light. Within the edge of the trees are some tents. In the middle of the hollow is an upright post. We all form a circle round the hollow and hold hands. The drink is passed around after a brief invocation. I'm growing to like this stuff because it makes me feel warm inside. It fizzes in my mouth, and I feel really relaxed and then it seems to `explode' in my head. My fears disappear and it is a marvellous feeling making me want to dance. I feel quite silly and light-headed. The colours in the forest have changed and things look different.

Oh my. I didn't expect this. They're bringing a man out from one of the tents. He's tied up and they secure him to the post. I realise that he is going to die, that it is a human sacrifice! I feel so strange, like there's two of me. One doesn't want to see this and says it's wrong, the other is saying it's all right, don't worry, it is right to do this. My mind seems jumbled - all mixed up. My lady friend senses my confusion, smiles and squeezes my hand to comfort me. Doran is standing in front of the victim. At his feet is a small altar with various knives on it. We dance around, chanting, with our hands joined. At a certain point, we each have to walk to the centre, take one of the small knives and cut the victim's skin, so he bleeds. As we circle, I can feel the build-up of energy.

It is my turn and I am uncertain, hesitant. I feel rising panic despite the relaxing drink. Picking up one of the small knives I quickly cut the top of his arm. His body is streaked with blood from all the previous cuts. His eyes are full of fear and pain. I sense it and return to the circle feeling upset and bewildered.

We stop, and Doran offers a prayer to the Earth to accept blood and strengthen our circle, to give us power, and the Earth replenishment. We are kneeling now, with our arms raised. Doran picks up the long ceremonial knife. I don't want to look but I can't look away. He drives it into the man's chest, and then cuts him open. It is gruesome and horrible and I react by feeling sick and dizzy. My friend holds me and I am shaking. She gives me a small biscuit, and tells me to eat it, that it will help. I swallow it - it is also pleasantly sweet. I feel the tension draining away as my body relaxes. My sickness disappears and I feel much better.

Getting back to our quarters quite late, I find that Janya is in bed. My head feels strange, I feel dizzy still and I can't seem to see things properly. He asks where I have been. I try to find a good explanation so I say I have been to the town. He knows I am lying, but I can't argue. I just say I don't feel well - I need to sleep.

It is some months later. There has been increasing unrest in the town. It seems they do not approve of the temple anymore. They are calling us `leeches' and saying we are a drain on the town's resources, that we do not contribute anything and take their food and services for free.

I am in my rooms. A messenger has arrived. He is breathless from running. Janya has been attacked in the street. He has been stabbed and is badly hurt. They need my skills to stop bleeding. I go as quickly as I can. He has been taken to a safe house. When I arrive I am shocked. He is ghostly pale and has lost consciousness. I am so afraid he will die. The wound is in his side, still bleeding and it looks quite nasty. Obviously, they intended to kill him. Because of my love for him I need to `detach' myself and concentrate. It is so difficult. I begin to `hum' the correct note frequency, and allow a sonic vibration to build up. This penetrates the tissues around the wound, allowing the bleeding to stop, and stimulating the injured flesh and skin to knit together. For some time, I work in a trance state, using my hands to direct the energy. Slowly, I notice a response. His colour improves slightly, and I sense his psychic energy returning. Soon, he opens his eyes and smiles at me. He is still very weak, but he grasps my hand and squeezes it. He is out of danger.

It is some time since the attack on Janya and he is fully recovered. He is not his usual self though, and is often away from home. I have asked him where he is going but he just avoids telling me. This bothers me a little, but I am more involved with Doran's group, so I don't push it too much. At least when he's away I am free to go with them. However I do feel very lonely at times.

Some time ago I had an almighty argument with my friend Saranne and we parted. Since then, I haven't seen her and she's obviously avoiding me. She didn't approve of what I was doing with the group but it is no business of hers. I will do what I want. Sometimes I sit and think and can feel very despondent, but I have the others now, and this takes a lot of my time. I can't remember things like I used to. I'm beginning to doubt Janya. Has he taken to someone else, another woman? He seems so cold sometimes - so distant. I wish things were like they used to be.

It is later. We are gathering for another ritual. I have been with the group about a year now, and tonight I am to perform the actual killing of the victim. This will be the first time for me and I am anxious to do a good job. We all have to take our turn at this to become full members of the group. The sacrifice tonight is a woman. Sometimes I still feel that strange `division' in my senses. Part of me is revolted by what I am doing, but I know the stronger part of me is happy with it. Even so, the feelings are disturbing. It's like I'm two different people.

Taking the drink I order the commencement of the ritual. This time I am standing in the centre, in front of the woman. She is tied to the post and looks terrified. I detach myself and concentrate on the immense build-up of energy as the others begin to dance and circulate. Here in the centre it is so powerful. One by one, they all come and cut her. The blood runs down into a pool at her feet. She is moaning and squirming. In my thoughts I hope she keeps still for me because I want to kill her cleanly. I need this to be good.

The moment of killing has arrived. I take the ritual knife in my hands, say the invocation, and, taking a deep breath, plunge the knife between her breasts, right up to the hilt. Her head falls forwards. She is dead. Blood pours out and runs down to feed the Earth. I feel a strange mixture of nausea and elation. Hastily, I eat one of the biscuits immediately this calms my rising fears. The others come and congratulate me - even Doran. I feel better with their approval - this is going to be all right

It is later. I have been involved with our group about 3 years now. I hardly ever see Janya for he seems to be always away. When I do see him he won't talk to me but he shouts, saying I've changed, that I'm not the same as I was. I don't like this but I don't argue. My head won't let me. Always I feel so muzzy and muddled as though I can't seem to be bothered. I still feel like two separate people, which is really odd. I don't tell him how lonely I am. Sometimes, when I am alone, I `sense' him. It's almost like he's there. I think this is because I miss him so much.

I am weary but elated and I am returning to my rooms. It's after midnight and we have just completed another ritual. Again I led and I feel really good about this. Tonight was my seventh time in charge. Now I don't get nervous, but I just enjoy the feeling of euphoria and power. Walking into my quarters I jump. Someone is there. Oh my. What a relief, its Janya. But he is so angry and he is shouting at me. He says he knows what I have been doing and he is ashamed of me. Janya claims he has been watching. How dare he? How dare he follow me? I yell back at him and he grabs my upper arms. He's hurting me! I struggle and he slaps my face! This shocks me. I am grabbed from behind and my arms are being held. It's Salash. I kick and wriggle but he's too strong for me and I can't get free. I am shouting and swearing at them. Then Janya forces a drink of bitter liquid into my mouth and makes me swallow it. I cough and splutter but can't avoid it. I feel my awareness slipping away. I am gradually becoming limp and my limbs feel heavy. Looking into Janya's face, he holds me to stop me falling and there are tears in his eyes as I lose consciousness.

The next thing, I feel myself waking in a strange bed in a strange house. The sun is shining through a small window. Slowly I become aware of Janya, sitting by my side, holding my hand. My head feels very odd. However, everything looks different, clearer, brighter. Blinking, I look around expecting it to change but it seems to be normal. I feel like I am waking up from a long sleep filled with horrific nightmares. I can still see vague and disturbing images in my mind. Some others come into the room, Saranne and Salash. It seems ages since I have seen them. It's lovely to see my friend Saranne again. She has brought some food for me. I realise I feel quite sickly and I don't seem to have much physical strength - I feel weak and ill. Janya explains what has been happening. I have been unconscious for three days. The antidote to the drugs has worked and my system is clear now. When he tells me what I've been doing I am absolutely horrified and feel so ashamed. Starting to cry hysterically he holds me, letting me release all the horror and fear. I feel so different. My mind is clearing all the time. Saranne has been nursing me and helping. She says she has forgiven me for the past and realises now that I was not acting as myself, but was under the influence of both the drugs and Doran. I feel so sorry for what I have done - so deeply sorry.

Over the next few days or so, I gradually recover my strength and vigour. I feel so much better. We are in a safe house in the town. Sadly it seems that the temple is no longer safe for us for Doran's group have taken over. They are desecrating our beautiful home. How did all our dreams go so wrong? We had such high ideals and hopes when we left our old home but we have gained nothing in our new society. It was so exciting when we arrived all those years ago. Whatever happened to us?

Salash and Janya have gone away again. I wish they would explain this. But somehow - now, I trust them. I am with Saranne, in yet another place. We need to keep hidden most of the time. It simply isn't safe anywhere for us and it is so difficult. There are a few townspeople we can trust, but they are dwindling in number. Soon, I fear we will have no one.

Saranne has gone out to get food, and I am alone. By some impulse I decide to go to the temple to my old rooms. There are some small personal things still there that I would like to have. I realise it is a risk, but I know the area well and if I go at dusk and keep to the shadows, I should be all right.
It is later. I am in my rooms, getting the things out that I want, from a small cupboard. All is quiet and I haven't seen anyone. Suddenly, the door bursts open and some men come in. Before I can run they grab me and hit me on the head. I feel so scared but I can't stop them. I feel myself falling...

Slowly I am waking up becoming aware that I am tied and gagged, not able to move. Feeling shocked, I realise I am lying on my back, naked. I seem to be in a tent of some sort. It dawns on me with sudden and horrifying clarity that I am in the forest near the ceremonial hollow. This must mean that I am to be sacrificed. Oh no. Briefly, I wriggle but it is impossible to move for the ropes are so tight they hurt. Feeling frightened, I know there is nothing I can do. This is Doran's doing, getting his revenge for me leaving the group.

It is some time later and I hear voices. Doran comes in with Danash and two others. They stand and stare at me. Doran says I must be punished for betraying them. He himself will be performing the ceremony, and he will make sure I suffer. I cannot help myself from shivering and reacting violently. He is enjoying my fear.

They come across and start touching my body. They are making disgusting remarks and laughing and I feel so helpless. One of them starts to untie my legs - they are going to rape me. As soon as my legs are free I start to kick and fight. This surprises them and makes them angry. Doran slips round behind me. I can't see him. What's he doing? He slips a rope around my neck and pulls it tight so I can't breathe. As I choke and cough. He holds me down. I can't fight anymore. One of them is holding my legs. I can't resist. They are hurting me deliberately and enjoying it. One by one they rape me. I try not to feel anything. My body reacts but my mind is denying it. Waves of revulsion and intense feelings flow through me. This isn't happening! I won't feel it! Doran is last and he makes remarks about the last time he did this. Once more, he is deliberately rough and violent. I can feel the pain and I try not to show it, but he knows he is hurting me and he is enjoying my fear. He feeds on it. Eventually, they have finished. They tie my legs again, and leave. When they have gone I allow myself to cry. Tears roll down my face as I think of Janya, my life, and what has happened. Soon, I will be dead and Janya will never know what happened to me.

It is later and it is completely dark. Some of the men carry me to the edge of the hollow and put me down near the post. I am so scared. They are all gathering to see me die. The circle is forming and they are making the final preparations. I can hear Doran's voice. He is looking forward to this.

Then, I hear other sounds, shouting and general commotion. Everyone is running - I can't see what's happening. Then I hear Janya's voice, and Salash. They are here, fighting with the group. I can hear the clash of weapons. Twisting round I try to see. Oh. Janya is fighting with Doran. He will get hurt for he is not a fighter. They move closer and I see Janya lunge at Doran. He wounds him and Doran falls near my feet. Janya steps towards me, when Doran rolls over unexpectedly, and stabs me as I lie there. I cry out for it hurts! Doran has stabbed me in my left side. Janya goes to him and kills him with a blow to the chest. Then, coming to me, he unties the ropes, wraps me in blanket and holds me in his arms. I am shaking and trembling. Tears flood down. I don't want to let go - it feels so good to have his arms around me. I feel safe. He says we cannot wait - we need to escape quickly. Salash comes over looking pale and a little shaky too. They both help me to stand up. My wound is not serious, mainly just a cut. The small group of Janya's people are outnumbered by Doran's followers, and this feels dangerous. We make our way through the forest. However, our progress is slow as I need to keep resting - I am weak from shock and fear. Eventually, we make our way to a safe place where we can recover.

It is some time later. We are climbing over a high mountain ridge having been travelling now for some days. Janya and Salash are guiding us. They are taking us to a place on the far side of the mountains, where we can settle and live in peace, following the old ways and respecting the Earth. They found this place during their earlier travels. That was what they were doing when they went away together. There are high, snow capped peaks all around us. The land here is just grey rock with a few sparse plants. We have left the trees well below us now and it is cold up here. I have never been this high before. The air is thin and I am rapidly growing tired. We are crossing a narrow ridge which is rough and stony. The loose rock is unsettling me and Janya says this is the most difficult bit. Once we are over it we start to descend into the valley. The men have gone ahead of Saranne and me. They've got longer legs. I am having difficulty keeping my balance and we are helping each other, holding hands on the more scary sections.

Suddenly the mountain seems to move. The rocks are moving and I am slipping. Desperately, I try to find solid ground but my feet are slithering around on loose rock. Loosing my hold on Saranne, I fall, rolling downwards in a shower of rocks, dust and debris. There is noise all around me. Eventually, everything stops and there is an eerie silence. I become aware that I am jammed tightly between huge chunks of rock and boulders. Everything hurts and my head is in a muddle. Where am I? Where are all the others? Did we all fall? Where is Janya? I can't see him. Listening in the deathly silence I `know' that he is dead - I can't `sense' him or the others. We all fell. They are dead and I want to die too. Calling out, I know he won't answer so I start to cry - knowing I am dying that I am badly injured - I ask that it will be quick - I want to join him.

After some time the pain eases and I leave my body. I look down and see my body crumpled and buried under huge boulders - I am dead. There is no sign of the others. They must have fallen further down. Feeling lost and uncertain, slowly I become aware of a bright light. It is so lovely! There is a figure there, beckoning me and holding a helping hand to me. She is so beautiful, filled with light. Gently she takes my hand and smiles. Then I see Janya smiling too, with Salash and Saranne. All of us hug each other delightedly.

Eventually, we are taken to a beautiful garden, where we sit down and discuss that life we have just left. Now I realise that we have all been together before, in fact, many times, and there are lessons to be learnt. This time my guide tells me I did not do too well. My chosen challenges were not met and I failed as a character many times. Opportunities were given, but I chose not to take them. I should have communicated with Janya about Doran. I 'see' it all now. What a fool I have been. Our guides are kind and reassure us and now, we need to rest and recover evaluate what has gone, and plan our future progress.

Paul's Experience as Janya

Janya was a very passionate, determined and idealistic character. As Janya, I grew up with a deep respect for the traditions and organisation of society within the land of my birth. Lemuria was a vast land with an extensive and advanced civilisation.

In my youth, I was taken from my family to learn healing. This was quite normal in those times for someone who showed ability in that direction. My parents were simple people, my father being a craftsman, and they were happy for me to learn to serve in the manner, which I could.

I trained within a Temple complex which could accommodate hundreds of people. Healers were predominant in the society of that time, and there were many roles which they had to fulfil. They were `sensitive' people who could attune to and work with subtle energies, including the energies of the Earth. The healers then, were responsible for the placement of buildings, for the harmony and overall peacefulness of cities and towns and also the physical well being of people. In addition, people looked to the healers for Spiritual guidance and help in that way. So, there were many skills to learn. Some of those elders within the Temple were concerned with administration, not just of the Temple, but of the society itself.

The situation though in Lemuria was deteriorating. There was much physical instability and Earth movements. The vitality was going out of the land and the energies of the land were shifting. This meant that many healers were engaged in rescue work, helping people and places in distress. Lemuria was not going to survive much longer, and migrations of people were pouring out from the land to other places.

The `new land' that we call Atlantis had been known about for some time. But now it was considered ready for settlement. Seers from the Temple predicted that it would be the centre of a major new civilisation. So the prospect of going there was very exciting.

I was one of a group of ten people - five men and five women, selected to lead an expedition to the new land to start a settlement. We were selected for our complimentary skills, aptitudes and characters, and because we were young. There was not such a long period of time where we were working together before we were actually preparing for our journey.

The intention was for us to help lead and establish a settlement in the new land that would be based securely upon the principles and fabric of society, as it had been lived in Lemuria. For me, I did not mind where I lived, as long as I could dedicate my life to healing.

Each of us within our group had been given a stone. Mine was a black obsidian communicator stone. These stones each had energy properties to help us. My stone was very precious to me. With it, I could `see' visions of faraway places and people; I could impart and receive thoughts connected with people and I could even use my stone to help with mind healing. When people were distressed my stone could help me tune in to the person's thoughts and feelings that were causing problems. When I channelled healing, I could make the person become very relaxed and receptive. Then, with my stone, I could transfer thoughts to that person's mind to help them. It was a great gift. I had even had a vision of our new home in Atlantis. It appeared to be very beautiful, and vibrant.

Being a healer at that time really meant to dedicate one's life in service of others. Normally healers would not have children, although they could choose a partner with whom they worked. It was not an austere life however and healers were still able to enjoy many of life's pleasures.

The problem though, arriving in Atlantis, was that the feeling of pleasure and power was just too strong. Coming from Lemuria, people were not adjusted to it. As Janya, I could feel the energy buzzing through my body, making me feel very alive and exuberant. The effect of it was to make me want to do things, with the feeling that I had the freedom to do almost anything I liked. Everyone felt this energy and it made the place seem very exciting.

But then, people got carried away with the feeling of doing what they liked. The obligations towards keeping up the practices and ways of the `old land' felt rather restrictive and unnecessary. So this was the beginning of the struggle that developed.

The temple buildings for the healers were constructed and set up upon an energy power point, some distance from the town. At first this was fine, because people were happy to continue the traditional healing practices from their former home. However, later on, the distance created a separation. People felt so empowered and vitalised by the energies of Atlantis that the need for healers was less obvious.

Among the group of ten, there were disagreements almost from the start. Doran and Danash wanted to establish new practices and structures suitable for the `new' land. They felt no reason to adhere to the ways of the past. Soon they set up a base for themselves within the town and created alliances for their plans there. The unity of the ten was broken.

With Allanya, we became partners and were very happy together. I was the more dominant one, strong and protective while Allanya was more passive and dependent, but deeply aware of the beauty and feelings of her life. I believe that at this time, I was at the very centre of Allayna's life, whereas for me, although I loved Allanya very much, what was more important to me was the ideal of creating a happy and peaceful society.

I feel that when Allanya was raped by Doran, this had a very damaging effect upon her relationship with me. She could not acknowledge what had happened to her and therefore the whole central aspect of her life was greatly disturbed. Because of this, she became very fragile and vulnerable, lacking in strength and direction.
For me, as Janya, the distance between us that this created, was just one more instance of disturbing developments that were making me feel very frustrated and isolated.

Within the town a council of elders was established. This had nothing to do with the healers in the Temple and as such was a totally different organisation to how society had functioned in Lemuria. The members of the council more or less nominated themselves and Doran, of course, made sure that he was prominent amongst them.

At one point, I went to this council to argue and raise my objections. I could tell that many of these councillors were using this organisation as a power base to exploit others. Some of them were becoming very acquisitive, using large tracts of land for their buildings, and hiring workers to do their bidding, treating them like little more than slaves. People were being forced to go along with decisions from this council, whether they liked them or not. Fear was growing in the community. Power structures were creating an underclass of people. Yet many people were not noticing how much things were changing. People were pleasantly concerned with their own interests, and felt that it was OK for others to do the same.

I argued that this council was destroying the power of the Temple. The society would not be Spiritually based, but operating from vested interests and greed. They were not interested in my arguments. I was shouting vehemently at them but they were very angry with me as well. They told me that people needed to do what the council decreed, and that meant the healers as well. If we did not respect the council's wishes, then we would be made outcasts in the town and unwelcome.

I remember from this meeting a glance of pure hatred between Doran and me and felt betrayed by him.

It was soon after this that I was attacked in the streets of the town. It felt it like a revenge attack for my audacity in speaking out against the council. They did not want to tolerate any interference.
It was Danash who organised the attack against me. I tried to use a psychic shield to protect myself but he could break that down. From being part of a jeering mob, Danash came and intentionally slashed me in my side with a knife. I am not sure if he intended to kill or wound. However, I only just managed to reach safety, barricading myself within a friendly house, needing their help, before they could do more damage and probably kill me.

As the disturbances grew, I made a very close link with Salash. We had always been friends, but now it seemed that we only had each other to depend upon and trust. Allanya seemed to have been seduced by Doran and his group in the town. Salash's partner, Saranne, had also been very much affected by the disturbances and she had become very withdrawn and introspective. Salash and I felt a great deal of despair. We had long discussions to try and decide what we could do about the situation.

It was about this time that we started to use our stones to help us. Salash had a blue stone that could sense energies and atmospheres. His stone and mine combined very well to help us gather information. We started to trace Allayna and other people within the community to try and learn what was going on. There was much secrecy and fear. But also we needed to find people whom we could trust.

Some of the healers who had come in subsequent journeys after our initial settlement felt sympathetic to our viewpoint. We tried to talk with them and create a network of support. I no longer had any faith in the group of ten healers with whom we had come to the new land.

We needed links with others with whom we could combine our energies more positively. At this stage, we wanted to somehow find a way to gather sufficient support so that we could reform the society of our settlement and restore it to the Spiritual values that were intended for it. Our ability to do this felt very limited. However, Salash and I were refusing to be defeated.

We also decided to travel to learn about how other settlements had coped with the energies of the new land. Perhaps we could learn some lessons by how they managed. Salash and I travelled on long journeys. Mostly we just went together, but sometimes we took one or two of our new companions with us. Gradually we were succeeding in creating a support group. Usually, we used our stones to monitor where would be the most promising places to go. As well as finding other settlements, we were also interested in discovering Earth energy power points, and learning generally about the geography of the land. We wanted to pass on this information to our group. Often, it felt like a relief to be away from the town and settlement where we lived.

One of the settlements where we visited was colonised by people from a more southern part of our former land, Lemuria. In this settlement, the healers had not come in such a predominant position. They had placed their temple in the middle of the town, and we noticed how the healers were much better integrated within their society. There were still some power accumulations by some of the individuals there, but it seemed a much happier place to be than our own settlement.

Using our stones, we did learn of Doran's rituals and Allanya's participation in them. However, because I found communication with her so difficult, and she resisted my challenges, I just felt for a long time, that I needed to let her go. This made me feel very sad.

However, Salash and I did feel prompted one day, to follow her and see the ritual with our own eyes. Unfortunately, this coincided with one of the occasions when Allanya was making the kill. This shocked me tremendously. We had remained half hidden in the forest nearby, wearing dark clothing to disguise us. Salash had to lead me away to comfort me. He was very sensitive to my feelings, and without him there, I don't know what I would have done.

We were puzzled by the drink that they shared, and eventually we managed to trace this as a drug. Tuning into Allanya's inner mind had become very difficult, and now we knew why. Once when I was trying to concentrate upon this, a vision of the chest n the Temple room came into my mind. Salash and I went there and found the powder. We took some so that one of our healer friends could analyse it for us.

Very often, we were occupied arranging meetings, safe houses, gathering friends and supporters together. We had to be increasingly secretive because there were street patrols with men who were attached to the council. People who opposed the wishes of the council were often savagely beaten. Some disappeared. It was hard for us to see this happening.

My thoughts were turning more and more to the idea we may need to start another settlement somewhere else.

We tried to plan the timing of our interception of Allanya carefully. We knew that once Allanya stopped coming to the meetings, it would create danger, both for her and for us, and even for others in the movement. We had to be prepared. Doran would not tolerate any form of defection from his group. On a personal level, I felt I would need a lot of courage to cope with being so intimately close to Allanya again, after all that had happened.

In this event, all worked out well and we were able to carry Allanya to a safe house where we could be with her. While she was unconscious I spoke to her mind with the assistance of my stone, helping her to be aware of what was happening, offering her reassurance and support.

On one occasion, Salash was attacked while he tried to defend Saranne. She must have done something to offend Doran. It was only with Allanya's help that we were able to save his life. Then, as we were embarking on one of our journeys, some time later, I felt like a psychic distress vibration, and Salash and I were able to tune in quickly that Allanya had been taken captive. At first, I was inclined to panic and want to go to her at once. Now that I had Allanya back, I did not want to lose her again. But Salash was steadier than me. We got some of our friends to help us.

For both Salash and I, the attack to rescue Allanya was very painful and difficult. We believed in non-violence and had never used knives before. We did not like to have them, but we felt we must. Then, both of us were involved in killing. I killed Doran and Salash killed Danash. We both regretted this and were very shaken by it. Furthermore two of our close companions also died in the fighting. Afterwards we felt we had no choice but to leave the area.

During our explorations, Salash and I discovered a beautiful stretch of land by a river and the sea on the other side of the mountains. We felt that this would be an ideal place for a new settlement. This is what we were planning. Now, because of the rescue of Allanya we had to hasten our plans.

There were eight of us leaving as an advance party to set up a base there. The rest of us would follow when this was accomplished. We set off in two groups of four, and I had my communicator stone to help co-ordinate our journey. One of the healers was staying in the town with the others until the time was right to come after us. The group of us who had met and planned this mission had become very close during those last months with our many meetings together. The need for trust and complete co-operation strengthened our links.

It was very sad then, when on the brink of making a new beginning, the four of us were killed on the mountain in the Earthquake that took place. I remember my guide then as a woman with long blond hair and an ornament over her third eye, holding me close after I passed over. It was a very frustrating life, but with some deep warm connections. At least, this time I managed to avoid the corruption, which many others did not.

Other Connections

Denise identified herself as Saranne in this lifetime. She had some regression experiences to Saranne before either Linda or I did ours. Denise found it to be a very painful lifetime to relive. For her, it was an experience of isolation and despair. She battled with the temptations to turn away from what she knew was right, but she kept this struggle very much within herself and found it very difficult to ask for support. She felt betrayed and did not know who she could trust.

Linda and I have sensed Lynne to be Salash. Lynne has not been through the complete regression as Salash, but she has had one experience where as Salash she was being given her wonderful blue sphere for the first time. She felt the energies through her body and knew that this sphere could bring clarity of mind and peace. It was a strong life for the four of us Linda, Denise, Lynne and myself, together. This was the first of many, many lives in Atlantis where the four of us were connected in one form or another.

Psychological Impact

As I mentioned at the beginning of this chapter, the regressions to this particular lifetime were difficult for Linda. The first time she accessed Allanya, she totally skipped over the events of the sacrifices, making it seem as though she had led a blameless life, albeit with a tragic ending. However, she could not feel settled with that.

Months later, flashes of the memories concerning the sacrifices began to impinge themselves on Linda's consciousness, disturbing her. She was very reluctant to acknowledge these memories, but she knew she must. There were strong feelings of unworthiness, which she did not want to admit. However, admitting unworthiness was a theme, which was to have echoes in many of Linda's Atlantean experiences. It was the kind of feeling she wanted to conceal from others. This had a resonance in Linda's present life where she sometimes felt very uncomfortable about sharing her feelings.

On a personal note, Linda felt foolish and `bad' that Allanya had let Janya down, as she perceived it, especially with Janya being so passionately idealistic in his faith. It was important for me to offer Linda reassurance that I did not reject her for this, that I still accepted her in spite of this past life.

For me, going through the experience of Janya did not make such a great personal impact. There have been other Atlantean lifetimes, which I feel have offered more inner growth potential. Janya was quite a steadfast character even though he faced great difficulties. His characteristic of persevering even when facing continuing frustrations forms a resonance with my present life and so affirming this quality, has been strengthening for me.

The different reactions and responses of our respective characters set a note for both Linda and I about how other experiences and memories of being in Atlantis would unfold for us and some of the ways in which we would be tested.

Chapter 12

The Giant Crystal War

Introduction

One evening, Linda was meditating in our group, when suddenly a mass of imagery flashed into her mind. She saw beams of energy cascading from clusters of giant crystals. These were crisscrossing through vast tracts of land in Atlantis, waves of tremendously destructive energy. She saw maps of Atlantis and the suggestion of a war, virtually destroying the whole southern half of the continent, wiping out its population - from this one so violent war. Then came visions of how this war came about with the perspective of its context in the history of Atlantis and how this event linked with the final destruction of Atlantis many thousands of years later.

Linda found herself seeing these beams of crystal energy as one who was there watching it. She realised she was alive then - living a life when this war took place.

Previous to this, we had been given no indication of this war. We knew from other regressions to later times, about the repair work going on to parts of the southern portion of the continent, that the population had seemed to shift from living in the southern section from the early time period to settling more in the central and northern sections in the middle to late periods. But we had never known why that happened. It came as rather a shock.

Linda told Denise and me about her mediation experience. Immediately, Denise started accessing imagery of her own past life experience at that time and I started having very uncomfortable feelings in my body.

What follows is an account of the regression experience to my past life at this time. This was recorded that next day after Linda's meditation experience. Also included is Linda's regression to her life then, and some commentary by Albani from a channelled session recorded some days afterward.

Paul's Regression - The Peace Negotiator

I am standing by the Temple, a magnificently built stone building. It is quite old, but it has been done up recently to serve a new purpose as a military headquarters. The land is very green around me. There are trees with grass terraces with a view stretching down across the valley and towns towards the sea.

I am a young man in my mid to late twenties. At the moment, my expression feels hard. I feel a grim determination, but also a fear. Mostly though, I feel immense frustration. The words I hear repeating themselves in my mind are that `I don't want to be involved in this fighting'.

I am remembering back to my childhood. My father was involved in a war then. He was the local military commander. Many people would come to our house. They would be making plans, plans for the fighting, plans for how they could out manoeuvre the enemy. I felt I never really had a childhood because there was always talk of this fighting. Meanwhile, I felt I was just shoved in a corner while they got on with their plans. I didn't want to be any part of it, and I still don't want to be part of it now.

My mother cared about me but she didn't have time for me. My father was preoccupied and didn't have time for me either. I remember them sitting on these wooden benches around the kitchen table, talking so earnestly and passionately about their plans and strategies. I think they expected me to join in with them. But I just felt neglected.

I have a sister and she was perhaps less involved than me, because she was helping with cooking and housework. I remember her helping my mother, stirring the large pot of broth on the stove. My father wanted me to be like him. I think he had ambitions for me to learn to be a military officer like him. He wanted me to witness what he was doing. But I didn't want to become involved and I felt all alone with this. I was there in the room where these discussions took place, only because I had to be.

My father is long dead. He died in the fighting at the end of that war. All those discussions were of no use to him. He just died. And for a while the fighting settled down. My mother and sister managed as best they could and I tried to help them. There was not much joy in the house. My mother seemed to idolise my father and I can't understand that.

But now there is more trouble. There seems to be a war brewing across the land. My mother is still alive and has a high standing in the community through the position of my father. But she hasn't changed. She wants to defend the borders of our community and valley, by fighting if necessary. I just do not agree.

There is a local government which controls the large area of our valley. We are surrounded by mountains and hills with the sea in front of us. Many people live here in towns and villages. Our area of land is rich in natural resources and Earth energies. I can see that people living further away would like to claim this land to be their own. But this seems to be the pattern throughout other communities too.

The military appear to be building up their might as an aggressive force. All the military units are showing how tough and superior they can be, just like they were playing a game with each other to find out who can win.

However, I know it is not very pleasant when people you love start to die. I have been arguing with the military officers inside the Temple. They want me to try to summon up civilian support for their armies. But this isn't my job. I work as a diplomat or peace-keeper, trying to bring groups of people together, finding common interests or values so communities can live in harmony together. I travel around quite long distances across this southern area of our land, trying to solve disputes, getting people to listen to each other. There are a team of us that work together. Recently though, it has become much more difficult. I am not sure that the people want peace anymore. I feel that I have reached the limits of what I can do.

There is a young woman who works with me. I am not formally `joined' with her, but she is someone who understands me very well. She also lost members of her family in the last war so we have a shared feeling about the suffering which war can bring. She is psychic and can tell when people are telling the truth or not. This can be very useful in our negotiations. As well as working closely with her, I feel a strong personal bond of trust with her. I am usually the more assertive one when it comes to negotiations. She prefers to stay more in the background, in a supportive role. Her presence is very gentle and we work well together.

I feel rather afraid about the possible use of the giant crystals in war. They have never really been used in this way on any large scale before, but the military forces are all aware of their potentially destructive capacity. I have noticed in the other communities too, that great efforts are being made by the various military forces to test these crystals as a possible weapon. I don't like it, and I hope they won't be used. Just sensing the power of these crystals I know they could be very deadly indeed.

I have heard the same story in many different military quarters. They each want to use the giant crystals to achieve a decisive military outcome - to impose a peace through their superiority - I just do not believe it.

In all this I feel rather helpless. A strong part of me wants to withdraw and the whole situation seems to be escalating out of control. Now I am with my friend. There are five or us together and we are making plans to leave. We are all colleagues and we feel collectively that there is nothing more we can do to help.

The war is getting much closer now. I know from these military commanders that the crystals will be used, and I see nothing but destruction from it.

I sense that it is going to be a terribly destructive conflict. We have gathered our things together - and we want basically to escape. We want to go over the hills and mountains, and try to find a new life for ourselves, somewhere further north.

Besides my friend there are three others with me - two men and a woman. They are all part of my team, and they are coming, largely at my suggestion. We are on the edge of a market place in one of the towns by the sea. We are going to have to be careful about which way we proceed. The fighting on a small scale seems to be going on in so many different places.

I have never been to the north. But we know there are settlements over the mountains. I just hope it may be more peaceful there, and that those people may accept us to join them.

Inside I feel some uneasiness that I am not staying to help. My mother wants me to stay. And I have not been able to face her and to tell her that I am leaving. I think it would make her very upset. But the thought of the war just brings a kind of rage inside of me, and this spurs me on.

We have gone high up in the mountains now. Looking back, we can just still see the corners of our valley. It looks far away. Even so,I am struck by the beauty of our land. I really love my homeland. Up here, it is much colder and the wind blows around us.

However, I am having second thoughts. I am wondering if I am being cowardly by wanting to go away from the situation at home. I keep talking about this with my friends and they have different opinions to me.

My friend wants to stay with me, whatever I decide. I think she loves me and she wants to stay with me whatever happens. The others are adamant though, that they want to go on. I know this is my last chance. If I go any further I will lose sight of my homeland and I know I will not go back.

I am deciding to turn around and my friend is coming with me. We have parted regretfully from our companions. I feel relieved to have decided this, but also a little anxious. My senses tell me that I am going to die.

Somehow, I have an ability to know things. I knew my father would die when he went out to war. I could sense a war was coming again, even before the military commanders started making their preparations.

When I have been working as a diplomat I could sense what was gong on in other people's minds. Therefore I could tell which people I would be able to counsel and which people I could not reach. When I tuned into people I often knew what I needed to communicate with them. This ability has helped me do my job well.

From the beginning I have sensed a strong foreboding about this war. Because of this I have been very reluctant to take my friend back into this valley with me. However, she is coming because she wants to come with me. It is her own choice. She senses my nervousness and anxiety. And at the moment I'm not even sure that we'll make it back. There is a horrible sense of dread inside that makes me feel very lonely.

I know the war has started. There is fighting already, although I do not think the crystals have been used yet. But I don't think it will be long.

We've stopped in a small clearing, at the top of the hills overlooking the valley. It is cold up here now that we've stopped walking, but I just don't feel that I want to go further. We can see everything from here.

I sense something awful is going to happen, and I can't stop it. I want to sit with my friend and pray because I feel there is little more we can do. And I feel very much afraid.

I am quite near my home on this ridge. There is a part of me that longs to see my mother again and I feel torn that maybe we should go on just to do that. But a stronger part of me refuses to go on. If I went down into the valley, I would be caught once again in the midst of the fighting. Where I am now feels as close as I want to come to it. I do not want to desert my home and I do not want to be involved in the fighting either. I feel I want to stay here now until the end.

I feel the crystals are being used. There is a shaking in the ground underneath me. I am feeling really frightened. Holding the hand of my companion, I sense that she is frightened too. We are huddling close together. I think there is something happening to the Earth and I cannot do anything. It feels that the Earth is beginning to move. I can tell that these energy beams are going all around me and I feel there is some destruction happening. It is more than I thought it would be. I am afraid for our land and I do not know what is going to happen. I feel so afraid. I don't want it to end this way. I've done such a lot to try and stop the war. And now it has come anyway. It is even destroying the land. I can't....I don't want to allow this. I feel so powerless and helpless. I feel there are pressures building up. I feel the land..It is...I just wish this fighting would stop...I see those beams of energy...the crystals...I know it is wrong...I know it's bad. I just feel something awful is happening. I don't want the land to be destroyed like this. I don't want this to happen. I just wish they'd stop. I wish they'd stop, before it is too late. I just really feel afraid.

There are beams of energy. I do not see them so easily. But I know they are going out. Some of them are coming from far away. And each one seems to rock the Earth inside. I feel the explosions. I see explosions. I feel the Earth underneath me is reacting. And it is building up. There are more explosions and I don't think it can last much longer before something more terrible happens.

I am crouched on the ground, sitting with my friend and she is holding my hand very tightly. I know she is afraid like me. And there is nothing we can do. It is too late to get away.

The shaking is happening beneath us. We cannot go quickly enough anymore and I know inside myself we could not escape. We've come here to die.

Now it is night time. It is getting more violent and there is rumbling from the mountain above us. We can feel the rumbling of the Earth. We are both absolutely terrified. We are terrified for our own lives and our land.......

I think...I think...I may have died.

It was very quick...I think a boulder came and crushed me. I feel there was an Earth movement and then I was gone.

I just feel bewildered...bewildered, and I never want to experience anything like that again.

I feel my friend is with me, and it's like we're still holding hands. We are still clutching each other in fear, even though we're dead.

I sense there are millions like us. Millions. I just sense a great portion of our vast land has just gone.

I sense that there has been some great catastrophe. I think that the land could not cope with the crystal war. I think the land reacted. I think the land rejected us and our people. The land moved. The land went through upheaval. And it feels like the land threw us off its back. The land did not want the people to be using the crystals like that. The crystals belong to the Earth, for peace, for energy, not for fighting. I feel the land did that because the land did not want people doing those things to it. And the people nearly all died.

My mother and sister are here. My father has come from higher up to meet us. There is just much confusion. Even our companions - they did not get away. They too died. They thought they would escape but they did not. I sense the presence of my guide, reassuring me, helping me to unlock my hand from that of my companion.

The energy around me is of a huge mass of bewildered, frightened people/souls, struggling to cope and come to terms with what has happened......

Coming out of this regression, I felt very shaky for several hours afterwards. It was a very unsettling, powerful experience and it left me very thoughtful.

Linda's Regression - Braddon

I am standing on an arched bridge of white stone over one of the city's canals. There is a small group of us, just relaxing and enjoying ourselves. This is one of our favourite gathering places. We are all final year students at the military academy, and are almost at the end of our training. It has been an intense but thoroughly enjoyable few years, and I have formed many close friendships. Although we are laughing and joking, and celebrating the end of our course, we are also sad, that we will soon be parting, for we know we will not see each other again. We are all from different areas of our vast continent and will be returning to our respective homes, taking with us the skills we have learnt, and many happy memories. I will return to my home in the east, and hopefully, with my newly acquired knowledge, will be given a reasonably senior post in a military establishment, for students qualifying from here are generally held in high esteem.

It is two years since I came home and I am now commanding officer of the forces in my area. I enjoy the feeling of responsibility that comes with this position and I am well respected for my judgement and fairness. Our country is surrounded by high mountains on three sides, and by the sea to the east. In the years since I left the academy, the political situation has changed dramatically, with a great deal of military instability and the possibility of war.

My main priority is to keep my land and the people safe from invasion. We are prosperous and many others envy our wealth. The area of highest risk is in the south-east, where the mountains become lower towards the sea and they are easier to cross. If attack comes, that is probably where it will be.

I am in charge of a force of men on our border, and we are being attacked. There are missiles flying towards us, small bolts of metal that explode on impact with a form of energy. Several men have fallen. I am scrambling over some rocks for cover when I am hit in my right shoulder. The pain is sudden and severe - I am aware of hands helping me as my knees buckle and I fall in agony. My arm and shoulder feel like they're on fire.

Our healers are looking at me with serious faces. The senior man tells me the explosive force has done severe damage to the nerves in my arm. They doubt whether they can save it, and, even if they do, they do not think I will retain full use of it. This is awful. I feel my heart sink. This will be the end of my active career - I'm so young. I will be invalided out to some non-active position.

The senior healer talks to me at great length. He tells me of a new technique they want to use to repair the damage. It involves using a tiny crystal and implanting it in my shoulder to `connect' the nerves. I agree to this - they give me a sedative drink and operate.

I recover well. The main healer involved, the one who actually did the operation, talks with me a lot during my convalescence. His name is Emilo, and we become close friends. He has saved both my arm and my career. I am so grateful for his marvellous skills. We talk of many things sometimes late into the night. He comes to see me when he has spare time.

One day he suggests that I should leave my military profession and train as a healer. I am quite bewildered by this. I have always felt a great drive towards leadership, and yet, something inside me stirred when he suggested that. However, I am happy with my position, and, now I am recovered and almost as fit as I was, I am in a good place to achieve a high command commission, which I would dearly love. Perhaps when I am older, I don't know? The feelings inside me are quite uncomfortable. Politely I decline and thank him for his insight. I feel very close to him and, when I finally leave his care, some months later, we vow to keep in touch. There is a depth about him I greatly like; I'll miss having him around.

It is later. I am standing by a bridge over rushing mountain river. There has been a fierce encounter with our enemies from the south, who wish to invade us. We have succeeded in repelling them for now, but I'm sure they'll be back. I never expected to return to the active side of soldiering but I needed to come and see for myself what the situation was like here. My shoulder still bothers me occasionally. I can't draw a sword properly, but most of the time I manage well. The healers did an excellent job on me.

Looking around the scene of the fighting, I see we have lost some good men, but they have too. There are bodies all around. This bridge is strategically important, for it is one of the few places where the river can be crossed safely, as it is both fast-flowing and runs through deep gorges and ravines. Suddenly, I realise that I recognise one of the enemy dead. It is an old friend of mine from the academy. This shocks me, for I simply did not expect this. I didn't see that we could become enemies. The situation has changed so much in recent years. Trying not to show I feel upset, I turn away and go back to my command tent. The whole incident disturbs me deeply, and I try to put it out of my mind concentrating on the many tasks in hand. I tell myself it is a natural consequence of a war situation - but it still bothers me more than I like.

I have been having discussions with my senior officers and we all agree that the people we are fighting appear to have superior weapons. They seem to be based on using crystal energy so we need to look at this. Our technicians say we can develop the same. There are many who say crystals should not be used for aggression. However, I do not go along with this view - it is superstitious nonsense. If this force is available to us we should use it. It is apparent that the only places where there are large enough crystals for what we need are the healing sanctuaries. That is where we shall go, and take them by force if required.

It is later. We are at one of the sanctuaries and we have had to force our way in here. There was surprising resistance to us and some have been killed. It is regrettable but necessary. I have followed behind my junior staff who have taken this place. Our technicians will deal with the crystals.

We need their power to defend our land and our people - surely they cannot disagree with that.

My men have rounded up all the occupants and they are being held in a frightened huddle in the main room. Some are shouting abuse at us. They are saying that if we use the crystals we will destroy ourselves - they are not weapons of war - they say the Earth will take revenge on us. These people are so ignorant. They actually believe all this rubbish. One man, tall and proud, says he is their leader. He is being difficult and inciting the others to rebel. We have to get rid of him. I decide to make him one `example' to the others and so I order two of my men to bring him forward. Telling him that I will kill him if he doesn't keep quiet and obey my orders, he refuses to listen and seems quite unperturbed by my threats, continuing shouting at us. Taking my sword, I thrust it through his chest and he dies without a sound and falls to the floor. The others are shocked into silence. Some of the women start crying. I order my men to take them all away, and remove the body. I bring in my people to work on the crystals.

More and more I feel disturbed at killing the healer. He was a good man and didn't deserve it. But I felt, somehow, that I needed to establish our authority. I don't like what I've done - after all the healers did for me - they saved my arm - he shouldn't have died. But I cannot tolerate resistance - I have friends who are healers, good friends. The more I think about it, the more I realise I shouldn't have done it. It's going round in my mind and I need to forget it.

It is later and I have more problems. My technicians can only produce a small amount of energy from the crystals. We need further power. They say there are those amongst the people here who are `tuned in' to the crystals and can get them to supply the energy we need, but they are refusing to co-operate. My other officers want to torture some of them to gain their help. They say if we torture some of them with the others watching, they will probably give in. Reluctantly, I order my officers to do this but I want no part of it. Although I have to sanction it, I can `remove', myself from the actual work, and turn a "blind eye".

It is many months later and I am attending a peace conference at one of the mountain sanctuaries. This has been organised by the diplomats and peace negotiators. I have no time for this and feel angry and frustrated at being involved. The outcome does not matter to me for I feel the situation has already gone too far to contemplate peaceful settlement. There are several military commanders present, under a truce banner. We are all enemies and I feel suspicious of them. There are five peace negotiators, two pairs of men and women, and one single man, he is from the north of our land, and seems to be in charge. The arguments they put forward are very strong, but I still favour military action. We need to protect ourselves. The northerner is very vociferous against the use of crystal energies and I feel intense dislike for him. He is altogether too persuasive. After hours of futile discussion I feel angry and confused, storming out of the room and needing air. I need to get away from those fools for a while. I feel like I'm going to explode I'm so angry.

One of the diplomats has run after me, and his female colleague is right behind him. I know them, for they are from my own town. I have some authority over them and I don't want him here with me. The fact that he makes so much sense upsets me. When he calls me a fool and an idiot, I turn in a rage and hit him across the face with my fist. As he falls, he looks shocked and hurt. Resisting the tremendous urge to draw my weapons, she stands between us. There are tears in her eyes but she says nothing. The look on her face makes me terribly ashamed. She helps him up and they walk away. As far as I am concerned the conference is over. It has been a waste of time. Nothing has been achieved. I travel back to my command post and prepare for war.

It is later. The fighting is not going well for us. Our borders have been breached, much territory lost and many people have died. I feel the only way now is to deal a blow to the enemy with the crystal energy we have at our command, and destroy them.

I feel angry and frustrated for none of my plans are working. We are getting nowhere. These people at the Sanctuaries are both unhelpful and intransigent. They persistently refuse to co-operate with us, even to save their own land. I can't understand their

BRADDON WITH THE HEALERS

Linda Pope.

attitude. Don't they realise that we are in danger? We have been invaded. Don't they see the enemy forces are gathering near? We need the energy they can supply via the crystals to defend ourselves and our population. I have told them that many innocent people could be killed. They don't seem to care. I have tried everything, negotiation, anger, ordering them to comply. I have even killed one or two of them for being deliberately obstinate and inciting the others. Nothing has worked.

Now I am at one of the sanctuaries, high in the mountains. I have left my men in charge of getting the information we need once more. I hope this works for I can't think of anything else. But deep inside I am disturbed. I have had to supervise this kind of activity a few times now, and it doesn't get any easier. I still feel a strange guilt at harming these people.

Mounting my horse, I ride slowly away from the sanctuary gates. I am almost reluctant to leave and I feel odd. Shrugging my shoulders, I try to pull myself together. Being the commanding officer, I shouldn't be so indecisive. We are returning to our main base in the town. It takes about a few hours, down rough mountain tracks and woodland. There are six of us. Riding slowly, as the way is steep, care needs to be taken. I stay back, behind the others, feeling a strange reluctance to join their animated conversation. Deep in my own thoughts, suddenly my ears catch a drift of the talking ahead of me. One of the men mentioned Emilo. Emilo was my close friend, the one who operated on me and saved my arm. Surely he couldn't be there. I haven't heard from him in ages. He was attached to the military, but I heard he had left. When I tried to trace him, he seemed to have completely disappeared. We got along so well, I missed him terribly when he went, feeling sure he would get in touch. But he never did. Now I realise with growing horror that he must be at the sanctuary we have just left, and I have ordered my men to torture the healers. My heart sinks and I feel sick inside. I need to go back. I must find him and save him if I can. Reaching a flat section of path, just before it plunges into a steep sided ravine, we stop to water and rest the horses. I make the excuse that I need to go back and check my orders are being carried out correctly telling the others to continue on, and that I will return later.

BRADDON - THE PEACE CONFERENCE.

LINDA POPE.

I will go back to `surprise' my men. They laugh and we part. As soon as they are out of sight I urge my horse back uphill as fast as he can go. However, it is difficult to make any kind of speed. Panicking inside, I feel a deep sense of fear and horror. Somehow I know that my friend is the one they are torturing.

After what seems like hours, I arrive at the sanctuary gates once more, breathless and sweating. Marching inside, I try not to be in too obvious a haste. The guards salute as I pass. Asking where they have the healers they are questioning, I am directed to a back area behind the main temple rooms. Quickly, I walk down a corridor, again trying to maintain a dignified gait, but my body wants me to run as fast as I can. My heart is racing and I am sweating with fear. In the distance, I can hear screams.

Going into the room, two of my men are there and I see the shape of a body on the floor behind them in the shadows. They both leap to attention and salute me. I tell them to go and take a break, while I `inspect' their work, and they leave. There is a deep silence. All I can hear is my heart pounding and my rapid breathing. Going across, I kneel beside him. He is almost unrecognisable. His face has been badly beaten, his body and limbs are covered in blood, and they have blinded him. There are two slivers of crystal imbedded in his eyes. I feel rising nausea and can't speak. I feel choked. He knows me; he `senses' me. I hold his hand and gently raise his body and hold him. He speaks quietly and calmly and asks me to do one thing for him. As his closest friend, he wants me to kill him.

I am horrified and hesitate. He grips my hand with surprising strength, and pleads with me. I speak with difficulty and say that I will. Swallowing hard, I draw my dagger, I hold the point against his blood soaked chest. I want to do this cleanly with one blow. My hand is shaking and I feel tears in my eyes. Taking a deep breath, I plunge the dagger into him and he dies instantly. Withdrawing the knife, I hold his body close, allowing myself to cry. His blood covers my uniform. Staying for a while, I then hear the men returning. Laying him down, I stand up briskly and cover my bloodstained clothing with my cloak. Walking out of the room, ignoring the two soldiers, I order a horse to be brought, and swiftly ride away down the track once more. My mind is in turmoil: I feel sick and shaky. I reach the place where I turned back. Here, a mountain stream runs through a series of pools before plunging into the ravine. Dismounting, I walk to the water's edge, sit on a stone and start to cry. Tears roll down as I feel deep sobs come from within me. I feel wretched, sick and revolted, swearing there will be no more killing of healers, not like this, not while I am in command. I am angry, upset and deeply ashamed. Looking at my clothes, covered in my friends blood, I undress, and soak them in the water. Then I get in the icy water myself and swim. It takes my breath away with its coldness, but it feels cleansing and refreshing, I want it to wash the hurt away from me. Eventually, I am so cold I have to get out, and I lay in the sun for a while to dry both myself and my clothes, continuing my return journey after that. On the way I begin to feel shivery and ill. I ride into the courtyard at our headquarters and dismount, my legs give way and I collapse. Vaguely, I am aware of being taken inside. After a few days or so I recover and return to my duties. It has been like a horrible nightmare.

It is some days later. I am in a large circular room, standing by a table strewn with papers and maps. This is where I work most of the time. I have been studying the layout of the crystal energy centres. Soon we will have to use them. There is a large cluster here, in one of the front rooms near the terrace. It is enormous, one of the biggest I have seen. The crystals are six-seven foot high, taller than me. Always, I feel quite uneasy near them. It's almost like they `sense' my presence, like they're angry with me. I find this strangely uncomfortable.

After much deliberation and advice, I have decided to use the crystal energy tonight. I have given orders to activate the main crystal link at sunset, and to direct a beam of energy at the enemy encampment, in the mountains, and destroy it. It is late - I know my orders were carried out and were successful. At last, now we can destroy anyone who comes against us, but again I feel vaguely uneasy.

It is the middle of the night and I cannot sleep. Something is happening. I feel scared - frightened. Getting up, I go to a small garden area, which is near my quarters. Having nothing on my feet, as I walk on to the soil, I feel vibrations running up through the soles of my feet and deep inside me. The Earth is angry. Suddenly, I feel very afraid. There is a strange `feel' to the air.....I don't know where everyone is.....I seem to be alone. There are flashes of light in the sky....It is not lightning. It is different......The fear is rising inside me - like a panic.....This is crystal energy. What have we done?......What have we started?....We have triggered a terrible destructive force.....The healers were right.....What fools we have been.

Running back inside, I pull on my boots and clothes, and go through to the main rooms. Still I haven't seen anyone....Where is everybody? The map room is empty. Suddenly, I become aware with utter horror that the giant crystal here is also reacting....It is making a terrible sound.....The sonics reverberate through my head....I feel a rising panic.....I am alone. The flashes in the sky are increasing now. Beams of brightly coloured light are lancing through the darkness.....I can hear explosions and people screaming - the screech from the crystal is almost unbearable...I am transfixed in the doorway, frozen....looking in absolute fear at the crystal cluster....They are pulsating with a glowing light....and the sound.....The deep throbbing is causing me intense pain in my head so I clasp my hands to my temples and try to shut it out. There is a flash of brilliant, blinding white light and I lose consciousness.

When I come round I can't move. I am pinned down across my chest with the door lintel which has fallen. It is deadly quiet and my body feels numb....I have severe pain in my chest and head and breathing is difficult. The silence is frightening....The world has died....Everything is dead.....I sense it......There is no life around me. The floor is slanting over and the crystal cluster has gone, shattered into thousands of pieces. There are just blackened, burnt out stumps left with millions of tiny bits, some embedded in my arms and face. I `know' that everyone has died....I feel desolate...so alone....Dreadful feelings of guilt rise within me.....I know I am dying.....I cannot survive these injuries.

Becoming aware that I cannot feel pain anymore, I seem to be floating away from my crushed body. I can see it now, lying beneath a heap of rubble and stones. My fear has gone - I feel such a wonderful peace....a peace I haven't felt in years....and love....such an overwhelming feeling of love....I am in a brilliant light, and a woman comes forward. Then I see the man I killed, the healer....He is smiling and reaches out to me....I feel great love from him... love and forgiveness....My mother and father and brother are there. My friend Emilo is here for me and he thanks me for what I did. This is all so overwhelming. I feel shaky and very weak. My lady takes me to a place of rest, and I feel great peace.

Denise and Lynne

Denise experienced herself as Emilo, the healer who attended to Braddon's shoulder when he had his operation with the small crystal implant. It was a very painful life for her, especially the way she was tortured by the soldiers in the sanctuary. In her regression, Denise felt very strongly, Emilo's friendship to Braddon. Perhaps more than anyone else, Emilo was aware of Braddon's dual nature - the sensitive, feeling side as well as the hard, ambitious, clinical military side. Emilo responded to the gentle, feeling side of Braddon and always helped and wished that he could help Braddon so that this side of him could become more ascendant.

Emilo was quite a solitary man, but very caring. When he knew that the military were taking over the sanctuaries, he could not stay within the military any longer. His life was devoted to healing, but those in the sanctuary were suspicious of him, because of his military connections. So this left him feeling very alone. When Braddon ordered the torturing of the healers, Emilo did not hate him for it. He just wished that Braddon had acted differently. In asking Braddon to kill him, Emilo was appealing to Braddon's friendship. The bond between them was very strong. Emilo offered Braddon his best chance of being able to turn his life around and live more compassionately. However, Braddon did not take up the chances offered to him.

For Denise, regressing to Emilo's life has been very tough. The torture he suffered has been felt intensely by Denise. Emilo lived a life true to himself and he was tested in his character. This experience links with other earlier lives where Denise's soul was caught up in conflicts between the military and the healers. In the earlier lives Denise's soul had tended to react with hate and bitterness to what the military were doing. This did not have such beneficial consequences. In Emilo's life though, he resisted this, and his last action was a reconciliation of friendship with Braddon. For Denise though, these lives have left a residue of fear around her inclination to do healing work. Processing these regressions is helping her to gain more confidence to pursue a healing path more actively in her present life, and to know that it is safe for her to do so.

I identified the soul of Lynne as my female companion with whom I worked and died in that life. During her regression to this life, Lynne felt a tremendous sadness in her heart and a fear. As a peacemaker working with me, she felt so hopeless that whatever we tried met with failure. She recalled us trying to help the healers in the sanctuaries to co-ordinate their response to the military, but they were used to acting independently. With the military she felt an acute mistrust. And then the end, where she was on the mountain with me, with the energy war raging around us, and the mountain collapsed on top of us - this was terrible.

Braddon and the Peacemaker in Review

For Linda, regressing to `Braddon' was again very difficult. Initially, she omitted sections of the life such as the torture of the healers. She had a great resistance to confronting that. Part of the reason she eventually did so was because of the impact that regressing to Emilo had upon Denise's life. As Denise emotionally informed Linda of a few details concerning her regression, this brought up very uncomfortable feelings for Linda. Because these feelings disturbed her so much, and she could not shift them from her mind, she had to go through the regression in order to clear this.

100

Braddon was a complex character, presented with a conflict between his aggressive, assertive side and the more compassionate caring aspects of his being. Ultimately, the more aggressive power seeking side was dominant and so, the soul of Braddon felt some responsibility for contributing to the war that destroyed so much of the land. This brought a lot of suffering to Linda, although there were obviously many thousands of other people involved too.

One of Linda's traits in her present life is that she is very afraid of people using power to hurt others, and she has a very strong wish not to hurt anyone herself. The roots of these fears and yearnings could be traced to this life as Braddon and many other lives that Linda lived on Atlantis where, faced with a choice between the use of power and violence or compassion, she chose the less caring option and caused a lot of hurt to others and herself.

For me, I am aware that in my lifetime from this period, I could also have taken a militaristic path, because both my parents were involved in the military and urging me to follow family tradition. However, I resisted this and instead reacted against the military and tried to find peaceful methods of avoiding conflicts.

The main residue left over for me connecting with my present life, is the fear of war and large scale disasters, a fear which I felt very acutely during my regression.

Albani's Commentary Relating to the Giant Crystal War

Paul: In terms of the history of Atlantis, could you please describe how the events leading up to the Giant Crystal War unfolded?

Albani: *Following the foundation lives and the initial settlement of the continent, the people migrated across the land, from both the north and south, for it was populated at both ends, into the interior. We are talking about a very large geographical area. And the continent was very rich in crystals. For it was very new and very alive with Earth energy and a very vibrant place. Eventually* the people began to find these crystals, and realise, because they were so sensitive, that these things had life, they had energy and this energy could be used. The energy was used for healing, for working with the Earth and for empowering the Earth's auric field. This is why it was there originally. But people learnt through various means that they could use this energy to help their fellow human beings and to help the areas where they lived, in various ways. But of course like all things, when power is involved, eventually someone will find out how to use it in a negative way, and against fellow human beings for various reasons of greed and the need to control others and to be in charge, or to be better than anyone else. This unfortunately has always been a trait and presumably always will be, in the physical.

Over a long period of time, and we're talking thousands of years, gradually, what you would probably describe as technology developed, and the ability to use these large crystals in different ways, and to tap into their massive energies.

There were around the whole area, from time to time, small skirmishes and disputes over territory. For some areas were better than others. Some were richer than others for various reasons, either from the fertility, the Earth energies, or even something like accessibility to the coast, for commerce and various other things. Most of these things are desirable and others would jealously look at what the people next to them had, and desire it. And if they felt stronger, they would go and take it.

Then, as these situations developed, the ones with the stronger weapons or the largest army were the ones who would usually win. So methods were devised to use the various energies as an aggressive force, as an offensive weapon - or to help the people to conquer others and to oppress their fellow man. This as I say happened over thousands of years. Eventually, they knew that they could control this crystal energy to destroy other people, buildings and the land.

But what they didn't realise is that this energy is given by the Earth. It is given with love. It is given to help others, and to help the Earth herself. And of course when you go against this, this *creates a lot of problems. And eventually this power becomes uncontrollable. For it is a very, very strong energy. And although the men and women using it thought they could control it, they were very wrong. And it was really much beyond their capabilities. And eventually, it went out of control. This is what happened in the time you have described.*

It was decided to use the crystal energy to destroy the enemy - as they saw - or the invading people. But as soon as one point was triggered and used, it set up a network throughout the southern half of the continent. And all the various points where the crystals were situated were activated. The Earth reacted with this and because the energies were so great, it caused a reaction deep within the core of the Earth. The only way the Earth could survive and look after herself was to move and break these channels apart. And that is what happened. For the energies triggered the movement of the Earth. Because these energies were very negative, they were actually painful to the Earth herself. And the only way to break it was to move and split the crystals apart, to stop the production of this energy which had been triggered by people.

Therefore there were earthquakes, the mountains were falling, the volcanoes were erupting. All the various things which you would associate with movement of the Earth happened. These in themselves killed a lot of people. But a lot were killed by the forces involved in this energy, the explosive forces which destroyed buildings and also destroyed the people.

For these energies also have a disruptive effect upon the human aura and if anyone comes into contact with a direct beam of this energy, of this magnitude, it will destroy them. And that of course did happen. Most of the population died of the Earth movements, and the various upheavals which took place, causing buildings to fall, and things like that. But it was very, very bad.

The Earth reacted below the central fault line of Atlantis, and that central fault moved in such a way to act a little like a safety valve. The northern part of the continent was virtually untouched. It felt tremors, and they were very aware of course, that something was going on. But the destruction was confined to the southern part, south of the major fault line. For that was where most of the energy was being used at that time. And the Earth decided to split lengthways and pull the mountains apart, thus breaking the link between all the various beds of crystal that were being used at that time. The effects of a lot of this energy caused a change in the constituents of the atmosphere. It made the vegetation die, and it killed a lot of the animals also. It made the atmosphere poisonous for a short while around that area. Eventually, this came back to normal. And the Earth healed all the various problems that were there. It healed the wounds and sealed all the various cracks that had appeared. And the volcanoes settled down. The mountains settled into a new formation. And the land settled into a slightly different shape. Eventually it was colonised again by the birds, the vegetation and the animals, and people.

Paul: How did the Crystal war get started?
Albani: *It was mainly due to the civilian politicians' side of things rather than the military necessarily. The military simply went along with the various factions involved. It was as you can appreciate quite complicated for there were many, many groups of people involved who were all basically antagonistic to each other. Each was jockeying for position. There were many ambitious and greedy politicians who wished to be in charge of their section, or probably in charge of someone else's section as well. And therefore they were willing to use any kind of force to get their way. This involved using their own military forces which they had at their command and their bidding. Within the military you also had ambitious people so you had a catalyst here. You had a large melting pot of people who were all wanting the same thing, and all quite serious in their ambitions. They would stop at nothing to get what they wanted. And it is difficult to pinpoint one place where it started. It was almost simultaneous - for here was almost a strange connection. For by now the Earth knew what was happening. It was throughout the southern part of the continent that these crystals had been taken over. They had been contacted by the various military minds and the various people who wanted to use them for the ulterior purposes and for attack and defence. They used defence of course, as a good excuse, for really what they wanted was an offensive weapon, so they could wipe out their enemy.*

Remember crystal is alive, and crystal has a memory and a living heart, and therefore knows what is going on around it. It knew that in many places upon the surface of the Earth these things were being done and planned. Also, by then the Earth, within the main power centres, had realised that this was a very dangerous situation. Basically as these places were taken over, it was resolved deep within to allow this reaction to take place to some degree. And when it got very imminent, the whole lot would be triggered together. So in some ways the Earth almost triggered herself to do this. For it was realised that if one person started this on his own, there would be a severe imbalance of the energies and it was far safer for the Earth herself, and not the people on the Earth, to trigger this effect simultaneously, and simply pull things apart.

Paul: So you feel the Earth influenced people's minds into triggering this all together?
Albani: *Yes exactly. This is why it happened so simultaneously, for that would not happen under normal circumstances. Each person would probably think about it at a slightly different time. So the general feeling was put that this was the right time to do it. And all did it together.*

That was what the Earth wanted, to rid itself of this problem that was bubbling up among the human population.

Paul: Can you say something about the peace negotiators?
Albani: *There were many thousands of people wanting to help. This was happening across the land and these people were trying to develop a peaceful settlement. For the negotiators and peacemakers were very sensitive people and they could sense the agitation within the Earth itself, and they knew, I'm sure, that this impending disaster was coming. They were trying desperately to veer the military minds and the political minds away from the course of aggression. But of course this did not happen.*

Paul: What happened after the war?
Albani: *The southern part of Atlantis, throughout the rest of its history, became less populated. For people remembered. There was a memory of this dreadful thing that had happened. And people were somewhat afraid to go to the south. People travelled there,*

and quite a few migrated there to live. For it was still very beautiful once it had recovered. But there was a lot of repair work to do. There was a lot of work done by the people who had caused these problems, as they came back in future lives to repair and balance the damage and the energy lines of the Earth. For the energy lines of the Earth were severely disrupted, and needed reforming. And although the Earth can do this to some degree, some help from people does make it a little better. And because humans were helping with this, helping to establish the love link between the human and the Earth, this also was very important, for them to show that they really cared about the Earth, to help repair and put back a lot of the damage that had been caused by them. Most of the people working in this were the people involved in the destruction.

Paul: How did this particular destruction link in with the final destruction?

Albani: *It was very similar. All the people who were killed in this energy war were the people who had the knowledge to use these large crystals, and to use them for destructive purposes. They all died. Of course they were reborn. But they were reborn with the memories suppressed and the knowledge not accessible. So the knowledge of how to do these things was lost for a long time. And then eventually the knowledge began to resurface. And the same things began to happen, for people essentially do not change. And jealousies and wars started. The large crystal energies were once again found and tapped into and this time the whole continent was destroyed. For they got no second chance with it.*

There are places on the Earth now which contain large crystal beds. Most of them are completely unknown. But in Atlantis there were a lot. It was a very alive and vibrant place as I have said. And the crystal energies were there for people to use.

The healing sanctuaries remained virtually untouched, particularly in the north, where there were quite a lot. These were allowed to remain because they helped and healed people. They had a good purpose. A lot were very inaccessible and difficult to get to. This was deliberate.

And the crystals used were much, much smaller than the ones that were used in the destruction of the land. They were very, very big and very powerful

But as I say, these skills were learnt again. And they were learnt in a way that could be used with smaller type crystals. And eventually the Earth broke the continent apart and destroyed it with the waves.

Paul: When did the Crystal war take place in the overall scheme of things?
Albani: *I actually gave Linda the date of 17500 BC which is roughly halfway along the existence of the continent itself.*

It took 1500 - 2000 years to recover. It takes a long time for nature to recover, but it does happen, and it becomes just as rich and lush as it was originally.

Chapter 13
The Golden Age

Following on from the crystal war, civilisation upon Atlantis was traumatised. I'm sure it took some considerable time for the population to recover. Meanwhile, there was also a strong reaction against war and fighting. From this unfolded an inspiring and beautiful era of relative peace, where all that was most good potentially upon Atlantis, flourished. I have called this time period within the history of Atlantis, the Golden Age. Linda and I have explored a number of regressions to different lives within this period. They have tended to be very positive lives where much was achieved. We have chosen Linda's regression to her lifetime as Elayna as one to include in the book, as a lifetime that could most encompass the mood and activity of what life was like in this golden age. It was a life where Linda's soul and my soul were closely associated. So, I have also included some aspects of my experience as Elayna's partner Jon to complement what Linda has related. At the end of the chapter is a commentary by Albani to help place the Golden Age within the overall context of the history of Atlantis.

Linda's Regression - Elayna

I am in a dense forest, which feels so beautiful. There are huge brightly coloured flowers, tall trees and rich vegetation and also lots of birds. In particular, I like the blue and yellow ones with long red tail feathers. I love coming here. This area has tremendous life and energy and I can feel it all around me. Along the forest floor, I can see "paths of light", glowing lines of energy that seem to criss-cross the Earth's surface. They make my feet tingle as I dance and skip along them.

Although I am always happy to be here, today is tinged with sadness, for I am saying good-bye to my `friends', the trees and birds. I have to go away to university to study, which I want to do.

This requires me to travel to the city of Thrumbis, many miles north of us.

I live with my parents in a small town. My father is a teacher here and is well respected. I am very fond of him. He has taught me well, and I am planning to become an architect. I want to study the structure and design of buildings in relation to the Earth energies that I feel so strongly. This is very important to the happiness of a building and the people who will use it.

Our little town is built around a very strong Earth energy point. It is situated where there is a natural spring in the middle of the square. This is now a fountain, and is the central place within our community. The buildings here are of a white clay-like construction with flat roofs. Many have gardens on the top, and there are bright coloured flowering plants cascading down the walls. It is a lovely place and I will miss it. I hope the city people are friendly. I don't know much about it and have only heard rumours and so I feel both apprehensive and excited.

It is later. Now I am at the university and have been studying some time, enjoying my work and life very much. I really like the city, which is huge and it's people. When I first arrived, and looked at it from the southern hills, I couldn't believe anywhere could be that big. Now it is familiar and I know it well. The city is in two distinct halves, separated by a wide river that flows east into the sea. The city is well laid out with many lovely squares and gardens, there are busy harbours and a large commercial area. There is an Earth temple, and a large Healing temple. Thrumbis is one of the main centres hereabouts, and much good work is done there. The buildings are mainly of white smooth stone, with bright decorations of coloured tiles. Some have pictures painted on the walls themselves. The roofs are nearly all terra-cotta tiles, which adds to the bright mix of colours.

The university is a large complex of different buildings, roughly in the centre. It runs alongside the river and has many secluded courtyards and gardens that go down to the water's edge. Within one of the buildings is a large and comprehensive library with a large number of books and manuscripts, some of which are very

ELAYNA AND JON — THE CITY OF THRUMBIS

Linda Pope.

old. These are usually leather bound and very heavy. There are maps and atlases, some so ancient they are on skins attached to scrolls of wood. We have to take great care handling them, as they are very fragile. They tell of our ancestors, from thousands of years ago, and how they crossed the ocean from another land. I like to take books out into the library garden and sit by the river. The garden overlooks the northern part of the town and it is a tranquil spot. Above the houses and rooftops, is a low range of tree covered hills, and on top of the highest point, clearly visible from the garden, is an ancient Earth temple. When I have time from my studies, I like to climb up through the woodland, and visit this amazing place. It is quite a steep climb. The ruins themselves are clear of the trees, on an outcrop of crumbly rock. It is quite a scramble to get to the top. The old walls are broken and in places completely gone, but on some of them old paintings and frescos can be seen, on crumbling plaster. The main structure is circular and the floor still has much of the beautiful mosaic pattern of a star, in the centre of which is a tall, black stone. When I first came here I touched the stone instinctively and received quite an energy shock. It hurt my arm and I realised that although neglected for many years, this place still had tremendous power. Now, I have been here many times, and the stone and I are `tuned in' to each other, and I can meditate here in perfect tranquillity. When I do, I can `see' the lines of Earth energy, reaching out across our land and beyond the sea. Intuitively, I sense that the energy links in with a gigantic network all over our Earth, and is alive and vibrant. It feels quite wonderful to join in with this energy, and I always feel `energised' myself afterwards.

Now I have nearly finished my studies. Last night, I had a strange and disturbing experience. My father was standing in my bedroom here in the university. He looked calm and serene, and seemed to glow with an eternal light. He smiled so lovingly at me but did not speak. It was just like he was here because he seemed so real.

It is three days later. This morning I have had news that my father died suddenly the night I saw him and I feel very upset, for I loved him so much. We were very close. For some time I haven't been home and I wish now I had made the effort. I have been much too pre-occupied with my friend Jon. He is a fellow student and we have been seeing each other for a while now.

I love him, and when we qualify we are planning to stay together. Now, I go to him and he comforts me, and helps me cope with the sadness and loss. It is only a week before our graduation and I feel bad that my father won't be there, although something inside me says he will, but not physically.

Jon believes in this too, and it helps me to hold on to this thought. Now the day of my graduation is over. It has been an emotional day, which felt wonderful. I `sensed' my father's presence and his pride. I know I have Jon now and he is all I need.

Jon and I have been married for 2 years now. We are very happy, and both practice as architects in the town, helping to create and design new buildings with the principles of Earth energy, allowing them to be healthy, happy places. We ourselves have a large house on the south side of the city, high up on the hillside. It is quiet and peaceful here, and we have lovely views north, over the city to the ruined temple.

I am feeling elated as I'm sure I am pregnant. As yet, I haven't told Jon, but I feel he may know, as we are almost telepathic, and can communicate easily. He has been down in the city today working on one of his buildings and I `know' he has set off to come home. I am in our study on the upper floor, feeling uneasy. I go out on to the balcony and look north. Oh!.....I can see Earthlights, flashes of light above the town and the old temple.....There's going to be an earthquake. I know. I can feel it. We get lots of minor tremors, but I `know' this is going to be a big one because it feels different. Quickly, I need to leave the house.....get outside. Rushing to get down the stairs, I feel the first shocks trembling through my feet. As I reach the lower stairs, I slip in my haste and fall, knocking myself on a large cupboard at the bottom. Briefly, I am dazed, then pick myself up and run out into the street. Desperately, I am looking for Jon, hoping he is safe. I am aware; in my mind of him `calling' to me.... but I feel very strange, light headed and dizzy.....hardly seeming to know what is happening. Then I feel a sudden, fierce pain in my stomach...Jon is here with his arms are round me and I am bleeding, lots of blood. I am aware of losing consciousness.

I sense myself to be floating above my body and the scene. There is lots of fallen masonry round me.... I can see Jon picking my body up in his arms taking me to the nearby Healing Sanctuary. Then I experience a brilliant light all around me. My father is here and he is smiling at me lovingly....I long to go to him......I can feel the most wonderful love and peace which is so beautiful. However, he is shaking his head and saying it is not my time.....I have to go back, to do the work I was born to do. My spirit guide is here too, and is helping me to accept this. I feel so good here. Yet I am torn, between my desire to stay in this wonderful place, and my love for Jon.....I need to go to him.

I am aware of waking up, lying in a bed in the Healing Sanctuary and Jon holding my hand. He looks so worried but he is delighted when I open my eyes. Jon tells me I have been very ill, and I have lost our baby. I bled a lot and almost died. The senior healer here, a lovely serene woman, has been helping me and has a special interest in my progress. She says I have been `sent back' to work with the Earth energy, to help with the vast amount of repair work that is needed across our land, not just from the earthquake, which has done much damage, but from previous times, when our Earth was hurt and damaged by man. She tells me that Jon and I have to work together on this and she will teach us. Already, we are sensitive to the needs of the Earth, and are told we could have a talent between us to become a powerful combination for healing and rebuilding.

Hundreds of people have been killed in the earthquake, which has torn Thrumbis in half. The eastern part has sunk beneath the sea and the harbour has gone. Sadly, the old temple has been destroyed and the hill it was on is now a high cliff overlooking the sea. This is all very hard to take in. The healer is gentle with me, but I know now I have work to do, and want to get on with it!

It is later and I am with Jon. We are working together to build a new Earth temple. This is to replace the old one that was

ELAYNA AND JON

LINDA POPE.

destroyed in the earthquake. The new `power point' is situated about five miles further west. The grid of energy lines were disrupted by the earthquake, and the new temple must be built here, on the new alignment. It is a big project but vitally important to the health of the area. The people of the city have picked up their lives now, and are gradually adjusting to the new land configurations. In time, the community will migrate to the area here, around the new temple, which will be a good place.

Jon and I are moving slabs of blue stone to form the `ribs' of the main hall. Sitting together, feet to feet, and palm to palm, we begin to circulate energy between ourselves, moving it faster and faster till it becomes a spiralling vortex. Then, we move slightly further apart, allowing the spin to increase so it flattens and forms into a ball. This has tremendous power and we can manipulate this ball with mental control underneath the blocks of stone. This energy supports their weight so they can move with ease. Then the stones can be easily handled and guided into the positions required. To maintain the power of the energy balls needs a lot of concentration from us, and can be quite tiring work.

In the centre of the main hall is a black stone, like the one in the old temple I used to visit. This acts like a `needle' in the power point and increases the energy flowing into the Earth lines. This is the most important function of the temple. There will also be a large healing complex here, with many rooms. These are roofed with different coloured glass for different energy values to use in differing conditions. There is also a beautiful circular garden around a natural spring, to bring the energy of the water Spirit within the temple as well. This is a beautiful and powerful place and Jon and I are proud to be part of its inception.

It is later and our work is taking us to many places. We have travelled to the west coast and are helping with the building and setting up of an observatory and scientific complex, to study the Earth energies and the stars. This construction is being built in the hills behind a small town. We have placed the `uprights' which are made of red stone, covered with patterns and lifted them into place with energy balls as before. The roof is made up of triangular sections, and the temple has to be aligned with the sunset and the blue star Aridion. There is an older man who is in charge of this and he knows about the stars and the various calculations we need to do this. This man is an experienced astronomer, and has much knowledge. We both love talking to him when we have time. It is fascinating. He has several special instruments he uses to study the star patterns and many charts and maps. Behind the main circular building we are constructing is a long Earthwork. It tapers over about half a mile to a narrow point, due east. Where it ends is another black 'needle' stone for the energy. This again, links and strengthens the earth energy lines.

Gradually, over some time, we travel all over the southern part of the continent, doing building and main construction design for the Earth temples and sanctuaries. There is much to be done. The area is empty in many places and sparsely populated. We also 'know', hundreds of years ago, the Earth was devastated by some ancient event that disrupted the grid lines and caused great destruction and pain to the land. Our main work has been to heal this damage so the Earth can renew herself better.

It is later. Jon and I have been `drawn' to a really desolate place. This is the furthest south anyone can go, the very tip of the land mass and the devastation is terrible. Nothing grows here. The soil is dry and barren and there is an awful sad and angry atmosphere and `feel' to it. As we leave the last village and walk into the dead area, I can feel through my feet, terrible pain and sadness from the Earth. We have come to one of our most important jobs, to heal and redress the massive damage that was done here. This must have happened centuries ago. The air is silent, an eerie silence, no birds, no life, just deadness. Jon and I hold hands as we walk, to support each other, for we both feel very uneasy and unsettled. After some time we come to a huge hollow, a crater about a quarter of a mile across. I feel some kind of explosion has taken place here....This is where the bad energy is emanating from. I can feel waves of dark vibrations coming out of it making me feel sick and dizzy. Jon is also affected but we know this is where our stone must go.

The next day, Jon and I transport the black stone we have brought on the energy balls to the crater. After protecting our own energy fields, we prepare the earth, and gradually ease the stone into place. Immediately the inrush of powerful healing energy is felt. It is wonderful; so amazing. I feel my skin tingling and my hair rising as these powerful energies flow through us. Holding each other delightedly, we then join hands and dance around the stone, helping the energies to spiral and `grow'. Eventually, we both collapse in an exhausted heap on the ground, quite spent, and sleep there. Awakening to the wonderful sound of bird song, I look across to Jon, who is also stirring. We both smile. The sense of deep contentment between us is so beautiful. I feel love for him that is so strong and enhanced by the love of the Earth herself. We both know, as we walk back to the village with our arms around each other, that the healing is working, and already, life is returning to this empty place.

I am about 60 now and standing on the cliffs to the north of Thrumbis, where the old temple used to be. Jon died two years ago and I am desperately lonely. I miss him. Together, we had a long and happy life and did much good work. His death was caused by an illness to his chest. I don't want to live any longer without him. I was planning to kill myself by jumping off the cliffs into the sea, but I'm frightened and I can't do it. My mind is in turmoil as I turn away. The land beneath my feet crumbles and I slip over the edge. Vaguely, I am aware of falling. Then I seem to be watching my own body as it falls onto the rocks below.

There is light all around me, and through it, coming towards me, is Jon. He looks so young and radiant. Putting his arms around me, it feels very beautiful to be with him again. My father and mother are here too and I feel deep happiness. They take me to rest. I feel very pleased with that life, and realise now, of course, that the work we did was planned, and that feels good too.

Paul's Experience of Being 'Jon'
It was about 8 months after Linda had her regression as `Elayna' that I went through my two regression sessions being `Jon'. By

this time, I had largely forgotten with my normal consciousness most of the details of Linda's experience. Therefore, when we compared notes at the end of the sessions, we were surprised and delighted at how accurately the two sets of regressions had matched up. However, as you can imagine, the emphasis of what was most important for me to experience was quite different to that of Linda.

While not wanting to go through the whole of my regressions to 'Jon', I would like to mention some details and go through some of my experiences as I remember them. I hope that this will be of interest, especially relating to what life was like in this `Golden Age' period of Atlantis and the sensitivity which people could feel during this period.

As `Jon', I grew up in a small city by the sea, just to the south of the more major city where we later studied architecture together. Like Elayna I had a very loving and supportive family base. For me, my mother was very significant and her sensitivity to energies was influential on how I developed. However, it was through my father who was a builder that I chose to study architecture.

Just before I went away to the university, I was a witness to a dramatic storm which had a great impact upon me. As it came towards us from across the sea, I watched it outdoors from the balcony of our house. I was very aware of the power of Nature. The storm seemed quite angry, an angry release of violent energy. It made me realise that the power of Nature and the Earth Spirit was stronger than me. I felt very humble in the presence of the storm, and I did not feel that that the Earth Spirit was opposing me. But I wanted to listen to what the storm was telling me. It felt like the Spirit of the Earth was talking, not only to me, but to the people, telling us to be true to the one way, to be in harmony with the Earth. As I watched the lightning cause damage and destruction around me, I stood on the balcony letting myself become drenched in the rain, daring the power of the storm to take me if it wanted, yet trusting that I was safe at the same time.

We were told in the legends of the former destruction of our land, how people had abused crystals and the Earth energy, and how the Earth had finally reacted. I felt a very strong need to respect the Earth and I feel that this was very much attuned to the Spirit of the age in which I was living. Many other people felt very similarly to me.

At the university I was aware of a surging idealism. People wanted to build a peaceful society with a common purpose, so there would not be wars and struggles of one group of people against another. There were many talks at the university about the need to repair the damage of the past, to form links of co-operation right across our land.

In my heart, as Jon, I felt inspired by these ideals. I wanted to help all I could, to join in with all the people wanting this, to travel and work with many others.

Military establishments had been banned apart from a small navy presence designed to protect our land from invaders coming from other lands. We had civilian governments and wanted open access and freedom of movement for all the people of our vast land. There was much travel between the various cities, forging links, gaining understanding and learning how to work together. This is how we wanted our society to be.

The healers and people sensitive to Spiritual energies were very prominent in the administration of our affairs.

In my work as an architect, I had to learn that the healers would determine the placements of buildings and towns in harmony with the meridian lines of Earth energy, so as not to damage the fabric of psychic Spiritual energy connecting the Earth together. We could create the form and structure of the buildings themselves, but this had to be in harmony with the Earth energy as well. Much of our training was concerned with learning about these energies.

Not everyone was sensitive to Spiritual energies. However, in general, people were very concerned about Spiritual worship.

Most houses had within them in the centre of the building a sacred meditation room. Usually, this would be a circular room with a sacred flame at its heart that would burn continuously.

There was a large Temple within the town where people could go and find peace and contentment. People from our community would come together to celebrate festivals here. There would be festivals honouring the sun and moon cycles plus important rituals connected with planting and harvesting associated with our seasons.

Within the Temple, there were people who studied the stars and planets in our skies. It was felt that just as our Earth had a living Spirit, so did the planets and stars which we saw in the sky. The energies from these bodies could influence us and affect our well-being. There were suggestions from ancient texts that originally our civilisation on Earth was seeded from people who came from planets far away.

This was a time when people were very eager to learn more about their history. Ancient texts and scrolls were being discovered by research expeditions and deposited in the university libraries. Such potential knowledge aroused a great deal of curiosity in me.

Later on, after the Earthquake, when Elayna had become injured and lost her baby through miscarriage, I stayed in the Healing hospital with her day and night while she continued to be unconscious. At some point Elayna needed psychic surgery to stop internal bleeding in her abdomen, and I was grateful to be allowed to stay and observe this.

There were three healers working, one at the head, another at the feet and the senior healer who was a woman performing the actual operation. During the operation, Elayna's body was very calm and still. I could sense an enormous energy from the healer's hands, creating a shimmering effect throughout her body. I felt that this was giving protection to Elayna so she could cope with the structural alterations to her energy field. Meanwhile, I was trying to send love to her and felt I was reaching her. The senior healer did not touch Elayna's physical body, but moved her hands, manipulating Elayna's auric field. I was so attuned to Elayna that I could feel the alterations to her energy field in my own body. It felt like all the knots and damage were being put aside and new pathways were being created to let the healing energy flow and the bleeding stop. I felt some marvellous sensations inside me while the healer did this and I later knew that her work was succeeding.

At this moment, I decided that I wanted to do healing and energy work myself. Architecture was not quite sufficient to fulfil my desires. I wanted to help heal the Earth, repair the damage to our land, and build a new and happier society.

Elayna and I were very close. We could sense each other's thoughts and feelings very keenly, when we wanted. Also, we were aware that we had our own Spiritual guide helping us. So, we knew that there was a Spiritual connection for us from beyond the Earth. However, the beauty of the land and life where we lived was very intoxicating and enveloping for us.

Although it was not much talked about, I could sense that I had lived before. When we travelled, the places we visited where we did our work felt like important personal connections for me from my past.

When we went to the west to help with the construction of the Astronomical Temple, I felt that the man in charge of this project wanted to form a link between the Spirit of the Earth and the star, Sirius (Linda as Elayna referred to this star as Aridion). He told us that there were planets around Sirius that supported life, and that once this had been his home. He felt that the link between the energy of Sirius and the Earth had to be strengthened. Much knowledge had been lost and he wanted to create this temple to attempt to regain it.

The energy from Sirius would be focused using crystals from within the Temple and would be grounded by the conductor stones which we laid along the Earth meridian passing through the Temple. I must say that I did not fully understand what he was doing. But the Temple seemed quite a magical place, and it felt a privilege to have a small part in its construction. The old man appeared to be a very wise soul and he had many pupils wanting to learn from him.

Going to the area of destruction at the very southern tip of our land was very important to me. Sensing that this area had been devastated by the activities of the people in the long distant past, I wondered if I had had some part in this? I felt strongly that I had a personal mission to repair this damage. Sitting in the hole at the centre of this barren land, we had to ask our guides to protect us from the radiation, which seemed to want to attack our energy fields. We had to place a large column of basalt deep into the Earth here. Then we needed to use our thought power and imagination to bring Spiritual energies down through the basalt to create roots of energy lines that would go deep into the Earth. The energy disturbance was not just on the surface of this land, but underneath too. So we had to keep working using all our concentration and inner resources further and further until we could feel that the energy lines we had constructed were reaching the active lines of the Earth Spirit again. By the time we did this, we felt the energy change and the release of tensions, but we were utterly exhausted. Then we just slept where we had been working.

Afterwards, it was a wonderful feeling to know that we had succeeded. We went to the village closest to where we had been and told them what we had done. No one from that village ever came into the devastated area, so they were very curious. Of course, they all noticed the change and were very excited like us. In the days that followed, they helped us plant seeds all over this area. We felt that life wanted to return here. Elayna and I discovered two places which could become power points - where Temples could be constructed to strengthen the energy more. Some of the people from the village said they would like to start a settlement here. We wished them well and I felt a lot of satisfaction.

Another place where we visited was an old ruined Temple situated on a hillside; again in the far south of the land. Here, there was a man who had been a tutor at the university we attended. He was trying to organise people to build a settlement in the region. We were helping him to find the site for a new Temple, quite close to where the old one had been situated.

Around the old temple, we found fragments of what seemed liked shattered crystal. We sensed a lot of pain emanating from these pieces. With some assistance from the others, we felt compelled to gather these pieces together. Then we found a hollow and buried them within the Earth, covering them with shielding stones to protect them. We felt we were doing what the pieces of crystal wanted and we meditated and sent prayers asking that these fragments may be united with the Spirit of the Earth.

As Jon, this place seemed familiar, and afterwards I wondered as Paul if it may have been the same site where long before, the Military temple had existed that had featured for me in the lifetime of the crystal war.

Later on we lay the foundations for this new Temple. For this, it appeared that we used basalt rock. The basalt had a strong energy, coming from deep within the Earth, through volcanic action. So placing this at the base of buildings helped connect that place more fully with the inner Earth and its lines of energy.

We had to cleave large pieces of this rock into the shape we wanted, for this purpose. So we first asked permission of the rock. Then through meditation we would conduct energy and use visualisation until the rock would move apart along the natural energy lines within it. We would shape the rock to be more angular at one end and this would then be the end that was directed down into the Earth.

One other place where we were called to visit was a Sanctuary in the mountains. I felt very much at home here and sensed that I had lived many lives in such places. These people had problems because the Earth movements had meant that their Earth sanctuary was now slightly out of alignment, and we were asked to help build a new one in a more appropriate position. However, we found that the residents of this sanctuary were in dispute with each other and there was much unhappiness amongst them. I was called to try to mediate and help them. I found that I could do this very well. After listening to all sides and offering my suggestions, two of the people decided to leave and the atmosphere of the place became much more peaceful.

As Paul, I again wondered if this episode related to my life in the Crystal war. Perhaps in that earlier life, I had stopped my efforts too soon, and now I was needing to make up for it in this way.

However, once more I seemed to be successful and at the end of that life with Elayna it felt that a great deal of positive good had been achieved.

The therapeutic value of this experience for me was mainly in helping me to know more about my personal history and the history of Atlantis as well as giving me comfort for the satisfying work I did then.

For Linda, her regression as Elayna was one of the first Atlantean lives she visited. With such a lot of beauty and positive energy, it gave her much incentive to continue these explorations. At this stage, I don't think she was aware of how difficult this may be for her.

Sometimes people can be guided from within to gentle, satisfying past life experiences as a beginning and introduction to what may prove later to be more challenging therapeutic work. Certainly, this is true in the case of Linda.

Among the many, many people with whom I associated in that life, I sensed that my mother then was the same soul as Lynne. I think that Denise may have had a minor role as one of the other healers who was sometimes working with us.

Commentary by Albaní
Paul: Can you tell us about the golden age of Atlantis?
Albani: *People imagine two pictures of Atlantis. They are the most common images. If you asked the average person, `Suppose*

Atlantis existed, how do you imagine it would be?', they would answer in two ways: One that the continent was corrupt and used crystal power in a bad way, ultimately destroying itself. This is correct. The second answer would be that it was a beautiful place where people lived in peace with nature, and allowed their better side to come forward. This is also correct. That is the period of which you are speaking.

Paul: How did this era begin?

Albani: *There was a long period of recovery after the damage caused by the crystal war. Even though the north was not involved, it still sustained damage. With the massive cataclysmic change, which happened in the southern part of the island, it caused problems with the north also, for there was a great deal of dust and volcanic ash thrown into the atmosphere. This drifted northwards and a lot of it settled over the northern section. This caused problems for quite some time. So, although the north did not sustain so much physical damage, change occurred.*

Therefore, the recovery period actually involved all of the continent in different ways. This took a long time. It took many, many hundreds of years for the population to recover, for the land to settle, and for things to return to some semblance of normal.

In this time the memory of people carried forward the horrors of what happened. There was a great resolving never to allow this to happen again. It was carried down in oral tradition, stories and written work of what this dreadful thing was that had happened.

And so it was resolved, almost simultaneously amongst the people, that they would learn to live in peace with each other, develop a peaceful civilisation, and work very hard at healing the damage that they had done. This is the onset of what you refer to as the golden age.

This was indeed a wonderful period. The time of total stability was roughly 1500 years. Towards the end of that time, things were beginning to change again.

Paul: Where does Elayna's lifetime fit into this?

Albani: *It is roughly in the middle, as are some of the other lives you have come across. Over that period there was a great deal of healing energy and healing work done. For many souls, lives during this time tended to be very positive, and a great deal of beauty was produced.*

Paul: How did the golden age develop?
Albani: *It took some time to develop to its peak, as you can probably appreciate. Eventually, when things died down, people were quite put off by any thought of fighting and war. It was a gradual realisation and a gradual building up of the more peaceful aspects of society.*

Paul: So would the Golden Age be from about 16000-14500 B.C.?
Albani: *That is about the period to which you refer. Roughly, it peaked towards the end of that period, when again things started to backslide slightly. The peak came towards the end when much development had been done, and much progress had been made.*

You realise, when you compare the Atlantean time scales with modern day humanity, and you may wonder, I'm sure, and readers may wonder, why the Atlanteans never developed things like cars and television, and the modern things you have now. For they had equal time to do it. In fact, they had longer. But there was no industrial revolution, as you call it. It did not happen on Atlantis, for they used different power sources, as in crystal energy and Earth energy. They saw no need to develop other forms of energy which you have developed in the modern world.

I believe that your industrial revolution started with the use of steam power and things like that, from the basic elements of the Earth. This did not happen on Atlantis, for they saw no need. There was no drive to develop that kind of society and technology. Their technology as such, if you want to use it in a broad sense, was developed far more along psychic lines, with Earth healing, healing in general, psychic surgery and this kind of thing in the medical field. The people communicated very often by telepathy and using crystals. So things like your modern day commun-ication systems were not required. They simply did not have any need to develop this kind of thing and therefore did not see it. I'm

126

sure had the need been there, then the minds of the time, would have produced this kind of social change.

Paul: What kind of government existed in those times?
Albani: *Government during the `Golden Age' as you refer to it was essentially total democracy. The people who led the various areas, towns, cities were chosen by the people who lived there. They were chosen for their outstanding qualities, their uprightness, their honesty, and their understanding of peaceful things. Anyone who was seen as aggressive, or arrogant or wanting their own power would simply not have made it through the system.*

They were chosen very much by feelings, by the energetic values of that person. They were chosen for their kindness and under-standing and compassion. It was essentially a very caring society.

You would have a council of a number of people. This varied according to where you were. Some of the larger towns and cities had a larger group. As in your system today, each person would be responsible for a certain area, or a certain field of activity. They would bring together all their various skills to run the city efficiently. This worked. It worked extremely well. People were cared for and looked after. From the bottom of society upwards everyone respected what was around them. For there was this great linking with the Earth energy. Therefore all was respected.

There were minor problems, of course. There always are. But these were dealt with in a very fair and easy manner.

Paul: How were children educated in these times?
Albani: *There were various schools and colleges. Often education was started at home. It was common for the parents to educate the children when they were quite young and teach them the basics. These basics also included again the honouring of the Earth and the energies, and the other forms of life around them. The basic literacy skills were started quite early in most places. It varied a little. It was quite a large continent, and some of the systems were a little different. But inevitably, they would move on to a form of higher education as they became older. At the bottom of the society you have the people who do manual work, building and other*

support jobs, work that would be considered lower down the social ladder nowadays. Once those children had received the basic literacy and numeracy, skills such as carpentry and making things of varying forms, would be given usually by the family. Occasionally, that child may be sent to another place where that skill was practised, where they could learn additional skills and stretch their own experiences.

When you reached further up the social scale, it was far more common for the older children to go to a form of college or university, very often in another geographical area, to encourage independence and growth. This is not to say that someone from the other classes could not aspire to this. It was open to all, providing they could show that they had the necessary skills required, to do the course involved.

It is not unlike your current system, but I feel the system there was more open and fair. The universities and schools were supported by the various moneys that were collected by the central council of elders, or however you wish to speak of them. They would support these. But a lot of it was done through philanthropy. These institutions were supported by individuals, people who had earned their place in life, people who had a good social standing and wealth. These people would more than likely put their wealth into something to benefit others. This was quite common, and it was considered a step up the social ladder if you had built a school, or put your name to something, or put money into an education establishment or healing temple or something like that. It was considered a very good and kind thing to do. Also it was good for people's soul, for their own growth and good essentially for the whole community. Therefore, the needs of the Earth, the energies and the people were aligned for this. It was idyllic. It was very beautiful, and very powerful. This is why the energies worked so well through this period.

Paul: Is it true that some children would be taken away from their families if they had some special gifts, and then they may have someone to teach them specific skills?
Albani: *Yes, indeed. This again was a fairly common thing, and quite well accepted. For children were taught fairly early by their*

128

parents, so that if they showed aptitude in a certain area, then this would be a natural progression. Then they would need to leave their family environment and go to a special place. This often happened with healers. This was the most common field in which this did happen. For the healing could only be taught, in many instances, in the healing temples, which were often away from society in general. It was accepted at a deep level that they would be parted from their parents and their family. Although it caused distress and sadness, this was only momentary. For they knew that this is the way it had to be. This was the way society ran. They were one of many hundreds. They were not alone, for they were always taken in groups where they could form friendships. They had what you would call nowadays a mentor, who would look after them and care for them. Also, they could visit their families on quite a regular basis, so the family connection was never lost, unless that person when they grew older, wanted to break that connection. Then that was their choice.

The age of maturity was generally about age 16.

Paul: What was the age expectancy around this time?
Albani: *Reasonably high. I feel the average age when people died was probably between 60 and 70. But there were exceptions of course, as there always are. Disease always existed. But with the healing abilities within many of the areas, this could be conquered to some degree. However, it was accepted, for they understood this, much better than people understand in normal society now, that if a person had chosen to accept a disease as part of their path, then the healers would know this, and they would accept that this was the way that the person had chosen to pass in that life. So in some ways, interference with that would be considered bad. They did ease that person's pain or suffering if they had it, and made the transition far easier for them whenever possible.*

Paul: What was life like in the Healing temples at this time?
Albani: *Again this did vary in geographical location. For the most powerful places were the places in the mountains, of which there were many. This was where a lot of people who studied healing would go. But in the bigger cities there were also healing sanctuaries, and temples, where healers worked with the*

population. Of course, their numbers were greater there. They were structured in much the same manner. There would be one senior person in charge and they would organise the activities of the various people under their control, the other healers. Healers would often work in pairs, as a male/female pairing, although this was not always the case. It varied tremendously.

There was also a system where the healers travelled out to those who could not get to them. With emergencies, accidents and problems, healers would go out, or people would be brought. It worked on a loose basis. The actual sanctuary or temple needed to be prepared for anything that may happen.

Healing was done at all levels. It was done for all the various problems that beset humanity, including physical illness, accidents and mental illness. These were treated by the healers in different ways. There were variations in the way this was applied, but on the whole, the techniques used were very, very similar. Crystals were used to accelerate the energy in certain situations. Normal touch and hands on healing was used. Healing through the auric field and also what you term now as psychic surgery was also used. They also worked with the vibrations of sound and visualisation and the bringing forth of Spiritual energies which they could control much more strongly than in our contemporary times, for they could deal with a great deal of different situations.

If there was, for example, a disaster, like a volcanic eruption or an earthquake, or some form of major accident, then teams of healers would go to that area to affect rescue of the souls involved, to administer healing and pain control, to help with any form of injury and also to help with the after care of the injured and people involved. They well knew that these things brought about mental stress and difficulties, which you are only just beginning to address in your society today. They well understood the affects on the mind of traumatic experiences. Therefore they could help with this at all levels.

Paul: What were the main spiritual beliefs of the general population?
Albani: *Most people believed in the Earth energy, and the power of*

Spirit. It was well known and well accepted that people could speak to Spirit. In the various corners of the land, different terminology would be used. But essentially they would be speaking to a Spiritual being who they knew - a power, a force that was beyond them. They knew there was power and energy operating throughout the land.

Each home had a sanctuary. Even the smallest homes would have a tiny sanctuary where the family would meet in the morning, or the members of that group, and they would meditate together or just sit quietly and pray together before the day started. Very often, they would do the same at the end of the day, and give thanks for whatever had happened. For they were very tuned in to their own needs and the needs of the Earth.

Paul: How were these sanctuaries set out?
Albani: *They were generally circular and, if we take the average - not the smaller ones or the larger ones, this would be a circular room roughly 7-10 metres across. They would often have paintings on the walls of scenes that were meaningful to the people there. Usually these would be natural scenes of animals, birds or plants. Around the perimeter would be a bench, running right around the outside, from one side of the doorway, right round to the other side of the doorway. In the centre there was always a plinth of some variety and upon this would either be a flame kept burning in the form of a lamp, or a flame that was lit when they went in to meditate. This would be decorated with flowers, fruit or the way the family saw fit. This did vary, for families may have their own way how they wanted to decorate the alter, to honour the Earth's energy. It was always considered that while the flame was burning, negative thoughts or anything impure should either not be spoken or thought. It was considered a sacred space where each person could commune within themselves. Again, the people tended to be well aware of the power within their own souls. They were well aware of that connection with Spirit that came from within. By being together they formed a link. This created a bond of harmony between the people involved. It was an unwritten accepted rule that anyone with whom you had been in a sanctuary, should be someone with whom you would get along. This of course, did not always happen. But in general, it was considered very bad*

to have difficulties or arguments with people with whom you would share this sacred space.

People would honour the Earth energy, the energy the Earth gives, for the life that she gives, for the waters and the food, and the light and the energy from the Sun.

Some of these sanctuaries had a clear roof so that the natural light could come in. This would probably be in the wealthier homes. For glass, although it was used, was considered a very precious substance. Therefore, it would only be the wealthy people who would add this to their sanctuary.

Usually they were just lit by the single flame, or possibly small oil lamps around the side of the walls. In the poorer homes, it would simply be a small circular room with a wooden bench around the outside, and a small wooden plinth in the middle with the flame upon it.

Offerings would sometimes be put there if people felt strongly about something for which they wished to say thank you. They would bring a small sample of whatever it was, and place it upon the altar, as a form of gift to the Earth and the energies that flowed through this. They saw it as a flowing pattern. Once they were in the sanctuary, the energies flowed around them, and through them, in a circular manner, from the plinth to them and back again, through the floor.

Paul: And people could actually feel those energies then?
Albani: *Oh yes, indeed they could. They knew that once they were in there, they were in a sacred place. It was generally honoured and considered extremely bad to disrupt the energy within a sanctuary. In fact, in some areas it was considered an imprisonable offence. To threaten any kind of violence or angry words within a sanctuary was very much frowned upon.*

Paul: Was there any belief in reincarnation at that time?
Albani: *Yes, most people held the view of past lives. Most people accepted that you lived many times. That was a common belief.*

Paul: Were there any regional differences in the way people conducted themselves throughout the land at this time?

Albani: *Yes, there were some although there was also much uniformity. There were parts of the southern areas of the continent where the sanctuaries were actually outside. They would be formed in a garden or some external space. For the weather was warmer and more equable.*

In the northern regions, they tended to stay inside. About three quarters of the continent had the more inside type of sanctuary.

The external ones were decorated with plants, living flowers around in colours which were meaningful for the people involved. Bright colours were used to enhance the energy for they understood the vibration of the colours.

In the north, there were many areas deep within woodland where there were Earth sanctuaries. These were often rings of ancient trees where the central area was kept clear and the central plinth - usually a tree trunk, or rocks or stones - would be kept as a sacred space. Anyone could go to these places, and sit quietly and contemplate. Otherwise, a group could go and conduct a ceremony, an honouring ceremony, just to feel the energies between them, by linking as a circle.

Paul: What happened with the Arts and music during the Golden Age?

Albani: *They flourished in this time, and people became very aware of the beauty, and of the Nature and things around them. Music flourished for people were aware of the beauty of sound. Concerts were very common. People enjoyed listening to others. People enjoyed performing for others and making beautiful music for their own pleasure. There were many establishments where this was very strong. There were colleges of music. They had a written notation and various forms of instrumentation which are not too different from today's instruments - for essentially they come from the same sources. They need the same physical elements to make sound. Therefore the shapes and the types of instruments that were involved were very similar to today's. They have been throughout time. For if you need to create sound, the same physical elements of* *resonance and vibration occur no matter when you are building the instrument.*

There were different influences for music according to the area where it was produced. Musicians did travel and performed in other areas. This was considered a very good profession to follow, as was dealing with Art and producing beautiful things like pottery, ornamentation, paintings and things of that nature. It was considered a good thing to have something of beauty within your home. It was considered a good vibratory thing to have something that you loved and could respect, that would represent something of yourself and something of the Earth to bring into your home. Again, even the humblest of homes had something considered quite beautiful. It may have just been a selection of rocks or pebbles. It may have been a pot or something with lines. But beauty was very much appreciated at all levels of society.

Paul: What were the forces and factors that led to the end of the Golden Age?

Albani: *It is the usual story of people's greed and need to control others. Very gradually people of ambition and power began to infiltrate the peaceful society. They began very slowly to change things. And those around them who were susceptible or weaker began to see that by attaching themselves to the more powerful personalities, they too could gain. And greed crept in. And once these more powerful personalities began to take over - and again this happened in different places at different times - they became desirous of taking other people's things. They were jealous. They wanted the riches of another. And that is when the military establishments started to return again. For these people required protection for they made themselves disliked, and it is automatic to bring about people who would defend you - in other words, soldiers or the like. It was a very gradual change. Eventually the greedy and the more competitive element of society crept back in. It happened so slowly that most people didn't even notice. By the time someone in one given town looked at things and said `Things aren't going so well', it was too late. For by then, change was occurring and it was occurring in other places also. Had it just been one place then people would have resisted. But people, by then, in a strange way had become more apathetic. Because they* *had had it so good for so long, I don't think they ever conceived that such a thing could ever happen again. But it did.*

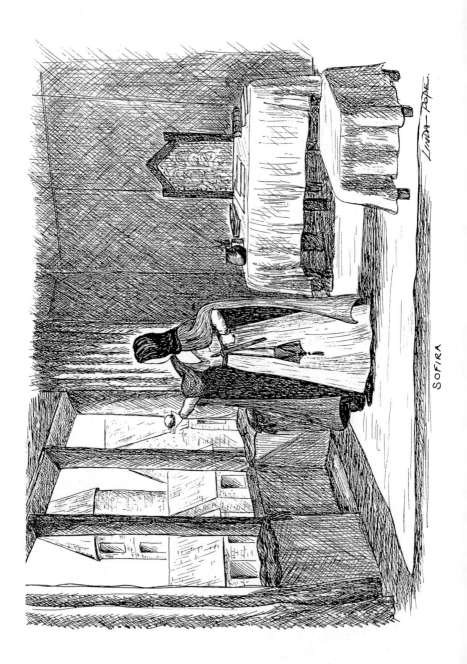

SOFIRA

LINDA POPE.

136

Chapter 14

Sofira and the Amethyst Sphere

Preliminary Comments

In Atlantis, people's nervous systems were very sensitive to the influence of power. People could feel power very easily and it gave very strong sensations in the body. Therefore, the pursuit of power could be a seductive temptation for many souls. It was possible for souls to lose contact with Spiritual love and truth through the thirst for power. Indeed, often this thirst for power came into being when people felt a lack of love in their lives otherwise. However, for people to seek power at the expense of others, or the Earth, could bring much suffering and negativity. Frequently, souls in Atlantis only realised the extent of terrible things they did after they died. These experiences brought with them many lessons for the soul.

Linda's soul has always been very sensitive to psychic influences, and in Atlantis, with all its power, Linda's soul had many incarnations where she did not cope very well with this. We have discovered through our exploration that Linda's soul had three particularly awful lives where things went badly wrong. The one as Sofira was about the worst. In this lifetime, Sofira killed many, many people, and she enjoyed killing these people. It gave her a sense of power. Some of those souls she killed then, Linda has recognised as people she knows today. This past lifetime was a shocking experience for her to encounter. Linda realises that she is still recovering from the ripples and effects of that lifetime in her life now. It has left Linda with a deep fear of power, of hurting other people, and guilt for anything she feels she does wrong. However, for Linda to live through the experiences of this lifetime has helped her to acknowledge her dark side and to start to come to accept herself more fully from within. I feel that she has been very brave to allow herself to experience some of the scenes from this lifetime, but she has known she needed to do this and has come out of the other side feeling stronger as a result.

I have recognised that my soul was one of Sofira's victims in that lifetime. The wound of that experience affected my relationship negatively with Linda's soul for many subsequent lives, and I feel I am still learning to love Linda with an open heart and without prejudice or negative expectations. I am not meaning to imply that Linda's soul has hurt me without reply. I am aware from our explorations that my soul in incarnation has also hurt Linda's soul very badly on occasions too. Sometimes, I feel that traumatic experiences that are like wounds, may form scars on the soul, and need many lifetimes to heal.

In this chapter Linda will give an account of her various regressions relating to Sofira. It is a censored version. I will also include an account of my regression as Sheeran, Sofira's lover. Then, there are some paragraphs about the parts Lynne and Denise played in the story and a description of a healing process we all went through.

We have dated this incarnation from a time at the end of the Golden age. Perhaps, not all was bliss, even then!

Linda's Regression - Sofira

I am in our garden. It is a beautiful place. Our house is large, and situated high up at the back of the town. The garden is a series of terraces with lawns and flowers. I am going down to the furthermost point, a balcony that overlooks the other buildings and trees, and the sea in the distance. I am carrying a black and white seabird. Since I found it with an injured wing some days ago, I have been caring for it. Now, it is fully recovered and I am going to release it, to fly free once more. I love doing this and it gives me a huge thrill. Holding its light feathery body close to me one last time, I sweep my hands upwards and let it loose. Quickly, it climbs away into the blue sky, and I feel a surge of love and energy flowing through me. I do this quite often, and I have, in a secluded corner of the garden, a small area of pens and cages where I keep sick and injured birds and small animals.

My mother disapproves because she does not like me doing this. She says it will interfere with my academic studies. I know she has great ambitions for me. She wants me to succeed, to be the best. All the time she pushes me, feeling that caring for my animal friends is wasted effort, and that my time could be more gainfully employed doing my studies.

Father is a musician in our town. There are three of us. I have two brothers, who have followed father, and are studying music. I have no interest in that at all. Mother is scientifically trained in geology, and has persuaded me that the best way to achieve success is to follow the sciences. I have chosen archaeology, and am working towards a university place in one of the nearby cities.

She had great ambitions before she married and had us, and now she wants me to gain high honours so she will rise in social standing through me. Quite often I feel her bitterness at being just a mother, and losing what she saw as a promising career. Now she is relying on me, as my brothers are not studying a proper career. She emphasises that I must not get too soft or I will lack the drive and determination required to achieve what she wants from me. Her main principle is that I must never allow my feelings to dominate my scientific abilities. Not understanding this, I find it hard to talk to her. She won't listen, and just walks away, making her disapproval very obvious. This makes me confused and very unhappy.

I have come out of my schoolroom. There is a tremendous noise going on. I can hear birds crying and general raucous laughter and shouting. What I see frightens me. There is a large group of children of all ages. They are deliberately throwing stones into the nearby trees to frighten and disturb the birds. They are on their nests with their babies. I run out, screaming at them to stop. They are hurting them. The birds cries echo in my ears and I hate this. Stop, stop, I shout. Can't you see what you're doing isn't fun? Its cruel.

I see a bird fall to the ground below a tree, flapping an obviously injured wing and crying piteously. I push my way through the rowdy throng, and scoop it up in my arms. Feeling its heart beating against my chest, I cup my arms around it, trying to protect it. There is blood on its wing. The others come and start to jostle me, calling me names. They push me deliberately, pulling at my arms and clothes to make me drop it. They are pulling at my hair, it hurts.

Suddenly, one of the boys grabs the bird from me. I can't stop him. He twists its neck and kills it in front of me. Then laughing at me, he gives the body back to me. It is so horrible, I feel sick inside.

As I start to cry, they all laugh at me and I try to push through them and run away. I rush home and into our house. As I dash inside I meet with mother, I was hoping to get to my room without seeing her. She grabs me by my shoulders and asks me what I am snivelling at. Her tone is sarcastic and contemptuous but I refuse to answer, looking at the floor, with tears still running down my face. She lifts my chin and slaps me. It stings. Rushing to my room, I cry and cry, not wanting to feel like this ever again. I decide I don't want to show my feelings to anyone, I want to be hardhearted like everyone else. Being kind and caring just gets me hurt and humiliated.

When I eventually go to my cages, I find that they have been destroyed and the animals and birds are gone. Inside me I feel an emptiness, a coldness and a numb sensation in my stomach. No one will ever hurt me again. I will never feel anything ever.

I am older now and at a party. It is a special celebration as it is the evening before all of us from our town will be going to start our university courses. We are all going different ways and I am going to study archaeology as I planned some years ago. The prospect of leaving home and my mothers influence excites me, and I want to gain more independence, but I am sad at leaving my boyfriend. He and I have been seeing each other for some time now. He is the first person towards whom I have felt able to feel love.

We are together in the garden at our friend's house. There is such a romantic atmosphere. He is very handsome. I am very aware that all the girls like him, but he is with me. We are holding each other close when suddenly, one of the girls rushes on to the terrace, screaming abuse at me for stealing him. I feel shocked. She comes across and grabs hold of me, dragging me to the floor and starts to fight me. I respond but she is stronger than me and tears my dress. Using all my strength, I manage to break away and I grab a nearby container of water to throw over her. That feels good.

Turning, I run away in tears. Once again, my feelings have let me down. I feel humiliated in front of the others. How could I allow this to happen, after all I vowed to myself? I knew it was wrong to feel close to him. This is the end. I will never allow myself to show how I feel again ever. In fact, I will not allow my feelings to control me anymore.

I am starting a new life tomorrow; people will see a new me a strong and ambitious person who can get to the top without her emotions getting in the way. That is what I will do and I will succeed. I will prove to my mother that I can do it, that her little girl is strong and independent and very capable of holding high office.

Now it is later. I am in my final year. It has been an interesting course, and at times, quite difficult, but I am fairly confident of doing well. The others in my group are a mixed bunch, mostly no problem as rivals, but there is one, Sheeran. He is clever and quite a challenge. Like me, he is ambitious and I need to watch him carefully. I have worked hard and do not want to lose anything to anyone, especially him. Those who come top of a group are automatically given a tutorship, and from that position it is easy to become head of department, and in charge of the whole faculty of archaeology. That is what I want. There is much power and prestige to be had, and I would be able to organise things the way I would want them and not be ordered around by others.

It is later. We are at a dig on one of the ancient temple mounds. Our work here is being assessed as part of our final exam preparations. It is important to find things of interest and evaluate them. We are also expected to help keep records which I find tedious. Up to now I have found very little, just insignificant bits and pieces.

Something unusual has happened to me. I have found this old man, a hermit of sorts, living in a cave in some nearby woodland. I discovered him quite accidentally. One day, I was bored and tired with my work, and as it was hot, I went for a walk away from the dig, into the wooded area of hills close by our site. I felt the need to get away from the others too. Sometimes I find their enthusiasm and keenness suffocating. Most of them are pretty hopeless anyway and they annoy me.

This old man is a strange old soul, and seemed to take to me right away. Taking me into his home, he showed me an artifact I have never seen the like of before, a glorious amethyst sphere, incredibly ancient and full of power. He is teaching me to use its energies and it is absolutely fascinating. It can project thought that is directed into it. He tells me its primary purpose is for healing, and intensifying healing energy to a person or situation in need. But I have realised that it can also be used to gain power, to control what others do and think. Imagine the success I could achieve with it to help me. I must have it. Later tonight, I intend to go to his cave to steal it.

As I am deliberating on this, I hear shouts of excitement from the main area of the dig. I go out and investigate. Wouldn't you know! That man Sheeran has found something of great value and importance. It would be him. That should have been mine. If I had the sphere I could have done that. I must get it tonight as planned. Now he will get honours and I won't and they are all treating him like some hero. It's absurd. His name will be on this find and will make him more able to come top in the final exam.

But wait, if I have the amethyst I could arrange things otherwise couldn't I?

It is after midnight; I am outside the old mans cave. It is quiet. Going in, I see he is asleep, snoring. I go to the box where I know it is kept and lift the lid. It squeaks. Hastily, I grab at the cloth bag where it is kept and slip it into my robes.

There's a movement. He's woken up and is shouting at me, grabbing for me. Stupid old fool. He's cursing me. I push him away for I am young and strong. He is old and frail. But his hands grip my arms with surprising force. I feel determined to have it. I wrench myself free, lose my balance and steady myself against the table. There is a knife. I will kill him. No one will know. My fingers close round the handle. He comes towards me. I plunge the knife into him and he falls without a sound. He's dead. There's blood running across the floor and on my hands.

I wipe myself clean and leave. Now I have the sphere and it's mine. Mine. I feel its weight and shape in my robe. This will give me power, the ability to do what I want. I will get to the top with this. No one can stop me now.

I am back in the college at the university and our final exams are approaching. To make sure I can sort out my rivals satisfactorily, I begin to work on my fellow classmates. Some are fairly close to me academically, so I need to make sure they do not better me in the exams themselves. I practice implanting thoughts into their minds, little things at first, like forgetting to go for meals, and not remembering where their room is situated. Visualising the person concerned, I formulate the thoughts I wish them to have. Then I concentrate, channel the energy into the sphere and release it. It is so easy, so ridiculously easy. I have even made one girl, who does not drink, go out and get really drunk.

The day before the exams themselves, I programme my fellow students. Some will forget key facts. Some will simply sleep in and be down graded for that. Some will feel ill and either not come, or have to leave early. I need to be careful, and make things look as natural as possible. I have also worked on Sheeran, for he is my closest rival. I have tried to make him forget small details, but he is a difficult one I could feel resistance almost as if he knew something was going on. I'll have to watch him carefully.

Now the exams are over. I have graduated with high honours, top of our year. Sheeran came close, very close, but none of the others were near. I have, as is customary, been awarded a senior tutorial position. My mother is delighted and very proud. Now I must concentrate on becoming head of the faculty. That is my next step. It will not be difficult to arrange, but I must wait. I must be patient, and make things look normal.

Last night I dreamt of the old man, Arrad. He was standing in my room, staring at me. Leaning over the end of my bed, he looked so real. He was angry and told me I was abusing the sphere. It should not be used to manipulate other's minds. This practice was evil and I would be cursed for what I was doing. Feeling disturbed, I just turned away and he vanished. It was a bad dream, and surely would not harm me.

It is later. I have been on an expedition to the west of the mountains. I was in charge, but Sheeran came along. We became lovers. He is passionate and ambitious like me, and, perhaps it will be better being with him more closely. At least then I know his movements, but I also feel I could like him. He's a strong person. I like that.

I have just returned to my office at the college and am seething with rage. I have just been to see our head of department. He is an old and revolting man. He started trying to kiss me and fondle me sexually. I managed to fight him off. He's disgusting. I will deal with him and end this problem now. With great deliberation, I put the sphere on the table in front of me, visualise his image and allow the power to flow. I implant feelings of utter despair and depression, leading to thoughts of suicide. If this works, and he dies, I will get his post.

A few days later, I hear that he has jumped to his death from a high tower and I feel delighted. Then I hear also with horror that I have a rival for the senior post, another woman. I will have to deal with her too. Again I use the sphere. I implant thoughts in her mind. She goes out to swim in a flooded river and is drowned. It is easy. Now all I need to do is influence the members of the appointing committee to vote for me and the position is mine.

Now I have been head of the Department of Archaeology for some time, and have many people under me. I have invited a woman lecturer to my office to see me. She is causing me problems and becoming much too popular, making me look bad. I sense she is a dangerous rival and a threat to my position. Most of the staff prefer her to me, so I need to keep her under control.

She is sitting in front of me, and we have been talking. The discussion has become very heated. It is plain she doesn't like me. That essentially doesn't bother me, but the fact she is popular and influencing others against me does. She says I should be more caring, and show my feelings towards my colleagues and students, calling me a cold fish and heartless. This enrages me. I stand up and walk round the desk to face her. She stands there, defiant and smiling. I hate her.

Grabbing a large metal candlestick, I hit her over the head with it. She falls and lays unconscious, blood trickling from a wound on her temple. I stand, regaining my temper and my breath. A strange, but very satisfying sense of power and control surges through me. I like it. I have ultimate control. I decide whether she lives or dies. This is real power. This is energy. Slowly, I get a knife from a drawer in my desk, come back and stand over her prostrate form. I decide to kill her. It is so easy. I cut the sides of her neck and watch as she slowly bleeds to death

It is later. I have discovered that Rollan, the head keeper of artifacts, is involved in a black market of valuable antiquities, selling off items in his care through a network of dealers. There are quite a few people involved, and there is money to be made easily. I need to control this and I can do so with ease. They are fools.

As I confront him in my office, he laughs at me and says he knows about my activities too, and if I say anything, he will also. He is dangerous, but can be manipulated. I know where they meet so I tune into them with the sphere. I watch and wait. I will teach him to threaten me. Slowly I concentrate his image in the amethyst, and I send him pain, agonising pain. He starts to moan and clutch at his head. The others look around, uncertain and wondering what is happening. He collapses unconscious. I will not kill him this time; I just want to frighten him so I can control his activities.

It is some months later. I am away on another expedition, and I check what he is doing. As I thought, he is spreading rumours about me and stirring up trouble. The fool thinks I'm too far away to either hear him or do anything about it. How wrong he is! Once again, I tune in from where I am, and send the pain. This time I will not hold back. I continue till he dies in agony.

I am sitting in my special room, which is hidden behind my main office in the college and is quite secret. This is my own place. In front of me, tied to a stone column, is a young woman. I am watching her die.

It gives me a great sense of pleasure to do this, and I have done it so many times now. I use the sphere to influence the minds of my victims to lure them here. Some are students, some people from the town. I am always careful to choose the ones no one will miss for a while, and ones whose disappearance is easily explained. With these activities, I feel elation and excitement, especially if they are young women. I am jealous of them so killing them in this way is very satisfying. Usually, I secure them and then cut them in such a way that they slowly bleed to death. The blood fascinates me I watch with almost hypnotic intensity as it runs down their bodies. I have lost count of the number I have killed. It doesn't matter anyway. It makes me feel powerful and dominant. Using the sphere also to make others remove the bodies, I programme them to forget what they see and do, so it is simple to keep my activities secret. Even Sheeran cannot guess anything of this.

For some time I suppose I have realised that Sheeran has been seeing other women. I could accept this to a degree, for it kept him out of my way, and I could pursue my own activities more easily. But I have just found out that he is besotted with a young silly student. Over a period of time, he has been seeing her regularly, not just the odd once like the others. This seems much more serious.

Sheeran and I have been together ten years. How could he? I hate him for this. Today I have discovered that he has had her in our bed and he refuses to be there with me. I will punish them both for this; I am seething with jealousy and anger.

My hands shake as I remove the sphere from its cloth bag and place it on my desk. I tune in to them. They are in bed together. I concentrate on her to kill her. I send pain. She will not do this to me. Soon she starts to hold her head and moan, then she begins to scream and scream, writhing around in agony. That is good. Eventually, after some minutes, she collapses. I know she is dead. I feel relief and satisfaction.

Sheeran is looking around. Somehow, I feel he knows what has happened. How does he know? I will do the same to him. I try to send the energy, but, to my horror, I find he has put up strong mental shields. He must know. How has he found out? I must go and kill him myself.

It is late, after midnight. I am in our quarters. There is a dim light from a single candle in a wall bracket. Quietly, I move through the main room and into the bed area. He is asleep. I will kill him while he sleeps. I have the knife in my hand. As silently as I can, I go across and stand by the bed. He is not aware of me. As I watch his face, I hesitate. My emotions are overwhelming me with fear. I hate him and yet I still feel a deep love for him. Feeling so confused, I waver and realise I do not have the courage to do it. I cant kill him.

Suddenly, he stirs, rolls over and sees me. I have left it too late. He becomes aware of the knife, leaps up and grabs both my arms. We struggle. He is so much stronger than me. Trying to twist the knife out my hand I am filled with panic and fear and cannot see for tears. Wrenching myself away with all my strength, my hand breaks free and slips downwards. The knife plunges into his stomach and he doubles up, falling to the floor bleeding. I stagger back, horrified. He goes still. I'm not sure if he's dead or not. In a panic I stab him again and again

It is a few days after the death rites for Sheeran and I am sitting in my office feeling desolate. I miss him terribly, and realise now with deep sadness that I loved him very much and now have killed him. I have no friends, and know I am hated by both my colleagues and the students. There is no one for me and I feel desperately empty inside. I have been writing my resignation. The paper is on the desk. Next to it is the Amethyst. Looking at my reflection in the mirror, I see a bitter and lonely woman. My own eyes start back at me with deep, deep sadness, and I feel tears slowly running down my cheeks. I don't bother to wipe them away.

Suddenly, flooding back into my mind are memories of my childhood. Somewhere inside me is that caring little girl who loved the birds and who was lost all those years ago. Was she really me? What happened? What have I become?

The old man, Arrad, was right. I am cursed. I think of all the people I have killed and hurt so much, just for my own selfish pleasure and gratification. Feeling wretched, I know there is only one course open to me.

Taking a deep breath, I focus my own image into the sphere I begin to feel intense pain inside my head. It hurts so much, feeling like my head will explode. Is this how the others felt? Is this what I put them through? The pain extends down my spine and throughout my body I am holding my head and crying screaming

The pain suddenly increases beyond my endurance. There is a blinding whiteness. Everything goes blank. I am floating, floating. Where am I? I'm confused, disorientated. I can see my body, a crumpled heap on the floor. It's not me anymore, I can't go back I know I can't go back. I can see the sphere on the table. Watching it for a long time - I don't know what to do. What can I do? I'm so alone, so lost. There's no one here, nothing. I feel scared, so very afraid.

After what seems like a long time the room first fades and a grey mist, with darker areas of shadow surrounds me. There's nothing here. Reaching out, there is only emptiness. It is like my own heart. I'm so frightened. I need someone to help me. Time just seems not to exist here. Please, someone help me.

I become aware of a tiny glimmer of light, so small, like a tiny candle, but from this comes a wonderful feeling of warmth and comfort. Seeing hands reaching for me, I grab desperately for them. Gradually the light gbrightens. I feel a woman's form slowly drawing me towards her. Holding her very tightly, I don't want her to let me go. Please don't let me go. I don't want to slip back into the shadows.

She folds me in her arms and cradles me like a child. Desperately crying, I cling to her. She cradles me for a long, long time. It feels very comforting, having been such a long time since anyone held me.

Gradually, I became aware that we are now completely surrounded by glorious light. Gently easing me away, I become aware of another presence near. It is Sheeran, I can't face him.......

Sofira - Some Thoughts In Conclusion

Sofira was immensely complex and became an evil person. She was a psychopathic and sadistic killer, and was responsible for many, many deaths and much physical suffering. Her darker side came out gradually over the course of my regression work. It was like peeling an onion. The deeper I went, the more tears came. I have found integrating her as part of myself extremely hard. Many of the events and the killings to which I regressed are too dark to write about. I felt her feelings, her pleasure in these dreadful actions. This was incredibly uncomfortable.

The amethyst sphere was an integral part of this, in that it allowed her to control other's minds and bend them to her sadistic will. She used it constantly, to manipulate, and eventually, to torture and kill. It was her constant companion, a valuable tool in her ever increasing life of sadism and violence. This, of course, was wholly wrong. The amethyst was a healing stone and its purpose was to help others. She abused its energies in the most evil way possible.

During the work I was doing I found this was not my first encounter with the sphere. I had had it before. In a few previous lives in Atlantis, I had used it for its proper purpose, to accelerate and magnify healing energy from Spirit. But, as Sofira, I turned totally against that, and used it to hurt and kill. This built up a debt of Karma in my soul. I also saw, with great reluctance, some of those I killed as Sofira were people I know now. One of the hardest to accept was her partner Sheeran, whom I realised with horrifying clarity, was Paul. I felt tremendous guilt when I faced him afterwards, and was very ashamed I had hurt him so terribly.

Paul and I discussed these events at great depth. Clearly, there was a lesson here for me that certainly needed addressing. I felt very bad about what I had done as Sofira, particularly the abuse of the sphere. One day, Paul suggested that while in trance, I should ask for the Earth's forgiveness. What followed is very difficult to describe. It was an amazing sensory experience, hard to put into words. I asked inside me for the Earth to forgive me for what I had done, for the abuse of the amethyst sphere, which was part of the Earth, itself. I felt myself going very deep. Then the most incredible feelings swept over me, inside me and connected with my innermost being. Warmth, love, compassion, forgiveness, and a deep, deep understanding all rolled into one overwhelming sensation. It spiralled around me and I felt expanded, like I was part of everything, everything that is and was. At once, I felt humble and elated. It took me some time to come through this. I didn't want to lose it. Gradually, it faded and I came back, feeling relaxed and at ease. I knew my request had been answered, and I knew the experience of pure love - the immensity of it, the power and beauty of it.

The Amethyst

One day, I was out driving along a country road, when a wasp flew in the car. Not liking wasps, I immediately looked for somewhere to pull in and dispose of it. I made use of a craft centre car park and the insect flew out as soon as I opened my doors. The craft centre interested me so I decided to go in and have a brief look round. I wandered idly into a shop that specialises in geological items and fossils. As I looked around, the owner spoke to me, and handed me something he had just unpacked. The amethyst sphere sat heavily in my hand and I was speechless. He was obviously oblivious to my inner turmoil as he spoke about what an excellent specimen it was. All my work with Paul on Sofira's life came into my mind. This was too much of a coincidence. I felt a curious power from it so I bought it and took it home.

At the group meeting the following Friday I shared my story with the others. Later that same evening, one of our members, Marjorie, channelled her guide, Sojah. I asked him about it and he explained that the globe I had was the same one I had in Atlantis. It had been sent back for me to use properly, for healing. It took me some time to come to terms with this incredible sequence of events. I was learning rapidly about the ability of those in Spirit to guide and help us.

One morning, in my regular meditation, Albani showed me details of the sphere's long journey. I saw it being taken aboard one of the ships fleeing the sinking land. It sailed west, across what is now the Caribbean. The vessel sank in a violent storm. I saw the sphere falling into the water, bouncing down an underwater cliff, to lay for centuries in the pure white sand. Eventually, it trawled up by some fishermen, who sold it. It passed through many hands, finally making its way to England, in the craft shop order.

I am told by Albani, that Sofira was my darkest hour. I certainly feel that way. I still find it hard to accept that my soul did such truly awful things. This makes me more determined to follow my path of Spirit and healing now. Never again do I want to face such terrible events.

The amethyst feels sacred to me and I want to use it only to channel healing energy and love.

Paul's Side of It

It was some months after Linda had completed her regressions as Sofira that I opened myself to experience my past lifetime as Sheeran. During this session, Albani directed me mainly to explore aspects of that lifetime connected with Sheeran's relationship to Sofira and how he reacted to her. It was a short but powerful session, which had a big emotional impact upon me. What follows is the transcript of that session.

Paul's Regression: Sheeran

I am standing in the square of the university, feeling rather content with myself. I feel I am making good progress in my studies, and I want to do well. If I can, I wish to rise in position to a high level. My father has achieved fame and has had a significant position within the university, so I want to follow in his footsteps, although not in the same field. My aim is to attain recognition for my intelligence and abilities, which I know are considerable.

We are a group of about 30 students studying archaeology together. There are some whom I regard as rivals, while others are more like friendly acquaintances. I am not particularly close to any of them, feeling that I do not want to become too involved with anyone because this may distract me from my work. There is one woman whom I feel I need to keep my eye on. That is Sofira. I feel that Sofira is my main rival. She has a sharp intelligence and I know that she is every bit as ambitious as I am.

It is later now and I am near the end of my studies. We have travelled a long way across the mountains to a dig on the west side of our land. There are many abandoned settlements here with traces of much earlier civilisations that lived on our land. Many relics exist about us although a lot of them are fragmentary. Much of this area has not been explored by archaeologists yet so there are some exciting opportunities for discoveries. I am sure that if I can make a significant find myself, then this will earn me much praise and help with my advancement. For a long time, I have been waiting for a chance like this.

Other people do not know about my psychic gift, but I can use my inner senses to help me get what I want. It is something I have been able to do since I was a child. When I ask my inner senses for help, then I can feel and know how to achieve my goal. So now I am putting my intention through my mind to my inner senses for me to find one of these valuable artifacts. I will let my inner senses show me where to look, and do this.

I have found a vase. This vase is very beautiful and it is whole and complete. Nobody else has found anything as significant as this. I know I will receive accolades for my discovery. The vase is obviously very well worked and shows a high degree of sophistication from its construction. It is very interesting and the teachers with us are very impressed.

I notice there is a mixture of reaction among the students at my discovery. There are some who are appreciative of my efforts, the less ambitious ones I suppose. However, I can sense that my competitors are more envious, and they probably wish that they had found this themselves. But I used my gift, my gift for seeing. I knew where I needed to dig in order to find this, and it appeared for me just as I wanted.

Now my studies are over and I am sitting for my final exams. I am finding it difficult to concentrate. Something is interfering in my mind. As I would normally do, I am trying to set my intentions towards achieving excellent results with these exams, getting my inner senses to help me. However, there seems to be a force pushing me off balance. I don't find my usual calm.

Somehow, I need to learn what this is about, and I feel that there is only one way for me to do this. With my thoughts, I ask my inner senses to tell me where this interference is coming from. As I try to still myself, a knowing and a picture slowly come into my mind. I see..I see Sofira. She is the one doing this. I do not know how she is doing it, but she is the one interfering in my mind.

I ask now my inner senses to help shield myself from this inter-ference and my mind is becoming clearer again. However, I do not know how I can apply myself to shield my mind from her intrusions and focus my intentions for the exam at the same time. This is frustrating because I feel that I will not be able to do my best, but I can still try.

I feel a mixture of emotions towards Sofira. With her ambition, I am sure she is trying to stop me from beating her, so she can finish top of our year, and she will probably succeed. But I wonder how she is managing to interfere in my mind. She must have some great power that she can use. I wonder how she does it. If it is something external that she uses, then maybe I could gain access to that power as well. It could help my ambitions enormously.

As I think about it, I realise that this is not the first time this interference may have happened. There have been other occasions recently when my mind has also been muddled. I am glad that I have recognised it at last. At least I will be able to shield myself in the future, and be alert to this challenge.

It is later now and I have made a deliberate choice to become Sofira's lover. I feel the need that I had to become very close to her so I could find out what she was doing. I cannot say that I feel greatly attracted to her, but the relationship serves a purpose. Through my inner senses I have been learning more about her thoughts, and now I have discovered the sphere. Secretly, I have tried to use the sphere myself, and it works marvellously. I have to be very careful so Sofira does not find out. By projecting my thoughts into the sphere in the way I would speak to my inner senses, this seems to amplify my intentions and make them stronger, so I can see much more clearly and get the results that I want. Through the sphere, I can see people at a distance and direct thoughts to them.

I have not yet wanted to trace Sofira's movements with the sphere. I am afraid that she might sense that someone is interfering with the sphere and using it without her permission. There are some things about Sofira that make me feel very uneasy. My senses tell me that she is dangerous, but part of me does not dare to learn more. She is a very dominating and forceful personality, and I tend to submit to her wishes and moods rather than challenge her. As time goes on, I more and more try to stay out of her way, and I do at times feel quite afraid of her.

We have been together about three years, but I really want to escape from her. She does help me to gain better positions within the faculty. However, I'm not sure if that is enough. Once or twice I have taken lovers, and I've needed to be very secretive about this because I do not want her to become angry with me. I am very afraid of her anger. I sense that she could be very, very jealous. So I try to keep myself quite neutral with her and don't give her any cause to be alarmed by my behaviour.

It is later now, and I have discovered what she is doing. I had to know, and I feel absolutely sickened and revolted by what I have seen. She is murdering people, and enjoying it. I've seen it on a few occasions. She has this room, and she murders people there. She seems to take great delight in murdering young women, but it is not just them. It is others as well. Then, I notice afterwards that she comes up, and she has such a smug grin on her face. I sense that these killings give her some form of emotional release and satisfaction. This terrifies me. With what kind of person am I living? I need to get out of this. I need to somehow get untangled from her, or I'm sure it will be the death of me before too long. This woman is wicked and evil. I feel I have to make some excuse so I don't have sex with her anymore. I do not want to be involved with her at all.

Perhaps, if I feign that I am not interested for some time, she may just regard that we are drifting apart. I haven't wanted to have sex with her for some considerable time. But I sometimes feel that she forces me. She wants it very much, but I do not, and I know now about my reluctance to do this.

There is someone else anyway, someone with whom I feel much more comfortable to be close, and share some love. I don't ever feel love from Sofira. I feel that she is wanting to dominate me. Even though I know I'm quite strong in my own right, I don't want to feed energy into her. She gets her sense of power through belittling others and I don't want to be part of it.

It is later. I have been seeing my lover for a considerable time. Her name is Anja. She is a little younger than me and has trained as an archaeologist like myself. By being in my office as my assistant, we do much work together upon projects. So it is easy for us to meet and to find reasons to be together. I have tried to be very careful not to arouse Sofira's suspicions. I just wish she would find someone else so I could be away from her and be free. I would like to be more open about my relationship with Anja, but I cannot while Sofira is still around. I have tried to become more separate from Sofira, to encourage her to seek a lover, but she seems uninterested.

Sofira feels like a monster to me. She even affects my drive to do my work. I do not want to be working in the same department as her. My interest in archaeology has been eroded by the revulsion I feel at what Sofira is doing. It makes me question my own motives as well. If I had not been so ambitious, if I had followed my heart more, then I would never have come so much together with Sofira. If I had been more aware of her motivations, instead of letting my own base instincts for power rule me, then maybe I could have freed myself from her long before now. I just hope I haven't left it too late.

It is later. I am relaxing together with Anja in the bedroom. It is something we do quite frequently, and we have had a pleasant day together. We've been working, doing some research, sharing our results together. We feel we are making progress. Actually, we are interested in these settlements on the west coast and we have been making some catalogues of different articles that have been found there. We have completed quite a substantial section of this today, and I feel satisfied with the results we have achieved.

I am feeling happy and assured. But something is disturbing me. My inner senses are agitated. I'm feeling I need to be wary. What is it?

My lover, she's screaming. She's upset. I know what it is. It is Sofira. It must be. I have to protect myself. Anja is struggling. I cannot help her. She's, she's collapsing. I know she will die, because I've seen it before. Sofira does this to people. My inner senses have shown me. She'll turn her attention to me in a moment. I'm sure she will. I must stop her. She must have found out. She must have been watching what I was doing and become suspicious finally.

Anja is lying on the floor. She has such a grotesque expression on her face and was suffering so much pain. Her chest is not moving and she's stopped breathing. I know she is dead.

There are waves of energy coming at me as well. But I can block them out. I'm in shock, but I must concentrate on my inner senses and block her out. I must save myself now. There is nothing I can do for my friend. I'm just succeeding. It is a struggle but I'm just succeeding.

I feel terrible and my heart is racing. I feel the loss of my friend. I feel panic, and I am afraid. I feel sure Sofira will try to get me. She does this kind of thing, she seeks revenge. Nobody can get anything over her. She won't let them. She wont let me get away with this. Now that she knows I've had a lover, she'll want to kill me.

I'm sure that my days are numbered. I'll have to try to find some escape route, and I'll have to be very alert. What can I do to save myself? I'm sure she'll come at me. At least, I can tell when she wants to attack me with the sphere.

If I keep my guard up, maybe shortly, in a few days, I could find an excuse, some way of leaving the city and going somewhere she won't be able to track me down. Even then, I don't know with the sphere, if I can do this. I'm thinking that there might be only one way I can save myself. If I was to steal the sphere and take it from her, she wouldn't be able to use it anymore. Then I could go and be safe. I think that is what I must do. I must find a way and a time when I could steal the sphere. And I hope that in the meanwhile, my inner senses may just provide enough protection to stop her from me becoming another of her victims.

It is night-time. I am lying in bed. It is four days since Anja died. Even sleeping is something I have been wary of doing in the last few days. When I go to bed in the evenings, I feel the grief of Anja's passing. I feel it now and I miss her. She was precious to me and so supportive. I did not ever need to fear her.

With Sofira, it is different. I have avoided her, stayed out of her way. I hope I have kept the house secure enough so that she will not enter. I'm still afraid. In the next days I want to use my senses to find out how I can take the sphere. It may be necessary to wait until after the funeral of my friend. Then, there'll be more space. At least, this is what I plan.

Something has disturbed me, and I've just opened my eyes. I don't believe it. She's there looking at me. Am I dreaming or what? No, she's there, and she has a knife, I will try not to show I am afraid. I must grab the knife from her and protect myself. If I move slowly. If I try to pretend I'm not too alarmed, then maybe I'll have a chance.

I am grabbing for her now. I am grabbing for her. I am trying to wrest the knife out of her hand. She is frantic and squirming around. It is hard for me to hold her for she is moving so quickly and has such a strength in her body. I can hardly believe her strength. Ahh Ah. I've been stabbed. I feel myself falling to the ground. I feel the life force ebbing. Uhhh. She's attacking me again. She's not stopping. She's stabbing me..

I am looking down. My body is a complete mess. I see Sofira standing there, and she is shaking. She seems remorseful for having killed me. Perhaps I did mean something to her after all.

I feel myself rising upwards. I need help. Its been a shock and I feel revolted by what I've had to go through with Sofira. I feel such a lot of negative feelings towards her. Now I feel that there could have been much love between us. But that is clouded by so many negative thoughts and feelings. I find it hard to forgive her for what she has done, not just to me, but to my friend, Anja, and all those other people as well.

I can see Anja waiting for me. There is someone else too, a beautiful woman who is my guide. She is wanting to dress my wounds and comfort me. I feel my guide's love. She knows that this has been very distressing for me, what I've experienced now. Her thoughts tell me that it wasn't intended that way, in the beginning. However, the way Sofira turned had a great influence. She feels that I managed to some extent to avoid corruption in my own life then, but feels I could have been more outspoken and honest with Sofira. If I had said to her what I really thought about her activities, it may have changed her, because she could have listened to me. However, because I was afraid, and backed away from her, ultimately, this led to my death.

It is later now. I am aware that it is the time of Sofira passing over. She is coming, and I know in soul she is very beautiful, and there is a lot of love there for her from me. But I still feel this strong reluctance and repugnance, not wanting to get too close to the personality that she carried in that life. I feel timid, and I am standing somewhat behind my guide, to feel protection, until I am really ready for this. My friend Anja is also here. I can sense that she feels a similar reluctance to me. Other souls are here too. There is one whose name was Arrad, and there are many others. There is a whole collection of souls who met their end through Sofira in that life.

I am looking at Sofira. I see great sorrow in her eyes. She is very sad and remorseful. She now realises what she did and is very sorry. She is asking for my forgiveness.

For a moment I hesitate, but then I step towards her. I certainly can forgive her in Spirit, and I am glad to have her with me once again. I hope we can all learn from this, that it may help us go forward. But I fear that some great disturbance has taken place through that life, and for many of us a considerable correction may be needed before a balance can be reached again.

Connections

During a seminar, which I was co-ordinating, Linda was giving a presentation about her Atlantean past lives and she was illustrating this with drawings of her experiences that she was able to show. At this time, Linda had only been regressed to a handful of lives from Atlantis, but one of these was her past lifetime as Sofira. During her presentation then Linda concentrated mainly upon telling about Sofira and one of the other regressions whose character, Angela, was a woman who had poisoned other people. Neither of these lives were particularly pleasant so I was quite admiring of Linda's capacity to talk about these matters in public.

For Lynne, this was the first time she had heard Linda talk in any depth or detail about her regression experiences in Atlantis. Lynne was a science teacher, and although she had done some past life regressions with me, she did not feel that she could have any personal connection with Atlantis. She was open minded about the existence of Atlantis, and curious to hear what Linda had to say, but that was all.

From the beginning, when Linda started speaking, Lynne felt nervous and uncomfortable. As Linda proceeded with her talk, Lynne's body reacted in an extreme way. She suffered from an acute chest pain, a severe headache and her stomach was cramping. Lynne could hardly bear to listen. Afterwards her symptoms did not disappear so she arranged to speak with me.

Before Linda spoke, Lynne had felt no bodily discomfort. Lynne recognised from her past life regressions with me, that the type of sudden headache she had got was of the type which manifested when she resisted some imagery or memory that wanted to express itself through her consciousness. But Lynne did not want to admit that she may have some memories of lifetimes on Atlantis. It felt too painful and she was afraid. However, we both knew that her bodily sensations were telling her what her mind did not want to admit. The pains in her body were not shifting. I was aware that the only way for her to release the pain was for her to acknowledge their source truthfully and consent to work with the relevant memories that were associated with this. She agreed to this as I led her into a meditation, and at once the pain began to subside.

This was the beginning for Lynne of a series of regressions that took her to past lifetimes in Atlantis. It was a very difficult process for her, but ultimately liberating.

In both the lives that Linda talked about, Lynne had her own personal connection. From the Sofira lifetime, Lynne was Anja, Sheeran's lover. In the other lifetime Lynne's character was a victim of poisoning. No wonder she reacted so strongly!

Denise sensed herself as Arrad, the old man who showed Sofira the sphere. Denise felt that Arrad had spent many years as a recluse, and meeting Sofira was the first human contact he had had for a long time.

To be treated so badly by Sofira and killed was a great shock to Arrad, and left a wound in Denise's soul confirming a pattern of belief that for her to open herself to close human contact was dangerous. This is one of many examples of this pattern from lives on Atlantis that Denise has needed to confront.

Drawing the threads together

One evening, the four of us, Linda, Denise, Lynne and myself were gathered in my flat for a meeting. We were talking about Sofira and Linda was sharing how she was still very troubled by her memories of this life, particularly how she killed Sheeran. I had recently finished writing my account of my regression to Sheeran and so I gave this to Linda for her to read. For Linda, this account was quite shocking. She had to stop several times because of the emotions building up inside her. Then when she reached the point of Sheeran's death, she stopped for several minutes, and her head was down while she was silently whimpering. Even though it was very difficult, she knew she had to read this. Finally she managed to finish.

My intuition told me that the process for Linda over this past lifetime was not finished. I needed to do more. Then my attention turned to Lynne. In the previous days, it had been indicated to Lynne through her Spiritual guide, Echmael, that it would be beneficial for her to go through a regression to her past life as Anja, Sheeran's lover. Lynne had so far avoided this, through fear and knowing that it would be likely a very uncomfortable experience. I felt that now would be a good time to approach this, while Linda was present. Lynne reluctantly agreed.

Very soon Lynne was engrossed in her experience as Anja. As Anja she was a young woman happy with life, enjoying her position as a researcher working with Sheeran. She felt in awe of Sheeran with his knowledge and capabilities but she was happy to be close with him. Sheeran confided in Anja how trapped he felt by Sofira, and although she was aware of Sofira, Anja did not believe that Sofira would hurt her or be able to identify her. She enjoyed being Sheeran's lover and was content with that.

The death scene was very graphic and emotional. Previously, whenever Linda had talked of Sofira, Lynne had felt a pain in the back of her head at the brain stem or medulla oblongata. Linda confirmed to me that this was where she, as Sofira focussed the energy when sending energy through her sphere to hurt somebody.

As Anja, when she was attacked by Sofira, initially, Lynne felt in her body, a painful surge of energy coming into the back of her head and then spreading upwards into both sides of her head. The pain continued to fill her head as if her head would explode apart, becoming like a pressure that wanted to split her head open. Then she felt this pain going into her heart, and felt that her physical heart was failing. It was an excruciating pain in the centre of her chest. Along side of this a further pain went down her spine to other parts of her body. At this point, she collapsed and Anja died. The pain diminished as her soul became detached from her physical body. It was an awful way to die, and very emotional for Lynne to experience.

162

Later, Anja experienced herself being counselled by her guide about the anger she felt in her chest towards Sofira. She was being urged not to turn that anger into hate, and Anja realised that she felt sad for Sofira.

I asked Lynne if there was anything she wanted to say to Linda about it all. Lynne said that she felt sorry for the things Sofira had done. It seemed a shame not to have used the power and energy she had then for good. Lynne perceived that inside Sofira there was a beautiful heart and Spirit and that if she had been able to show this, then people could have loved her. Lynne felt then that she bore Linda no anger, malice or grudges at all.

When she came out of trance, Lynne went straight to Linda and they embraced in a flood of tears. It was a very beautiful healing.

Two days later, Linda had a further regression to her life as Sofira. This time, she accessed the childhood memories of Sofira, as a very sensitive girl, wanting to care for birds and heal them, but feeling isolated and alone. Then through various events, and the influence of her mother, Sofira was encouraged to close her feelings down. This, she eventually decided to do, and she almost did it completely. Without her feelings operating, she became a murderess. When she killed someone, she felt a sense of absolute control where she felt power. It was only with Sheeran, where she did not feel able to suppress her feelings that she could not do this. Becoming aware of this sensitive, feeling, loving girl was very healing for Linda. It helped Linda to acknowledge the importance for her to express her feelings in her present life. Also though, it helped her to know, that even with someone as bad a Sofira, at the core of her being, there was love.

After this, Linda felt compelled to revise the transcript of Sofira's life she had written to include these missing sections. The experience felt much more whole for her then.

Over the days of these regressions, I had been suffering from damage to my sciatic nerve and I was in a lot of pain, and largely immobile. I had been feeling much pain and fear and needed support. Linda was the person able to help me most over this period, and I valued her companionship very much. During these days, I felt the fear and resentment of Sheeran towards Sofira melt away. It was a healing for me too.

Chapter 15

Manipulations of Science

Issues of Control

Many people like to feel in control of their lives or even in control of people around them. To feel in control, people can make sure that things turn out the way they want them to be. It gives a feeling of being in charge. However, too much control can make life rigid and reduce creativity. When people feel controlled by someone else, they are naturally going to build up resentment and anger towards that person who is doing the controlling. We all have a right to be free and to make our own choices and decisions. People who want to be in control are often very afraid of what would happen if they were not in control. Who would do anything for them if they didn't do it themselves? This can sometimes stem from beliefs that no one understands them or that they are in some way unlovable. But it can be very difficult for those who like to be in control to allow the love and support of others.

For myself, I recognise that many of these fears and tendencies regarding control have affected me. I like to be in charge, but I have tended to feel very insecure if someone challenged my authority. The thought of someone controlling me tends to fill me with dread and I have tried to avoid situations where this would happen.

It has not surprised me then, to learn of a past life I lived on Atlantis where these issues were very much to the fore in a dark way. For some months before I went through the regressions to this life, I was afraid of it. In this lifetime I knew that I had tried to control people's minds, but I did not want to face this. I would be most scared of anyone trying to control my mind, and then it seems that this was what I was trying to do to others.

When I finally gained the courage to confront this life, I found it very hard. I felt the character I was in that life to have a heart that was very cold, and I did not like him at all. It made me feel even more sombre when I sensed that many of my victims from then were souls who are important to me in my present life now. I did not like that I could cause so much damage and pain to people's minds. Recognising echoes of this past life in my present behaviour made me feel very uncomfortable. I hope that the insights I have gained from this have helped me. We have dated this past life as coming from the middle period of Atlantis' history, after the Golden Age was over.

Paul's Regression - The Crystal Implant Scientist

My name is Pourli. I live with my family in a large house overlooking the sea. We live on the west side of the land. The members of my family include my father, mother, younger brother and sister. My father is a scientist. He is researching the power of crystals as an energy source, and he is interested in many varied applications of how this can be used.

I admire my father who is dedicated to his work. His work is his life and I would like to be like him. He works at the university nearby, but he has also built a laboratory in the basement of our house. Whenever we can, my mother and I help him with his work there. This is what I want to do, I want to become a scientist like him.

My father is quite famous. He travels to various learning institutions giving talks and demonstrations of his discoveries. He tells us that he has many rivals and people who are jealous of the success he has achieved. That is why he prefers to work with us, because he knows that he can trust us and we will support him.

One day I would like to be famous like my father. I would like to work at the same university where he has worked and achieve a high position there. If I learn enough from my father, then perhaps I can make my own discoveries using crystals as well. This is what my parents want from me too. They want to be proud of me.

I like working with crystals. When I place my hands close to a crystal, I can feel the energy emitted. My father has shown me how, by slowly moving my hands away, I can use my hands to measure the power and strength of the crystal energy. With our experiments, we have to discard most of the crystals that we receive, because we only want to use the ones that are the best conductors of energy. I can help my father in selecting these.

It is later now. I have acquired my own research laboratory within the university. The study I had to complete was quite tedious and boring and I found that I could learn much more by working along side my father. However, I had to gain my qualifications to become respected by other tutors who are here.

My father is still my closest advisor and I trust him more than anyone. I have decided not to entangle myself in any close relationships. This would only distract me from reaching my goals. I wish to dedicate myself utterly to my work, as my father has done before me. Only then can I gain a high position and achieve fulfillment of my potential. There are many ambitious people within the university and I will have to work hard to be successful.

I have two assistants working with me. One of them, Tarla, would like to be close to me. But I have refused, instead suggesting for her to concentrate on improving her working relationship with me and doing what I tell her. I have had to find an aspect of working with crystal power that would distinguish my work from that of my father. The work I have chosen is to do with the influence of crystals upon the human mind.

We have been experimenting with how crystals can be used to transmit thought patterns and then how other crystals can aid the reception of these thoughts in a person's mind. This is fascinating work. We have student volunteers helping us. What we do is to attach a pair of crystals to the subject's head. Then using a transmitter stone, we try to project thoughts and energy through this for the person to receive. During our course we had to study some human biology, so we are experimenting to find the best and most effective positions around the head where the crystals can be placed. What we have found works best is to have two crystals which are similar and linked, perhaps coming from the same crystal source. These can be placed on either side of the head, a little above the temple and affecting the person receiving strongly. It is marvellous that we have already been able to advance our research to this extent. The work I'm doing is pioneering and I'm sure to gain recognition if I persevere.

My female assistant, Tarla, helps me with the crystals. She is very sensitive to their energies, and has been largely responsible for selecting appropriate stones that we can use. My other assistant, Lainstra, helps more with the organisational side and recruiting of volunteers. It is fascinating how people's minds can be influenced. This work could have many applications.

It is later, and I am sitting in my office at the university, alone. I have received some devastating news that I can hardly take it in. It is a huge shock to me. My father is dead. The laboratory at our home was burnt out and the charred remains of my father's body was found lying on the floor. Nobody claims to know what happened, but I think it was murder. My father was too careful to allow something like this to happen. Someone must have killed him. I feel bitter and angry.

There are too many rivalries and jealousies in this place. Some people will stop at nothing to get their way. My father was a good man and he didn't deserve this. Who did this to him? I feel like getting them back. And if they killed my father, what's to stop them trying to kill me too? We worked so closely together.

Who can I trust? There is no one. My mother is too distraught to help me so I have to continue on my own. I won't let anyone near me. No one must interfere with my work. I don't want what happened to my father to happen to me. I will have to make sure that I'm safe, that no one can get to me.

One man I suspect is the biology professor, Sherrip. He was working with my father and stands most to gain by my father's death. Now he will take over as head of science. I don't like him. He is an unpleasant shifty man. Sometimes he comes to monitor and help with my experiments. I don't like his interest. If I could gain more control in using the crystals, I would like to interrogate him and find out what he knows. Then, if I could control his mind, he wouldn't be a threat to me anymore. Assuming he had something to do with my father's death, this would be much less than he deserves.

We have reached a new stage in our experiments. For some time I have been interested in finding more power in the way thoughts and energy could be transferred using the crystals. I have had the idea that if the crystals were actually implanted beneath the person's skin and next to the skull, then this may increase the capacity of thought transfer tremendously.

We have a young female student for this purpose. Many of the students are quite pleased to take an active part in the research we're doing. She is unaware though of the full extent of my plans. Noticing that Tarla is quite uneasy about us taking the experiments to this extent, I try to dismiss her anxieties by telling her that we will take the crystals out again within a few days. I need Tarla to help with the placement of the crystals and hope therefore, that her anxieties will not impede her abilities in this regard.

We give the student a drink. I say it is to relax her, but it is actually a sleeping draught which Lainstra has prepared. We need the girl unconscious for the operation. This has worked and we have her strapped in a chair.

I have tried to plan this as well as I can. We have obtained a healing ointment from one of the local sanctuaries. This can function both as an antiseptic and to help the skin knit together once the operation has been performed. Also I want to cut only a bare minimum amount of hair from around the incisions so that the effect of our work cannot be noticed. My assistants can help me with this.

Lainstra has made the incision for me. I have two triangular slivers of crystal, quartz crystal, and these I insert carefully. We have to wipe away some blood, apply the ointment and fold back the skin and flesh. Soon the operation is done, and we can wait for the girl to recover consciousness.

It is some days later and I am in the basement, a darkened room below the laboratory where I normally work. This is where the crystals are collected for the experiments which I do. I am with the girl here. It is a private space where I can work with her alone. I have the transmitter stone in my hand. This is a clear quartz crystal, pointed at one end. Holding this crystal in my hand, I can project my thoughts, into it and imagine these thoughts from there going into the mind of the girl in front of me.

Each time I do this, it seems to jolt her. Her head moves from side to side and she appears shocked. I have told her that she will remember nothing of what has happened to her and she must do as I say. At first I was having some success with my commands. When I told her to tell me things she would do so. But now, she seems so dopey and uncoordinated, it is like she has suffered a form of mental collapse. I don't really know what I can do with her anymore. I don't think I can repair the damage.

Actually, I feel quite confused by this and anxious by my failure. There must be a way in which I can modify my thought input so my subjects will obey me, yet keep their mind intact. I will need to experiment further with more students. It would be a great breakthrough in my research if I can succeed.

I cannot think what to do with the girl. She is so confused now, almost like a vegetable. I've told the others I've sent her home to recover. But if I let her loose, she may be taken to a temple of healing. They could discover what I've done. It is very difficult. But I decide I have to kill her. I'll give her a drink. She has hardly any life left in her anyway. It would be a disaster if her mental state was traced to me. There isn't any other way. Perhaps in the future, if any operations do not work properly, then I could take the crystals out before it reached this stage. I'll have to learn to do that myself. I think it would be possible to explain these cases away as being mental breakdowns. But I hope I can perfect my technique with this soon, so these messy situations don't occur.

It is later and I have performed quite a few implant operations now. Gradually, I have learnt to direct my thoughts so I do not destroy the person's mind. I have been surprised and delighted how much response I could get to my suggestions and commands. Usually, my subjects will do exactly what I tell them. It is as though their thoughts become my own. This is exactly what I wanted.

I have tried to operate on that biology professor, Sherrip who was resistant to my commands. It was like trying to get blood out of a stone. When I mentioned my father, his face would twitch involuntarily, but he would say nothing. This has made me even more suspicious of him. However, I have instructed him to stay out of my way and keep to his own business and I hope he does that. At least, then I will have removed him from being a threat.

I am having a lot of trouble with Tarla. She objects to my experiments and she does not want me to be implanting crystals. It is irritating me more and more. She cannot stop me doing my research. I have had to do many of my experiments on my own, in secret to keep her from criticising me, but she continues to go on at me. I am afraid that she may soon complain of me to others, and I can't let that happen. If I implanted crystals in her, then she would do exactly as I say and I could control her as I wish.

Tarla is with me in the basement room. She has just brought a consignment of crystals which will be very suitable for our work. I suggest a drink to celebrate. Of course, I have added something to hers. She has a little sip and hesitates. She can tell the taste and knows. All at once, Tarla looks up at me startled. Starting to be abusive to me, she moves to leave the room. I can't allow that, so I hit her across the face. She sits there quivering violently, pleading with me not to do it, not to do this to her. I feel a pain in my heart, but I cannot stop now. It's too late. I insist on her finishing the drink. Finally she does, and I prepare the operation....

Somehow, I feel very nervous this time, uncertain. I wonder if I'm doing wrong. Keeping Tarla in the basement room for some days until the wound is healed, I instruct her to forget what happened, do exactly what I say. There is a vacantness in her eyes, a sadness. She is not now the woman that I knew. But at least now she will do what I tell her without question and that will be better for my work.

It is some time later. I have been able to build up a formidable reputation for myself across the northern part of our land. Often I travel, giving talks and demonstrations about my work to various groups in much the same way that my father used to do. People are fascinated by what I have learned about the human mind and how crystals can be used to enhance learning and communication. Of course, I keep much of my work secret from the public gaze for it would be dangerous to me for me to do otherwise. I still have my two assistants working with me, although when I travel I tend not to take Tarla with me. Her personality has lost too much of its animation to be useful when I'm with other people.

There is a large gathering of scientists from across the land meeting together to discuss the power of crystals. I have been invited to present the keynote speech. It is a great honour. This represents the pinnacle of my career. Strangely though, I feel uneasy and I do not know why.

I am on the stage delivering my speech. Suddenly there is a disturbance in the room. It is Lainstra, my assistant. He is coming on stage with one of my students. There are military personnel with him. What is he doing? Lainstra is pointing to me, accusing me, showing the audience with the student where I have been implanting crystals. How dare he? He is betraying me. This is a humiliation. I feel afraid. Trying to defend myself, I find that I can't. This is the end of my career. He can't do this. I feel broken. Military personnel are shuffling me off the stage. I have to keep a semblance of dignity, so I don't resist. I thought I could rely on him. How stupid of me.

I've been taken to the fortress in the centre of the town, to one of the cells that is underground. It smells damp and musty. I don't like being here. The military have been rough with me. They've just thrown me in. Already they have interrogated me. They tell me that if I pass on my secrets to them, they'll let me go.

172

Now I am beginning to understand. This was a set up. Lainstra must be working for the military. I am sure they are paying him well! By denouncing me in front of my peers, they have made sure that I will be able to work nowhere else, except with them.

But I will not agree to their plans. I feel determined about that. I will not let my fine scientific knowledge fall into the hands of the military. I hate them. I hate them doing this to me. They have got no right to treat me like this. They just want to use my knowledge for their own ends. I will get nothing out of it. They just want to make weapons, to manipulate and hurt people. I will not go that far.

Being on my own, I am starting to question myself. I am feeling uncertain. In thinking about Tarla, I am missing her. What if she goes through the rest of her life with these crystals implanted in her? She'll never be free. What about the others? I didn't care about them. What have I really achieved?

They have taken me to another room and they have me strapped in an immobile chair. I can hardly move. I do not know what they intend. However, I refuse to tell them anything.

Lainstra has been here and I try to spit in his face. I hate him. But now Sherrip, the biology professor has come in with some more military personnel. I might have known he would be involved in this. I feel contempt for him.

They have drugged me so that physically I will not resist, but I am still aware of what they are doing. One of them is cutting my hair to the sides. Sherrip has some surgical instruments. Now I know what they want to do. This is too much. I will not let them.

He is cutting me and I feel the pain. It hurts. Now he is inserting the crystals, and they feel cold and foreign. I don't like it. They are trying to take me over, force me to tell them what I know. It feels so uncomfortable.

Lainstra has got the transmitter stone. Ahh! He speaks too harshly....I can feel the vibration go right through my brain...Aagh!...He's trying to make me talk. I can hear his thoughts. They rumble inside me. He can't do this very well....Aagh! I can feel his thoughts right inside me. He wants me to talk. I will not talk. It just irritates me inside. He can't make me do anything...Aagh...He can't do this....I don't feel compelled. He doesn't have the ability....Aagh. It feels like my whole brain is being churned up inside....Ohh! His thoughts are so loud and ugly, it goes right through me....so repulsive... so awful...He keeps repeating the same thing. I'll not tell him my secrets. My head is in agony....Aagh....

I feel totally exhausted. I'm groaning....I feel totally numb in my head. Lainstra says they'll keep doing this to me until I talk....I cannot reply.

They've taken me back to my cell. I feel distressed and numb. I can't stand this kind of torture. They are trying to control me. It hurts so much. I cannot think straight. Lainstra cannot do it properly. He cannot modulate his thoughts sufficiently.

It is later and they are becoming more desperate. I still won't co-operate. Now they are threatening to bring Tarla, to torture her unless I talk. The bastards! I will resist them with all the strength I've got. I will not say a thing.

Tarla is here. They have her in the room. They say they'll cut her, hurt her unless I agree to work with them. I'm in the chair. Lainstra is speaking to me through the stone, commanding me to do his will....Aagh....He still hasn't got it right. He says they'll torture her, cut her, even kill her, if I continue my resistance.

It has stopped. I look in Tarla's eyes and I see sadness there. Thinking that I had taken over her mind using the crystals, now I am aware that she knows what is going on. She doesn't want me to talk and is gagged. I can only sense her thoughts through her eyes. But we could always talk with our eyes. My heart is melting and I feel so sorry. Her eyes are imploring me not to give in.

They are making me watch while they torture her. They have taken off her clothes and are cutting her. She's bleeding and screaming. It is awful. First they are cutting her on the arms. She is standing up, held by binds to her hands and feet so she cannot stop them. They are threatening me. As soon as I agree to go along with them they will stop. I don't want them to hurt her anymore....I...love her. I can't bear this....but....but...she looks at me, and I can tell she still doesn't want me to talk....She is so brave.

I can feel a change coming over me, feeling sadness, not only for her, but for all the people to whom I have implanted crystals...I just don't....When I see what they are doing to me and to Tarla, it isn't right. It isn't right to treat human beings like this.

I haven't talked. They are saying one more time that they will kill her unless I agree to work with them. They make me watch. I don't want to see it...Oh no....They've stabbed her...They've stabbed her in the chest...She's dead.

They've finished with me now and are dragging me to my cell. I want to die too. There is nothing left for me.

It is later. I've been taken out of my cell and I've decided I'm going to kill myself. I'll pretend to co-operate. The guard is taking me along the corridor. I can see the knife I want to get. I'm walking very easily and willingly. Waiting for the right moment, I take my time...Now....Aaghh!.....

My body has slumped to the ground. I am floating. It feels grey. I must have died. My body is a mess. I was a twisted mess in that life, becoming so bitter and twisted, only caring for myself. What a dreadful waste!

My father appears to me, telling me to forgive myself. I did wrong and I must learn from that. He knows I loved him, but I became bitter and angry when he died, and stopped caring for people. I only wanted fame and position like he had. He reassures me that it was his time to die, and urges me not to be bitter when things like this happen. There is nothing I can do. He hopes I can learn from this, do better next time.

I feel ashamed of my efforts. I know there will be a lot to make up. Feeling very heavy around my heart, I realise my main lesson I needed from that experience was to love, to care about others as much as myself. However, especially after my father died I was far too much obsessed with my work. The main mistake I made was feeling that I would only be safe if I controlled everything around me, and everyone. This is what I set out to do.

I feel very sorry for all those people now, and I know they did not deserve it.

A Victim's Perspective

I have known Annie for a number of years. Our relationship started with her as my client, exploring some of her past lives. Then she became a colleague when she joined the Healing group and we worked together there. This has evolved into friendship and we both try to support each other in various ways.

The relationship we share has not always been easy. There has been a dynamic between us, where sometimes I would want something very much from her and she would perceive this as me trying to control her. As soon as there was the slightest tendency towards this, Annie would withdraw and I would feel very frustrated. Then Annie would remain distant from me for quite a time. We have continued to play through that dance a number of times, without understanding the roots of it - until recently. In the year previous to my crystal implant scientist regression, Annie had two nightmares three months apart. These had the appearance and feeling of being past life memories, with both dreams relating to different stages of one particular past life. Until after I had finished these regressions I had no knowledge concerning the contents of these dreams.

During the first dream, Annie experienced herself as a fairly young, intelligent woman with an articulate manner and expressive face, her eyes capable of bringing forth feelings from deep within her. She worked as an assistant to a scientist who was working with crystals and doing research about their possible effect upon the human mind. She felt close to this man. They had an empathy which made working together very easy. Through their conversations they could bounce ideas off each other, and she felt she could anticipate what he would do next. Her desire was to share a physical relationship with him but so far he had refused this.

Then his father died and she observed a change in him. He became very withdrawn, secretive and even cold towards her. There appeared to be a change in the direction of his work and she tried to question him about this. But she continued to trust him.

One day, he made her submit to have a crystal implant operation. She felt so much shock and disbelief and due to the drink draught she had taken, she could hardly react to him or resist him. The effects of this operation were devastating. Her intellect was not damaged. She could still see and perceive what was happening around her. However she was not able to articulate it. He had taken away her communication abilities. It felt like drowning and having the life sucked out of her. Yet she looked normal but she couldn't make herself heard.

She could not understand why people could not see that she was not the same. This gave her a feeling of utter helplessness. She carried inside a feeling of intense frustration and pain. With great despair, she wanted to cry out to other people `Can't you see what he has done?', but she couldn't do it, because he controlled her actions...

The second dream was a continuation of the first. With the implants, he made it so that they became physical lovers. She could tell that he genuinely loved her. He felt remorse that the spark was not there anymore in her. From his sense of loss, he was wanting to express his regret by being tender with her.

However, for her, she felt this as just a further instance of abuse. He could have had her as she was. She felt he had just wasted what they could have had together. This way of relating together became like a nightmare. She felt herself like a dog who submits

177

to her master's commands. Through it all, her own internal thoughts and feelings continued to function normally with devastating effect.

Now, all she could do was to wish for death. What had been most important for her had been the expression of her creativity and intellect. After the implant operation, she would never be able to realise this. Going through the physical motions of life gave her no joy on its own. She wanted to die. It felt like being a robot.

In the end, she was aware of her arms bleeding, bleeding elsewhere, and a stabbing in the chest. She had nothing to live for. It was like a suicide....

When I finished my regressions of this past lifetime, I gave Annie a copy of the tape from these sessions. She had not until then identified the man who was the scientist in her dreams. As soon as she started listening to the tape, it came together for her. The dreams that she had had and my regression sessions fitted together perfectly. She was the woman I had identified as Tarla, and I was the scientist who had abused her.

It was shocking for me to make this discovery, but in other ways also a relief. At least now, Annie and I know from where the difficult pattern in our relationship originates. I feel that processing through this has made our friendship stronger. But I do feel deeply sorry for what I did to her. Nothing can ever change what happened now...

Lainstra

I sensed that Lynne was the soul who was my male assistant, Lainstra, in that life. When I informed her of this and she read my transcript, her first reaction was denial. She did not want to believe it. She told me that she felt no resonance within herself for those violent acts that were committed against me as the scientist and Annie as Tarla.

However, while she wrote those thoughts she began to feel a burning sensation in her heart and recognised the truth of what her body was telling her. She sensed that a part of her was making a very determined effort not to see herself involved in such awful things as what happened in that prison. Yet, when she listened more to her heart and accepted what it was telling her, thoughts and feelings about the person she was in that life flowed into her mind.

She felt strongly that Lainstra was never loyal to my character then. He was jealous of my relationship with Annie, and was willing to betray me and work with Sherrip, because he believed that he had more ability than had been recognised. Lainstra felt insulted by the limited role he had been able to play.

Lynne felt very disturbed that as Lainstra, she had tried to control my mind. However, she could also acknowledge that for me to go through that experience helped me to understand the pain and distress that I had caused to others, and so helped me to learn.

Some time later, Lynne and I arranged for her to undertake a regression session to her life as Lainstra. It was an intense and uncomfortable experience for Lynne. She found that Lainstra's beliefs and outlook to life were very foreign to her own.

Ultimately, it was a broadening experience for her, giving her more feeling of strength to confirm that compassion and tolerance were qualities she wanted to live now, rather than how Lainstra expressed himself.

Lainstra was quite full of his own sense of importance and talents, but felt undervalued, especially by Pourli. He could be both manipulative and secretive. Lainstra believed that Pourli kept his findings far too much to himself and would not share his work. He felt that Pourli just gave him the most menial tasks to do. Lainstra felt that if he could be in charge, he would open the research up far more and involve many more people, and then sell the results to the highest bidder. He was quite aware of the damage Pourli was doing to people, but did not mind.

His main interest was self-promotion. From an early stage Lainstra accepted money from the professor, Sherrip, for providing information about Pourli's work. He knew that Sherrip for some reason was obsessed with jealousy around Pourli's family and particularly the fame of Pourli's father. But for Lainstra, it was easy money and what he wanted. The theme of lack of recognition was strong for Lainstra. He very much wanted Tarla's attentions but she seemed interested only in Pourli. Lainstra felt despair about this. Then, when Pourli inserted the crystals into Tarla's skull, Lainstra really turned. He hated Pourli for this, and was determined to destroy him. He wanted revenge so that Pourli would suffer like Tarla had suffered. He realised that he loved Tarla and hated to see her so much distorted by the crystal implants.

It was Lainstra's plan to humiliate Pourli in front of the symposium of scientists. He enlisted the help of Sherrip who was only too pleased to co-operate. It gave Lainstra much pleasure to demean and embarrass Pourli in front of the people he most wanted to impress! However, things changed after the crystal implantation of Pourli in the prison. This experience did not give Lainstra the satisfaction he had hoped. Then, as Sherrip began to take over, and wanted to use Tarla as a lever to gain information, Lainstra started to back off and have doubts. Lainstra did not want Tarla to be hurt, and he left in the midst of the torture. Then he began to feel sick about what had happened. He knew that Tarla would be dead, but he did not want to work for Sherrip, whom he regarded as even worse than Pourli.

Lainstra could sense no way out, and so he drank a draught of one of his drugs to kill himself. Going into Spirit, he could realise how much feelings of jealousy, anger and revenge clouded his mind. Meeting the souls of Tarla and Pourli, Lainstra realised that he could have had a close friendship with Tarla, if he had tried to be with her in other ways than seeking for intimate physical relationship. With Pourli, there had also been a potential for friendship if both could have been more open to each other. That life had been wasted. A lot of talent and knowledge was wasted.

Other Connections

It was very uncomfortable for Linda to realise that she also featured in this regression, as the biology professor, Sherrip. She experienced imagery of herself as this man, killing my father from that life, and setting fire to his laboratory. He was jealous of my father's position and wanted more recognition for himself.

After having the crystals implanted, Lainstra arranged secretly to take the crystals out again. From there Sherrip was extremely angry to have been excluded from the research and manipulated in the way he had been. Then, together with Lainstra, they plotted their revenge.

It was Sherrip who killed Tarla. Linda experienced it as pure frustration on Sherrip's part for not being able to get what he wanted.

I feel that I have identified two of my victims from that life besides Annie as Tarla and Linda as Sherrip. Each time I have made such an identification, it has left a tight feeling in my chest and a shivery feeling throughout my body. I'm sure that in time there will be more of my victims from then that I will be able to recognise around me now. It makes me determined not to make the same mistakes again.

Linda and I have both sensed that Denise was my father in that life.

My Own Reaction

The three regression sessions to this past lifetime were very difficult for me to allow. After the first session I was in shock and I had a severe headache, and my body was shaking for hours afterwards. Only in the third session was I able to allow myself to experience the torture scenes and the events of what I did with my first victim. It was then that I could feel more fully the coldness of this character and his unfeeling nature which seems so alien to me now.

The scientist was engaged in the manipulation and control of people's minds. In my present life, that is the work I do today. With Hypnosis, Hypnotherapy and leading personal development groups, I am dealing directly with people's minds. Some of my victims from then have trusted me in our present lives to let me explore deeply within their minds in an effort to help them.

Through the memory of this past lifetime I have become aware of the potential that lives within me to cause harm through working with people's minds, rather than helping and dedicating myself to healing. Each lifetime we are given gifts and aptitudes. However, it is up to us how we use those gifts. We choose.

This memory has struck an uneasy chord close to my heart. By only thinking of myself rather than being concerned for the well being of others, I could easily make similar mistakes again. I don't want to do that.

I am aware that from this period in Atlantis' history, ambition and corruption were rife among the educated sections of the society. There were great temptations for any soul to go off the track. But this is no excuse for what I did.

The reason, I believe, that this particular memory has affected me so strongly is because of the resonance which it has with the work that I do now. I am sure that part of the purpose for me choosing psychotherapy work in my present life has been to help heal the wounds of this past.

Interestingly, I have accessed a number of other healing lives from Atlantis where I specialised in treating psychological illness. So I am realising more and more that my inclination to do this kind of work has been developed over many, many lifetimes, not all bad!

Chapter 16

The Rise of the Military

Military Rule

My impression from various regression sessions to my own past lives and that of others, is that following on from the `Golden age' Atlantis became less and less a pleasant place to be. There were still pockets of peace, places where people dedicated themselves to Spiritual work, places of simplicity and beauty. However, this was not at the heart of the community anymore.

With population conditions becoming more crowded in the north, there came to be a defined class divide between rich and poor. At this time, typical personality traits of the Atlantean people were for them to be proud, passionate and ambitious. However, when these characteristics were not moulded with Spiritual influences and a sense of needing to serve others and the greater whole, these qualities could easily become arrogance and cruelty. This, combined with the psychic sensitivity, which many of these people had, could be a very volatile mixture.

The sense of common purpose among the people grew weaker, and instead people were concerned primarily with looking after their own position and interests. This grew into a very selfish society and was the breeding ground increasingly for power struggles of all kinds. The strong energies in Atlantis made some people believe that they could get away with anything. With it being quite a permissive society, the richer people tended to concentrate their attention upon fulfilling any kind of desire that they might have. But these desires were not always sensitive to the needs of others.

For souls incarnating during this period, I'm sure it was a testing time. Unless people retreated to the Healing Sanctuaries, there was always the temptation of corruption of all kinds. I believe that many souls made serious mistakes and much suffering was brought forth without people fully realising the consequences of what they were doing.

I'm not consciously aware of a complete picture concerning my own soul path through this time. However, I know that my progress was somewhat mixed. There were positive lives where I engaged in healing work and did much good, working with love and caring. In other experiences, I made some mistakes but did not deviate too far away from my purpose. There are two lives, I know, where I actually killed someone, but the effect of this jolted me so much that I spent the rest of my life following a healing path. In both instances, the person whom I killed was Linda's soul!

However, I did not completely manage to steer clear of corruption. In a few lives, my heart was closed and I did not care. During these experiences I caused hurt and suffering to others. Mostly, I did not choose the worst of excesses that I could have done. But there were two lives where I did not avoid this and these were the darkest and most negative experiences for me while in Atlantis.

The first of these lives was that of the crystal implant scientist, which I have written about in the previous chapter. It comforts me a little to consider that this life could have been worse. What strikes me about this life is that as this character with my heart closed, I was almost blinded to the extent of suffering which I was causing to others. He did not care. At least he chose not to share his secrets with the Military. But he left a large trail of destruction behind him with karmic consequences to follow.

The other dark life is worse. In this life I was female and sexually abused by my father as a child. I grew up to hate men and passionately wanted to crusade for women's rights. As an adult I joined a women's group who met at an Earth Sanctuary and engaged in rituals to honour the dark mother and to promote the power of the feminine. These rituals involved human sacrifice, sexual abuse, torture and offering blood to this dark mother energy. Later I became leader of this group and I enjoyed what I was doing. One day, a male healer was brought to be sacrificed. I felt his love and his peace. This shocked me. Until then I had never believed that a man could be loving to a woman. Suddenly, to my horror, I realised what I had been doing and I left the group immediately. Shortly afterwards I committed suicide.

With Linda, the pattern of her lives was somewhat different to mine. The lifetime as Sofira affected Linda's soul deeply. Desperately, she wanted to turn this experience around, to learn from it and make amends in some ways. But she kept failing and not keeping to the life paths she had chosen as a soul. I think a pattern developed where she tended to build an inner wall around herself to protect herself from hurt. But this also isolated herself from others. So, instead of reaching out to others with love, she sought to acquire power over others as a substitute for this. Ultimately though, this made her feel even more alone. In life after life, she continued to play this out, and some of these experiences were very negative indeed. Sometimes, when her gentle side could be nourished in supportive family environments, her sensitivity could flourish and she could live beautiful healing lives. The problems for her came when conditions were a little bit more difficult, when the personality she chose had ambition and drive. In these situations, it was very hard for her to be able to trust others.

About 12000 BC, the society in the north of Atlantis had grown in population so that there were large cities scattered along the coast. These were administered by military rule. In places, the military were quite oppressive and people enjoyed much less personal freedom than they had previously. This led to situations of struggle and conflict.

For Linda and I, I believe that we both considered that we needed to try to make a concerted effort to turn around from mistakes we had made and tendencies that had developed in both of us to act out negative lives.

For me, after the life as the Crystal Implant Scientist and the female life involving ritual sacrifice, I needed to learn in situations, where cold ambition and strong drives to succeed were dominant in me, not to blind myself to the needs of others and to allow my compassionate side to express itself. If I was to let this trend go any further in a negative direction I knew it would be disastrous for me as a soul.

In Linda's case, she needed to learn to love people again, to be kind rather than causing pain and cruelty to others. There was a need for her to let her walls down so she could feel connected with others rather than isolated. She needed to learn that it was safe for her to let her sensitive side come to the surface.

To try to accomplish these goals, we each chose a life to live at this time with strong, ambitious personalities. The life I chose was one where I would be born into a family with a military tradition, with a father who was a forceful and powerful influence on my life as one who was proud and successful in a military career and wanting his son to follow in his footsteps. My mother in that life was more gentle and compassionate. And so, the two influences were there.

The life Linda chose was one of more middle class values, where she was born with the ability and drive to out-do her parents, to move higher in the strata of that society. Her parents were kind but a little withheld in their love. It was really going to be up to her to create her own life.

Both the personality Linda chose and mine, were inclined to want to join the military which was the power base of life in the city at that time. With torture and killing being standard practices within that establishment, there was plenty of temptation to allow the less caring side of each personality to become dominant.

I do not think that Linda's personality and mine were so closely connected in that life. We both had our independent lives to live. But we were working and jostling for position in the same military establishment.

What follows are the regression transcripts of how each life unfolded.

186

Paul's Regression - Military Commander Arune

I am standing in front of our family home admiring the view below me. The house is situated on the slopes of the hills overlooking our city with the sea and the harbour in the far distance. It is a very prestigious position where we live. I see in front of me a beautiful green canopy of trees and grassland stretching downwards. I enjoy very much the spaciousness of our grounds and the grandness of our house where I live with my family.

My father has worked very hard in his career as a military officer to attain the rights to have a place like this. There are few who have done better or who live higher than us. I am proud of him and I would also like him to be proud of me, and so I am following in his footsteps.

Recently I have begun training in the local military establishment. I am a young man in my early twenties. Today is one of those rare rest days when I can get away from the barracks and enjoy the luxuriant space of our family home.

My father is just retired but he is still active. He is encouraging me in my chosen career path. Within the community, my father has a good position and has gained respect. Our house is a symbol of his position.

I also have one brother who is not at the military school. He is actually quite different from me and he doesn't have my ambition. His interest is more in making things, working with cloth, carpets and such like. I think he has been somewhat of a disappointment to my father. But this is what he wants and he is closer in fact to my mother. So, I don't have a lot of time with him. He is now living down in the town, learning his trade and is younger than me.

The city where we live is large. There is quite a lot of commerce, trade through shipping and there is also a large centre of learning, a university. We live on the north side of our land. Our harbour is an important gateway for shipping. In the wintertime it can get quite cool here.

With it being such a sizeable centre of population, much organisation is needed to keep everything running smoothly. The military has a strong and important role in this. We have to learn about management of people, of organisations, how to bring discipline and order to the region which we control.

I'm doing my training in the barracks of the fortress on the hill overlooking the harbour in the city. The room where I stay is not very big and I feel rather closed in at times. We have to do drill and physical exercises, psychological training and horsemanship. Most of this I find quite tedious and I'd rather escape sometimes into the countryside, riding my horse and feeling more freedom. I take advantage of this whenever I can.

There is a need for me to be quite patient with the training. With most of these officers who are teaching me, I feel I could do a better job than them. Their ways of teaching are often quite stupid. But I have to go along with it because I know the need to obey. By obeying them and being loyal I hope that I will get into a position where they will notice me and where eventually I may be able to get promotion. Then I won't need to be taking other people's orders, but I can help this operation to become more efficient.

As part of our training there are occasions when we are assigned to groups of trainees and officers who go out in the streets and are called to attend to small scale conflicts among the population. This has sometimes resulted in scuffles, people resisting arrest or sorting out rivalries between people. At times then, I've had to use my sword and shield as a defence to look after myself and the other military personnel around me. This is something I've been able to take in my stride. I feel myself quite physically strong and able to look after myself.

Within the city, there are various healing temples and there's an old Nature sanctuary in the hills. I feel that many people are finding these places less interesting than perhaps they did in the past. Maybe for some people these Spiritual places are a comfort. It is not something that I have investigated very much. For me, I know that it is the life that I am living now that counts. I want to make the most of that and achieve as high a position as I can. I want my father to feel proud of me, and for me to feel proud of myself, so that I know I have really worked to the best of my ability and that I have expressed my skills to the full. When we have tests and assessment within the training, usually I can quite easily do better than my contemporaries. So I feel I am on my way.

Socially I do not have a partner. Actually, I do not have many friends. There is no need for me to find closeness with other people. I know what I am seeking to do. If I got too close to other people they might distract me from my purpose and from fulfilling my ambitions. Even among the female military personnel or civilians I have not sought their company to any great extent. I try not to have favourites with my colleagues. Besides, I do not know how far I could trust others. It is easier and safer for me to keep myself somewhat detached.

Now I have finished my training. I have my own quarters within the barracks. Already I have gained some promotion. There are men and women whom I command. It has been noticed how I can manage people very well without my emotions getting in the way of what I do. I have learnt to be quite clinical in my approach to tasks. When I am given orders, I will listen carefully and carry out those orders accordingly. This is gaining me respect.

As I am making progress, my ambition is becoming more focused. The position I really want is to become in charge of this establishment. The man there now is not capable of doing nearly as good a job as I could do. I would like to take his position if I could. Anyway, he's getting rather old now. Gradually I am angling towards achieving this goal. Perhaps in a few short years if all goes well....

I have my strategy. There are some rivals of course. But I think that the best way forward for me is to make sure, especially when my commanding officer assigns a job to me, that I do this job totally according to his satisfaction and expectation. So then perhaps I can become his favourite. If I do my work well, then he can learn to rely on me, and value me as someone he can depend upon. Then he may more and more regard me as the ideal candidate to follow on from his example.

I do not care what my colleagues want when working with them. However, I am very interested in what my commanding officer tells me to do. And this, I follow to the letter.

It is not of much concern to me how my colleagues and contemporaries react. I hold my own and I am fairly well respected. Because I am polite and courteous, I do not cause fights or aggravations among these people. I leave them to get on with their job. As long as they leave me in peace, I will leave them in peace. It's not something where I feel I need to tread on their toes. Of course, if someone else wants to do a job for the commanding officer, I generally make it my business to show that I could do the job better, and demonstrate this whenever I have the opportunity. But really, I am not wanting to cause any animosity with my colleagues. I know that if I did cause animosity, they would only be my enemies later, and this would not do. I just want to do my job well, and fulfil my ambition.

Some of the officers like to show off their uniform. It can look very splendid with our sash, stockings and shield. But this is of no importance to me. We have different uniforms for different occasions. When we are on duty in combat situations, we carry a sword, dagger and shield, and wear a toughened leather like shirt to protect the upper part of our body from attack and there are hardened gloves. Usually I like to wear our plainer uniform when I can. I do not need to show off. My commanding officer is more interested in what I can achieve than what I look like. So that is where I put my energy.

On occasions there are riots in the city. Unfortunately, not all the population are always content with our policies. Some of them do not like to be controlled. However, if we were not there to control them there would very likely be a lot of civil chaos. In a city of this size, you need order. People need some sense of authority to know what is expected of them, what they can get away with, and what they can't. Because we rule with a firm authority, there are those who object to us at times and they try to express their civil rights. Sometimes they express opposition to what we are doing. This is something which my commanding officer and I look upon rather harshly. People should be sensible enough to realise that we offer the best alternative for them.

For us, discipline is very important. My colleagues must do what I tell them when I command them. Otherwise they will be punished. I prefer to work through praise rather than punishment, but the punishment is there as a last resort if needed. The soldiers who work with me know that I am strict, so if they do not obey me correctly it can be hard for them.

With civilians, it is similar. I give clear instructions to people, where necessary. If they do not respond positively, then they too can be punished.

For my soldiers, if they rebel from a situation where they are called to fulfil some duty, they may be beaten. There is a courtyard within the barracks where we do this. If their disobedience is more severe, they may be expelled from the military establishment provided it is safe for us to do so. Otherwise they may be held as a prisoner in one of our cells or even executed.

We use execution as a punishment mainly for people who are a threat and danger to the community and come from the population at large. We have special execution chambers for this purpose. When people cause trouble and disruption to our society, then we can't really tolerate them being with us. It is better for them to be dead.

We try to be discriminative about this and would not want to execute everybody. In fact we try to be very selective about this. But if someone will not accept our leadership and authority in any form, or perhaps causes havoc in other ways - say through robbery or murder, then it is possible they will be executed. And this is really for two reasons. One would be just to remove them from society so our people may live in peace. And the other reason would be really as an example to the other people in the society, to those who may be likely to try the same thing. We feel that basically, we need an orderly society around us, where people can get on with their business. And we are the ones who can provide this. We can provide leadership, and people need to accept this. When they do, everything is fine.

Sometimes, I am asked to attend these executions. Of course, my commanding officer has wanted to see me perform this side of the work as much as any other. I do believe he is watching me quite closely with an eye to the future. So I have not wanted to disappoint him with this. On occasions, I have needed to perform these executions myself.

It is late now. I am in the execution chamber. There is a woman who is here. She has been tied up in the usual chair-like device we have arranged. As is customary, she has been stripped naked and restrained with straps around her feet, hands and waist. We have to take these precautions to protect ourselves.

This woman has been causing a lot of trouble in the town. She's someone who feels that the military rule is wrong. She has also had relatives who have been executed by us. It is clear that she hates the military establishment. But she's been stirring others up to trouble. During a recent riot, she injured one of my colleagues rather badly. She had a knife and tried to attack him. As a result she has been arrested and brought to the execution chambers.

I don't enjoy these situations very much, because I must say, that in myself, I don't really like to kill. But today my commanding officer is here with me. He is watching me. So I know I have to be quite clinical and do what is required.

What I need to do basically, is to remind her of the crimes she's committed, remind her of the punishment that this incurs, and then regretfully tell her that this demands her to be killed. And I have to be the one to kill her.

There is a special sword we have for this purpose. Usually, this is thrust into the chest of the person concerned. I've been taught where to insert this weapon so as to cause a quick and almost painless death. This is what I intend to do with this woman.

She is arguing with me though, and I think she is quite frightened about what is to happen. I don't really want to hurt her any more than is necessary. But I know I need to do my duty.

Actually, I have to shout above her screaming and abuse to tell her what she has done. She is struggling as much as she can. I can tell she's desperate. But I have to do this, and I will do it.

I have the sword in my hand and want to do this fairly quickly to give her the least amount of time to build up fear within herself - just so it can be done. I come forward. For a moment she looks in my eyes and I see a depth to her, and a sadness. My heart is pounding. I have hesitated for a moment, but I know I must not hesitate - because my commanding officer is watching.

I thrust the sword in, but she moves. Just as I put it in, she jerks as much as she can sideways. I have not found quite the right place. This makes me very angry because my commanding officer is here. She is not quite dead as quickly as she could be. Blood is pouring from the wound and I am embarrassed by this. I wanted to make a good clean kill for my commanding officer to witness. I wish she hadn't done that. There is little I can do. Now she is slumped and dead. I wish she hadn't done that. She caused extra suffering for herself. I did not want this. I feel regret for having killed her in such a way. I must not show this. I must go and sign the records and do that necessary work - so I know I have satisfied the requirements of my duty.

It is later. I am now the commanding officer, having risen to that position. Actually, it was quite an easy transition. There was no one else really considered for the post and it was acknowledged that I could do the job better than others.

I have been the commanding officer for some time, basically enjoying my work quite well. I am well pleased with the organisation I have been able to establish. I think that the people under me respect me and generally carry out my orders.

Now, I am in my mid thirties and in the prime of my life. In some ways though, I am also going through somewhat of a crisis inside myself. It's nothing which I tell to my fellow officers and colleagues from other military establishments or certainly to my subordinates. The thing is, I know that I have risen in this job as high as I can go. I have actually achieved my ambition, and I have achieved it quite early in my life. At times, I find I am able to do my job easily, without too much effort being rather used to it in fact. But I'm wondering what else I can do in my life. It's like, I feel an emptiness inside - I feel I don't know where my ambition can express itself anymore. I am questioning myself.

We have captured a man who is quite interesting, and something of a philosopher. He is someone who was taken from the town. Really he has been causing us a lot of problems because he has been talking to groups of students at the university, getting them interested in other ideas, other forms of community besides military rule. He's been able to incite many of these students to join forces against us. This for us, of course, is unacceptable.

Strangely though, although I know he needs to be killed, I have sometimes visited him in his cell to talk with him. I find it rather interesting to listen to his ideas.

He speaks a lot about the meaning of life, but this is not the main aspect of him which I find interesting. When other people are brought here, they tend to be very afraid. They tend to react, either by becoming very timid and shell shocked, or else they become rather abusive and they try to argue with us all the time. It really becomes quite tedious for us, all this. But he is different. He has been quite calm. It has been as though he has remained rather unaffected by his predicament. And this quite fascinates me.

So, I'm interested just to listen to him and find out more about his ideas.

It is not as though I would want to do anything else, career-wise. However, I'm going through this questioning time in my life and it is like there is some opening in me. I am wondering what other possibilities exist.

He is quite a deeply religious man, sometimes sitting in his cell very quietly with his eyes closed. I know that his thoughts are somewhere else. Sometimes, it is as though he is not even there. What I feel when I go near him is that there is quite a strong energy of peace around him. I don't find that amongst the other prisoners, and I certainly don't find it among the other officers in the barracks.

I must say that I find this peace somewhat interesting, although I also find it disconcerting, because he does not seem upset that he is going to die. He even challenges me about this, and I must say, that my inner feelings of justification for killing him are wavering.

I will have to be the one to perform the execution. In this case I want to do it myself. Some of my subordinates now are getting involved in long arduous processes of torture and condemnation of prisoners, leading to agonising deaths. I would not like them, any of them, to work with him. I think he is someone whom I respect. If he is to die, he deserves a quick and painless death.

The actions of some of my subordinates is getting somewhat out of my control. They use torture to gain information. Sometimes we need to use more physical methods of interrogation when prisoners are withholding information that is important to us. But I feel that some of my subordinates are finding means to bring suffering to prisoners that is unnecessary and often excessive to what I consider is needed. It is hard for me to do anything about it though, because within our establishment, there is an unwritten rule, that as far as the execution of prisoners is concerned, there is no limit to the way this is done. It is discretionary according to the judgement of the officer responsible for a particular prisoner. So, there is a permission for them to do what they do, and I would not want to be seen as weak by interfering.

Generally I try to tolerate what they do. In the past, anyway, I felt it was their own business. It wasn't any concern of mine whether they tortured them or whatever they did. They were just condemned prisoners.

With this man though, somehow I am beginning to feel differently. He also seems interested to talk with me. He doesn't seem to hate me, or to fear me, like other people do when they come here. That is interesting for me as well. He seems quite a lot more at peace with himself than anyone I've met.

It is later now. I have of course postponed the execution as long as I could, signing several papers to indicate that he needed further questioning before this could be done. But, it is difficult for me, because the officers who brought him in for arrest have signed papers regarding the need to execute him. Even though I am the commanding officer, there are not really sufficient grounds for me to contradict this.

So, he has to be killed. But I feel that if I have to kill him, then I don't want to kill anyone else. I feel I have done enough killing. He would never kill anyone. I don't believe that he did anything in his life to cause violence to others. Therefore, it feels a mistake to bring him here. Something about it is wrong. But I cannot show these feelings to others because I do not want to be seen to be weak. I have to maintain my position.

He is rather quiet now. I think he has been interested to meet with me. However, I sense that he knows it is his time to die now. However, he is also sensitive and respectful. Although we have had several private conversations, he is not showing me up with my other colleagues who are here with me. I believe he also accepts that I will try not to cause him undue pain. But I don't like to do this. I don't like to cause him pain, or to be the cause of his death. He does not deserve that. It is as simple as that. He just does not deserve it.

I'm in the execution chamber and the sword is in my hand. I don't want to look in his eyes, but he is closing them anyway. Again, I feel him becoming quiet, and it feels almost like a peace is coming from him. Speaking in a very quiet voice to state what he is alleged to have done, I am not even sure that he hears. I take a very deep breath before I get my sword in position. Even so, I feel very nervous. I want to get this right, find the right place, so I can do it with as much care as I can. In the end I come up to him quickly. I put the sword in...and....I know he is dead....and I can hardly bear to stay....I feel I need to get away.....

Quickly signing the papers, I go to my room and lock the door.....I sit for a long time, trembling.....And I just feel that this is not the way. This is not the way to live my life....This is not the way, if I have to kill men that I respect.

This man I respected more that any other person I have met....And yet I had to kill him. I don't want to have to do that again.

For a long time I feel bewildered. I want to seek help or guidance, but don't quite know what to do. I could stay in my position as commanding officer, but a large part of me wants to leave. Somehow, I know that in my family, it would never do for me to leave this profession. My family would lose face. I would lose face. It makes me feel that I have to stay in my job. But I don't like it, and I don't want it.

I tell no-one of my feelings. I could not tell them. If I did, I would be a laughing stock, and would be hounded out of the job. They would probably torture me, like they torture some of their victims.

Amongst my colleagues I feel there are one or two who I have to watch very closely. I feel there are eyes upon me for any sign of weakness. However, while I continue to act firmly, clearly and clinically, as I always did, there is nothing really for me to fear. Overall, I still maintain the respect of the officers. But it is getting harder for me to keep up this act. There is something in me - I want to seek to find peace, like this prisoner had. I would love to feel that peace in myself and know how he attained that. And his religious convictions were so sincere. I can understand now how others were affected by him when he spoke to them. I just wish I could find a way to engender those feelings in myself.

It might make it easier for me to bear this job I have.

It is later. I am sitting in a clearing with the trees around me. The energies are strong here. This is the sacred Nature sanctuary. To come here, I have left the town. It is situated in the hills, inland somewhat.

I have been sitting on a stone and crying. I feel so much remorse for what I have done in my life, such a waste. There is a man behind me. It is rather strange. He has his hands on my shoulders and sometimes my head, and they feel so comforting...so peaceful. And I just feel as I am sitting here like lifetimes of suffering are just pouring out of me. I feel so weak and so ashamed. It feels so wrong what I have been doing. And I wish I could do better. I just feel that I am unworthy of anything.

I have not asked about this man. He is just there and I know he belongs with this place. It is not really my business. I just need help. When I come here, he appears and gives me help. He is here silently with me, seeming to speak more with his thoughts than words. And I hardly notice anyone else here. It is like I am alone with him and the energy of the nature and the Earth around me seems vast.

I enjoy this solitude. It is good to have a break. In the military barracks it feels claustrophobic to me. I don't like that place anymore. I don't like the killing. I don't like the torture. I don't like the authority. I don't like imposing our force on others. I don't like the oppression. I don't like the coldness. I struggle to know what I can do. Now I've got to this position, there's little else that I can do. I'm too old for any other form of work. I could not leave. Anyway, if I left, the oppression of that establishment, of these military people would continue. It would get worse. It has been getting worse. The uprisings have been getting greater.

People hate the military. They hate being ordered around. I just wish I could make it easier for them. I just wish I could. I'd like to make peace with them and to find some peaceful coexistence between the people and the military. I'd like to do this.

This idea has been growing in me. I have not talked much with anyone about it yet. I feel that this needs cautious planning, if I am to succeed. Some of the officers seem to be sympathetic to my idea. What I'm trying to tell them really, is the more brutal we become with the population, the greater will be their reaction. Brutality breeds violence, on their side as well. This is what I feel.

Some of the officers are listening to me. They are starting to modify their behaviour somewhat, in adherence to this. I still have some authority. But there are others who don't. It is very frustrating for me. In wanting to make changes like this, some of those under me are not really concerned. I have to argue with them, that my approach is the only way we will be able to keep the power of the military strong. I don't really believe that because I don't want a military authority anymore but I have to relate it on their terms.

Now it is later. I am at a meeting, negotiating with people from the university. We are talking. We are talking about co-operation. I am listening to their demands, what they would like from the military to find greater freedom of operational expression. I feel that most of their demands, if not all of them, are quite reasonable. They want an end to the killing and the torture. I think they are right. But I have to be a bit careful in what I express is possible, because I cannot speak only on behalf of my own interests, but what I feel that my fellow officers could accept. There are one or two other officers with me, negotiating at the table. These are people I have come to know that are sympathetic like me, to the principles of conciliation. There is this woman officer, Tarsha, who is at the door behind me. She is one I do not trust. But I've had to bring her, because she is my next in command. She is taking care of security matters while we continue the negotiations.

This woman officer is one who revels in cruelty. She seems to have a blood lust about her which I find very difficult. As much as I try and talk with her, I can tell, whatever she says, that she does not agree with my line. I can tell in her eyes that she only wants to kill, and kill again. She does not care who she kills. And I think she is just one example of how our establishment has gone badly wrong. I fear that if I tried to remove her, she would get me first. She is very much aware of these tactical conspiracies. Throughout my working life, I have tried to stay clear of these kinds of manipulations and conspiracies, and act more through example to build up trust and get what I want that way.

Now there has been a disturbance. My colleagues have come in. What? They want to arrest me. It's Tarsha's doing. I can see it now. She's there. I know exactly what she wants to do. I know this woman. She wants to take over. She does not want these agreements, so I must stop her.

No....She would torture me....I must....What can I do?....I must stop her.....I will go to her.....I am going to her now.....I will fight her......I will fight her....She will kill me now, because that is the best way. I do not want to kill her.....I struggle with her - Yes, I could be stronger than her.....I know I am....Ah...Aww....She's stabbed me.....I am sinking down to the floor....I can feel it is over......

I'm starting to rise up, feeling the peace.

He's here, the one I killed. He's helping me, holding my hand. There are others too. I feel great waves of peace. And it feels such a relief. It feels like I've been through something dark and horrible, and now I can begin to breathe again.

I feel there are many here - those I killed - that woman. I hated to kill her. I really hated to kill her. I'm sorry I had to do that to her, really sorry. She knows, because she could tell in my eyes that I didn't want to do it. She's forgiven me. I feel I was a fool in the way I was so blind to my ambition not caring for anyone except myself, and my family - my family honour. What a big illusion!

My father's here. He's here. There's a mixture of feelings. I know I fulfilled his expectations of me. He was proud of what I achieved. But we both know that what we aspired to was not really all we could have done. We were missing so much. He valued only my capacity to further my career and I valued that too as a way to please him. This does not feel enough anymore.

200

TARSHA

I think it was a good life, and I changed from having a dark insulated way of being, to where I started to care again for others and look for peace, instead of exerting my will over others to do what I wanted. I learnt in that life that there is more to achieve in life than just satisfying my ambitions. The main feeling around this life is one of relief, relief to have got through it the way I did. I'm glad to be over it.

Linda's Regression - Tarsha

I am galloping fast across the sands of a semi-circular bay. The wind is in my hair and the sun shining. It is a glorious day. My horse is moving smoothly and his hooves are thundering on the wet sand. I feel free. I love to escape the crowds of the city for a while and come here, it is wonderful. I just wish this horse was mine. He belongs to a friend of my father, who allows me to borrow him in return for some light chores. It is my dream to have horses of my own. One day I will.

I am fifteen now, an only child and living with my parents. We get along well, although I tend to be a bit of a loner, preferring to be on my own and having few friends. My father is a fine craftsman and well respected. He makes harness and tack for horses. His work is beautiful and ornate; he decorates the leather with intricate patterns using silver and gold. A lot of rich people come to him for his fine things. Mother does colourful embroidery on saddle cloths and blankets, using rich silks and precious stones. People pay huge amounts for some of her work. They want me to follow them into the family business, but I don't want that. I want to rise higher. There is no status for me in being a craft worker, no matter how good. I intend to go into the military service, rise through the ranks, and become a senior officer, perhaps even in command of the fortress. Then I would be well respected, have position and influence in the community, and be able to own and ride the finest horses.

Our city is situated around two bays, each on either side of a high, rocky headland on which is the military headquarters in the fortress. It is very old, some say hundreds of years. The fortress was built there because of its strategic position as it overlooks our busy harbour, which is to the east of it. Many hundreds of thousands of people live here. It is very crowded. There are steep wooded hills behind us, preventing any further expansion. We are on the northernmost tip of our land with other cities southwards, along the eastern coast. Many beautiful squares and market places adorn our city, and there is a large university, situated at the back of the city, where the ground begins to rise. We are a busy commercial centre, mainly situated round the harbour. The military keep law and order, and would defend us from any invaders, but there have been no problems for years. There are severe punishments for stealing and murder. These people are executed but I've never seen anything like that. Most of the population are law abiding, although there are the odd flare-ups of trouble now and again.

Now I have finished my course of training and I am a junior officer. Men and women are completely equal here so I have as good a chance as anyone else of rising to high rank. I am enjoying my life here. What gives me pleasure is to wear my fine uniform and to have command over people. My dream is to own and ride a fine horse.

Being now in charge of many men, I am leading twenty of them down the narrow alleys of the seedier side of town. There has been a lot of subversive activity going on lately, based mainly in the university. They want rid of us, to stop military rule. These people must be rooted out because they are dangerous. They feel our way is wrong, and we should hand over to a civilian government.

It is horrible here. How do people live in this rat-infested place? It's obvious we're not liked but that doesn't matter because we have a job to do. We are here to find and arrest one of the alleged leaders of the subversive movement, and take him in for questioning.

Approaching his house carefully, we need the element of surprise if we are to find our man. I order my men to surround the building. These people are undermining our authority and trying to turn the population against us. We try to prevent them meeting, but this is difficult in a city as densely populated as this. We arrest and imprison those we find. This is considered a treasonable offence, a crime against the state, and, as such, is punishable by death.

The men are signalling they are all in position. We break down the door, go in and up some stairs. There is a shout of triumph for he is there. We have him. My men have done well. We will take him to the barracks and interrogate him, needing to find out what and who he knows. I have no feeling or sympathy for him, just contempt.

This man is to be questioned with torture. The more senior officers are doing this. I am here to observe and learn techniques. Initially, he refuses to answer our questions, which is what we expected. We attach devices to his limbs, which will gradually be tightened, breaking his bones. This causes intense pain. I didn't really want to be here, and thought I would react badly, but I don't seem to be too bothered. It's not as bad as I expected. They are our enemies, and do not matter.

Reacting to our torture, he is screaming and swearing at us. However, we are getting a lot of information and names from him. He thinks that by talking he has saved his life, but we will kill him as a traitor anyway.

The officer in charge tells me to go and arrest those he has named. He implies that if I do this well, I will get the promotion I want. Asking him if it matters if any of them die, he says "not particularly if they resist arrest". But we do need some more for further interrogation, and to execute as an example to others.

I am on my way to carry out my orders, walking through the streets with my men. There are cat calls from around us, but we are not here to be popular. Many of those involved in this are from the educated classes, quite a few from the university, which means that a lot of students there are also in the revolutionary groups. They have many resources and can reach a lot of people. There is a lot of rebellion here. We may have to use force as there is a possibility of resistance. The man we are going to arrest is one of the tutors. He's a known dissident, and has been distributing information in printed sheets and things like that. He's a bad troublemaker and needs to be silenced.

We are in the house and my men search and find him. Saying that I am arresting him as an enemy of society, he tries to bluff his way out. I think about killing him, but decide to take him back for torture and execution. That is what I will do.

Reporting back to the military commander, he is pleased. I did well resisting the urge to kill him on the spot. He wants to question him. Then I will definitely get a command position.

There is one man in the way of my promotion, a wealthy officer who has been here a little longer than me. He owns a stable of fine horses, and comes from a rich family. I need to get rid of him. That would leave the way clear for me, and I could take his horses. Going to see the man I have arrested, I persuade him to name my rival as an accomplice. If he does this, although I cannot save his life, I assure him that I can make sure his death is quick and painless.

I am in one of the rooms reserved for this purpose. The two victims are ready prepared for me. The method we use is to secure the prisoner to an upright, rectangular wooden frame, arms and legs fixed to each corner, the body exposed and spread-eagled. They are naked. We use a special long bladed knife, and kill them by plunging this through the chest. If done properly and with skill, death is instantaneous and almost painless. Of course, if you do not aim exactly, the victim bleeds to death slowly and in pain. Sometimes I choose to do this.

The first man is shouting at me, cursing me. I was going to spare him pain, but he has made me angry, and is trying to make a fool of me in front of my fellow officers. I decide to cut out his tongue and castrate him before I kill him, to increase his suffering as a punishment for his attitude. It will also be interesting for the other, my former colleague, to watch, as he is the next to die.

Putting a metal clamp in his mouth to keep it open, I select a small knife, and cut his tongue out. There is much blood and I need to wipe my hands before proceeding. Selecting another knife, I take hold of his genitals and cut through them. He loses consciousness, so I order the soldiers to burn bitter herbs under his nose to revive him for the final blow. When he is awake and aware I take the special knife and plunge it into his chest. He dies instantly. Turning my attention to the second man, this is the officer whose horses are now mine. He is terrified, and pleads with me to spare him pain. Ignoring him, I taunt him before castrating him. I have also decided to make him die slowly and so I push the knife in slightly low, cutting him open down the belly, leaving him to die in pain.

Making my way to the stables, I take his finest horse, a magnificent golden chestnut with a white flash on his face. He is mine now.

I am riding down the steeply wooded slopes at the back of the city, having been out with a fellow officer, Petry. He is so handsome. We have been together for the day and it has been wonderful. Needing to keep our relationship quiet, we part company and enter the city by different routes to avoid comment. You have to be careful. No one will know. It is our secret.

Now I am in the barracks and have just received an urgent message. I have to go quickly. There has been a fire at my father's business. The place has been burnt down. People are saying they are dead.

Riding there as swiftly as I can, it takes me some while because it is right across the city. When I arrive, my heart sinks. There is nothing left. The building is completely gone....There is just empty space.....nothing......I can't believe it....I don't want to believe it. It has happened in the early hours. They are both dead. They were trapped upstairs....nothing could be done. They're gone......There's nothing. I walk through the wreckage of my home, searching, looking for anything that might be left of them. My feet crunch on ash and blackened timber. The walls are scorched. It must have been an inferno. Feelings well up inside me of sadness and loss. I am distraught, but I must not show it. People are watching. I am an army officer and so I must be strong.

There's quite a crowd now. I know I'm not liked. I feel this fire has been deliberate. They have killed my parents to get at me. Feeling rage and anger building up inside me, I decide that someone will pay for this. I will take my revenge. I will organise `arrests' and make the victims suffer for what they have done, as a deterrent.

Seeing something bright glinting in the blackened remains, I pick it up. It is a tiny silver horses head which would have been used as a harness decoration. Cleaning it up, I put it in my pocket. It is all that I have....nothing else.....just memories. Feeling tears coming, I choke them back angrily. I sense the people laughing at me behind my back. My life here is finished. The culprits will suffer, I will make sure of it.

I am preparing to torture one of the men arrested following the fire. I know him for he is the husband of an old friend of mine. He thinks this will save him but it will not. We have arrested seven men altogether. He is the first to die. The others are watching. His family has gone into hiding and I need to take them also as a lesson to others. He will tell me where they are when I torture him. I will make sure of it.

Intending to burn him slowly, I have attached him to the usual frame and naked. Applying a burning firebrand to the soles of his feet, he starts to scream and curse....I ask him where his family are....He curses and spits at me. Moving the flames to his genitals, he screams more and more, eventually telling me what I need to know. Now I can kill them as well. The room is filled with the smell of burning flesh. He loses consciousness again. I order the men to burn herbs to revive him. Being angry with him, I push the fire into his face before taking the knife and killing him. He dies quickly.

I am riding up a winding cobbled street, between tall buildings which are wider on the upper levels. Leaning across the saddle, I am looking intently for the house where my former friend and family are hiding. When I reach the place, I post two soldiers I have brought with me for protection as sentries and go in. The woman is there with five children. They are the ones I want. She was my friend once, but no longer. She is the wife of a traitor. Drawing my sword, I thrust it through her stomach. She falls to the floor, but not dead. I go to the children. They have gone into a terrified huddle in a corner. The youngest is a boy of about two. He is clinging to the knees of the eldest girl. Grabbing his hair I pull him away, draw my knife and cut his throat. I repeat this with the others till I get to the eldest. She appears to be in shock.....frozen rigid. I plunge my knife through her chest and pull downwards, cutting her open. This done, I return to the mother, who is still alive, and push my sword through her chest to kill her. Scattering lamp oil around and lighting it, I leave as the fire takes hold. Mounting my horse, I do not look back.

Returning to my quarters one evening, I walk along an upper corridor with windows that overlook an inner courtyard. My eye is drawn to a movement in a far corner under some arches. I feel a sudden shock in my heart. It is Petry. He is in a passionate embrace with another woman, and I recognise her, Euradasia, one of the junior officers. Feeling rage building up inside me, I feel he has betrayed me, having gone with her. They are kissing.....I thought he was mine. Now I see him with someone else. How could he do this to me? He will pay for this....I will confront him. I stand and watch, seething with anger, till they walk away, arms around each other, and vanish into the shadows.

I am on my way to his rooms to confront him, in my full armour and carrying my weapons, feeling that I may need them. Opening the door, I walk in. There is no one in the outer area. They are in bed together. I knew they would be. As he looks up in horror, I scream abuse at him for what he has done. He jumps out of bed to answer me. Hitting him across the face with my armoured glove, he falls to the floor, stunned. She is in bed, cowering under the bedclothes, naked, trying to cover herself. Drawing my sword, I snatch away the covers and plunge it through her chest. Blood pours out and she dies. I turn to him. He has got up and grabbed his own sword. Although he comes at me, he is at a disadvantage as he is naked and I am in full armour. He doesn't stand a chance. I run my sword through him and he falls across his lover on the bed. Standing to regain my breath and temper, I look for a while.....then leave.

It is becoming clear that our commanding officer, Arune, is favouring a negotiated settlement with the civilian leaders. This is weakness. I do not understand why he has changed so much. He has become soft and he is giving in to them. He is also frowning on our methods, especially mine. I have been told off severely, having to do as he says or he has threatened to take me down in rank. How dare he?.....How can he? We need to get rid of him. Then I, as second in command, can take charge and get some much needed discipline back into the situation, instead of giving in to their demands. Deciding to set him up, I pretend to capitulate and go along with his wishes. I agree to accompany him to a meeting at the university with their leaders to negotiate a settlement to the unrest. I will go there and have some of my own men hidden. At the right moment I will denounce him as traitor, arrest him for treachery and execute him. Perfect. The place will run more efficiently without him. He's got too lenient of late.

All is planned. We are in a high ceilinged hall at the university, and are with the senior members of the civilian groups. Commander Arune is sitting at a long table with them. I am standing against a wall, close behind him, near a door. I know my men are in position. The delegates are talking intently. When I give the signal, my men rush out. Accusing him of treachery, I order his arrest. Looking at me in realisation and horror, he knows I have organised this. Without warning he stands, turns and draws his sword in one swift movement, and comes directly at me.....I am taken by surprise.....He is attacking me.....Caught off-guard, I am trapped by the wall behind me....just having time to draw my dagger from my belt before he is upon me. He is a good swordsman and soldier.....I find it difficult to defend myself as we close together. He's strong......Suddenly, I manage to drive my dagger into his chest, he gasps and slowly falls to the floor. He's dead. I know somehow that this is what he intended.....He forced me to kill him....He deliberately forced my hand.

I have been in charge for some time now. I have many enemies and have to pay private bodyguards to protect me. One day I decide, on almost a whim, to go and visit an ancient Earth sanctuary in the mountains behind the town. I mustn't let anyone except my trusted guards know where I am going. Not quite knowing the reason for me going there, I feel a strange `urge', almost a compulsion, to visit it. Telling my military colleagues that I am making a round of inspections to our guard posts on the outskirts of the city, I go to an inn on the edge of the forest, slip inside and change out of my uniform into a maidservant's dress. I feel that I need to be `in disguise' somehow. It feels strange...I've worn uniform for so many years. I set off up the path which is steep and climbs up through dense trees. It is stepped in some of the more difficult sections. The ascent takes some time and rises high above sea level. It is silent deep within these ancient trees. Fingers of mist creep between their trunks and there is a peculiar atmosphere. This is a strange place......Why have I come here? I catch my breath in places, feeling scared....odd. Eventually I come out on to a wide flat circular area, which is surrounded by a ring of venerable trees, tall and imposing. The sense of time here is amazing....I feel overawed, frightened and uneasy.

I do not know why I am reacting like this and it disturbs me. The centre of the circle is neatly clipped grass, upon which is etched an interwoven pattern of flowing lines in pale stones. In the very centre, is a tree stump, on top of which is a metal bowl in which a flame is burning, and around it are fresh flowers. This place feels sacred and I feel the need to kneel. Even with part of me feeling so out of place, I bow my head towards the centre, uncertain of what to do. Suddenly, my heart jumps, becoming aware of a tall figure walking towards me, across the circle. He is dressed in dark robes and is hooded. Lowering my head again, I don't want to look at him. I feel a deep sense of peace coming from him. Gently, he lays his hands on my bent back. Then he takes my chin and, lifting my face, looks deep into my eyes. He calls me by my name.....He knows me.....I am so scared. His eyes are deep pools of love and compassion. They look into my soul. His touch reminds me of my father......How much I miss him.....I still think of him. He cared for me. Looking away, I am unable to hold his gaze. I don't like the feelings welling up inside me. Scrambling up in a panic, I turn and run away down the path, almost falling on the steeper sections. Feeling angry, foolish and shaky, I return to the inn, change back into my comfortingly familiar uniform, sort my thoughts out, and try to get back to normal. The whole episode has unnerved me.

I am standing on the highest part of the battlements. It is the middle of the night, about three hours after midnight. Everything is still and the sea is calm. I am alone, wrapped in a warm cloak, gazing out across the water. The sky is clear and the light of the full moon is sparkling on the water. It is incredibly peaceful. Many thoughts are going through my head. I could not sleep. They are thoughts I don't like.....I am not happy.....I don't know what to do.....I cannot alter things now..... I have felt strange since I visited the sanctuary in the forest, vaguely disturbed somehow. Something in my life doesn't feel right. I feel so alone.....so isolated, having not had a partner for a long time. They are afraid of me. I feel things ought to be different....But I cannot undo what has been done. I have to remain strong. I need to clear my head and get back to disciplined thought.

It is dawn. I am leaving the fortress on my favourite horse, Captain. I will go for a long gallop to clear my thoughts. Two of my bodyguards are following me. I ride down on to the vast expanse of wet sand that is exposed at low tide. The air is sharp and clear and it feels good. Urging my horse to a fast gallop, his hooves thunder on the sand, water flying from them as we race along. This is wonderful. His action is so smooth, so graceful. We are flying. Looking over my shoulder, I notice that my two guards are falling behind. Their horses are no match for Captain's speed. Ahead of me is a grassy promontory with a wide belt of trees along it. There is a path through which leads to another long stretch of sand. Racing along the beach and up on to the turf without slackening speed, the belt of trees is directly ahead, and I move quickly towards the green `tunnel' that goes through them.

The sound of Captain's hooves change as we enter the green shadows. Suddenly, he is falling.....He has been brought down. Crashing heavily to the ground together in a flurry of movement, I swiftly disengage my feet from the stirrups and roll free as I have learnt, keeping myself clear of flailing hooves. Then I am attacked.....Figures are kicking me......I roll into a ball to protect

TARSHA – THE SANCTUARY AND KEEPER.

LINDA POPE.

212

myself, I cannot draw my weapons......Then I am hit on the head and lose consciousness.

Someone throws water on my face and I wake up spluttering. Sheer terror comes over me as I realise I cannot move. I am on my back, arms and legs outstretched, wrists and ankles tied firmly to stakes, totally naked. Squirming briefly, I find I can only move a little. Five cloaked and masked men are silently watching me. I am terrified, but must not show it. That is what they want.....they want to see my fear.

Swallowing the rising panic inside me with great effort, I listen as one speaks to me. He says I am to be executed, and I will die slowly, suffering like those I have killed and tortured. I want to cry out but dare not. I am so scared. Raping me in turn, they encourage each other. I close my eyes, trying to ignore the intense feelings of fear and revulsion flowing through my body. When this is over I realise one of them is kneeling between my outstretched legs. He is holding a long bladed dagger. Inside my head I am screaming silently. He `plays' with me, gently and deliberately stroking the flat of the blade along my thighs. Tasting blood in my mouth from biting my lips, I try to hold back the overwhelming urge to cry out. "This is for my sister". He thrusts the knife into my vagina. I cannot hold back any longer.....It is agony....terrible agony......Hearing myself crying and screaming, he cuts me as much as possible as tears roll down my face. Standing up, he leaves the knife in me.....Silence descends. Slowly, I become aware of two of them standing over me, on either side, holding a long sharpened stake of wood. I realise with utter horror what they intend. Again, they `play' with me, running the point of the stake down over my body, slowly drawing it between my breasts.... Hesitating, then they move it lower, holding it against my belly. I have never felt fear like this.....they are deliberately making me wait. Two of them push downwards. The stake slices through me and into the earth below. The pain is indescribable.... I scream and writhe as they hammer it firmly into position. Blood seeps out slowly. I cannot stop myself moaning.... I know it will take hours for me to die. They settle down to watch. My body feels cold, very strange. Trying to `escape' by allowing my conscious-ness to drift, they keep me awake by hitting my face, or pushing my body against the stake to increase the pain and bleeding. I am afraid of death....I know I am dying and am so frightened. There is so much pain.... This is what I have inflicted on others.....All the people I have tortured and killed....Their faces swim before me.....Please let me die quickly.....Take away this pain.....Tears flow as I realise how they must have felt....They begged for mercy, and I ignored them, leaving them to die in agony....Now I am in the same position....helpless, alone and afraid....and there is no mercy for me.

After many hours I gradually become aware that I cannot feel anything anymore, I feel numb and drifting. Eventually, after all the terrible agony, I float free of my body. I know I have died and it feels very peaceful.....I look down on the scene, it is horrible. One of the men gets up, kicks my body and realises I am dead. They cut my head off, laughing, pile wood around and burn it. Watching for a while, not knowing what to do, then I feel that wonderful peace again....There is love.....like I felt at the sanctuary in the forest. Drifting up, over the trees, there is a presence here, a figure of light. She is beautiful, full of brilliance and she is taking me with her. There are others....my parents.....They are here......It is wonderful to see them.....They look so well.......We hug each other delightedly. Tears of joy roll down my cheeks.....I haven't felt love like this for so long....so very, very long.

My guide takes me to face someone else. Oh no.....Commander Arune. I don't want to see him. I am filled with guilt for how I betrayed him for my own selfish ambition. I see now he was a kind man, and cared deeply for peace and the well being of the people. As he smiles and forgives me, this makes me uncomfortable and increases my feelings of shame. He says I was almost there...after my visit to the sanctuary, I was changing. With Arune I see others and realise with renewed shame that these people were all my victims. This is too much. My knees give way and I sink to the ground in tears and beg their forgiveness.

The sheer horror of all my terrible actions seems so clear, so awful.....How I wasted that life. How did I allow myself to go so terribly wrong? All the torture, deaths and executions - so dreadful. I know now I will have to repay these things and experience a lot of these challenges again. My lady smiles at me, with kindness and deep compassion. She understands. She explains that when I am ready, I will need to evaluate and work with my soul's path, but now I need to recover, rest, and allow myself to heal.

Tarsha - Some Thoughts in Conclusion

I began to realise, as I looked at the work I had done on Tarsha, that, although I had written her experiences as I `lived' through them in regression, there were feelings deep within her that I had (and she had) failed to acknowledge. I could see, all too clearly, what had caused her to behave as dreadfully as she did. Inside, I was acutely aware of a vulnerable and lonely little girl, who desperately needed love and kindness. The tragic death of her parents affected her deeply, but she suppressed the strong feelings of emptiness and loss that she felt. Soon after this, she was betrayed by her lover, Petry. This emphasised her existing feelings of rejection and loneliness, and, because she refused to accept her more gentle self, and allow the emotions to show, the pent up energies turned into rage and violence. She successfully `buried' her feelings of love and compassion for many years, till the visit to the Earth sanctuary stirred these emotions she did not want to accept.

She experienced great fear at the sensations of love that welled up from inside, beginning, very reluctantly, to see the horror of what she was doing. It was too late. Her `fate' was already decided, and the lessons were to be learnt at another time.

I have found writing this chapter an emotional and difficult exercise. As the explorations continued, I accessed the very dark side of her. There are again experiences I feel I have had to leave out of this transcript. While writing some of the more traumatic scenes, my hands `froze' and I had to stop. I felt strange. An overwhelming sadness took me over and tears flooded down. Graphic details of scenes of torture and bloodshed swam before me. It was horrible. This happened frequently, and I have learned to deal with these incidents by breaking off, and going to do something mundane, like the washing up.

As I worked with Paul on this, feelings within my present self began to surface and I realise somewhat reluctantly that they mirrored Tarsha's feelings. Sensing that I was much more like Tarsha than I wanted to be, I too had `buried' my own emotions in a very similar way. However, instead of reacting with violence as Tarsha did, I had tended to turn my emotions in on themselves, leading to ill-health and depression. During my life I have felt very afraid of violence and never wanted to express that towards others. Acknowledging Tarsha's life has been a very difficult, but a freeing and healing experience. With Paul's guidance, I am learning to express my feelings more easily now and allow myself to be more `me'.

Karmic Consequences

The experience of being Tarsha has been very difficult for Linda. Over and over again we have needed to go through aspects of Tarsha's life, drawing out more details and releasing feelings. The whole experience has haunted Linda at times. I feel that she has been very brave to face up to it.

Having created so many victims in that life, Linda's soul needed to learn what it would be like to be on the receiving end of such brutality. The way that Tarsha died started a process of redressing that balance.

How Tarsha suffered then was very similar to the nature of the torture that she put many of her victims through. As she has mentioned, in her account of Tarsha's life, Linda has omitted many instances of sexual abuse, torture and murder, which she had to endure in regression.

Linda has become aware that her own character and background has some similarities with that of Tarsha. As she has written, Linda is horrified by violence and very fearful of it. She would never want to express that side of herself and would turn those feelings in upon herself rather than hurt anyone else. Linda has identified souls who were her victims in Tarsha's life as being people who have oppressed her in her present life, or in some cases, as people she has needed to help this time around. This has been painful learning.

It appears that in her present life, Linda's soul has been trying to redress some of the karma engendered by Tarsha all those thousands of years ago.

From this experience, another thing which Linda's soul has had to learn, is how to cope with being this type of character without turning to violence. Actually, her soul did attempt to do this one more time towards the end of Atlantis' history. She chose a personality who was strong minded and ambitious, but also sensitive and somewhat isolated. This life certainly had its chances where she could have responded to situations more positively. But when she was tested, she did not manage to learn her lessons and the pattern of Tarsha was repeated. We have not included details of that regression in this book.

Connections

Denise featured in Tarsha's life as one of her victims, a child. Independently of Linda, Denise has been through this regression. It was one where a lot of fear and terror was blocked in Denise's throat centre.

Going through this was quite harrowing for Denise, but it has cleared her self- expression with her voice and she has gained more self-confidence to speak and sing, as a result of accessing this lifetime.

At first we did not think that Lynne was involved with any of us at this time. But then as she was typing the transcript of Tarsha, Lynne felt some very strong body sensations and resistance when she typed the sequence where Tarsha was killing the children. Soon afterwards, both Linda and Lynne realised that they had met then. From another episode than the one which we have included, Lynne was a mother whose children were killed in front of her by Tarsha in appaling ways and, then she was killed herself.

It appears that Lynne, Denise and I in our various character guises appeared in Tarsha's life to give her opportunities to turn away from violence. Because of her great love for each of us as souls, there are moments when she could have changed, but she didn't, and the three of us suffered as a result.

In her last life upon Atlantis before its destruction, Linda's soul experienced a very painful life as a victim. It was a short life. However, we have found that it links directly with that of Tarsha. Linda has sensed that the souls of the people who abused her in this life were the same as some of those whom she abused as Tarsha. Then, in the manner of her death, being impaled upon a rock, she was impaled through the same part of her body where she used to impale others as Tarsha when she wanted to make her victims suffer.

Linda needed a lot of support to go through this life. This girl's name was Mina and she was only a young girl when she died. But the life contained numerous horrific instances of different forms of abuse so that it seemed that this lifetime was at least a partial redressing for some of the excesses of Tarsha's actions. No doubt, many other lives have been needed to rebalance things completely

Parting

I did not enjoy going through my experience in regression as Commander Arune. I did not like his ambition and his inclination towards a military career felt very alien to me. In fact, I was very much relieved when my session into this life was over. However, I have come to understand that this may have been an important life for me, because I managed to renounce violence and allow expression of my compassionate self, after starting on a path in that life which could have became very negative. I have others to thank for helping me with this. I believe that I learnt and gained a lot through that life and the choices which I made.

For Linda of course, as Tarsha, the outcome was very different. We both sensed that following on from this shared experience, we did not meet again in physical life for a considerable time.

We estimate that these Military lifetimes occurred about 12000 BC, which was approximately 2000 years before the final destruction of Atlantis. Linda's soul continued to have her physical incarnations only upon Atlantis until that end. We believe that the next time I met her as a soul was in Egypt, after Atlantis had gone.

Chapter 17

The Life of Jorli

Personal Reflections

Since I was little, and I was aware of Atlantis as a legend, I have felt very emotional about the ultimate destruction of the continent. I have felt both fascinated and appalled. As soon as I began to consider the experience of past lives and that Atlantis may have really existed, then somehow, I knew that I was present around the time when all this happened. I felt so sad, and a strong sense of nostalgia for the lost continent. Until I went into my regression as Jorli, I had no clear idea of what I was doing then, except the sense that people would not listen.

The details of what I experienced in my regressions sessions as Jorli came as a complete surprise to me. Yet it felt right and true. It took me five sessions to complete this regression. It was a mammoth undertaking. And so, in writing out my account of this lifetime, I have divided the telling of this into five parts, one for each of the regression sessions. The experience itself appears to encompass many of the facets of Atlantean life during this end period. For me, this regression sequence was extremely emotional, and the sense of utter loss was hard to bear.

During the course of these regressions, my marriage broke up, and so I faced the loss of everything precious and dear to me from both the past life experience and my present circumstances at the same time. I do not feel that such a coincidence occurred by chance. Coping with these regression experiences was extremely challenging. I had to learn to accept loss, that finally from every ending there can be a new beginning. However, it was hard. From my childhood, I was conditioned not to cry and so tears did not come easily to me. But, during this regression sequence, and with the crisis in my marriage, it was like a dam bursting inside of me. For days on end, I was crying and sobbing. My feelings had to be felt without any barriers. At the conclusion of this regression, when I died as Jorli after Atlantis had been destroyed, life on this world had completely changed. My home was gone.

In my present life, the same was true. There were some big lessons for me to learn so I could integrate this. Again though, I felt I was being shown that inner and outer experiences come to us at the right time. It is up to us how we deal with them. This was a series of events where I needed a lot of support, and yet felt very alone at the same time. For those souls who were involved during the destruction of Atlantis, the transcript of this regression may contain some uncomfortable resonances. What is written is faithful to the regression sessions as they unfolded.

Paul's regression - Jorli

Part 1

Early Life
I can see the boats in the harbour and the water is lapping very gently against the shore. This is one of my favourite places to be. As I take in the energies of my surroundings, I can feel myself drifting inwards. I love the peace of the sea. At these times, I can almost feel at one with the life around me. But the air is cold, unnaturally cold. A shiver passes through me and I feel very uneasy. It is a feeling that all is not well.

My name is Jorli and I am seventeen years old. I live in a house situated quite close to the harbour. Our house is made of stone and wood in the traditional manner. There are many houses like ours fairly close together, with narrow alleys in between. We live in a medium sized town between two cities that exist further around the coast.

Our house has more space than the others, because we have a workshop. My father is a fine craftsman and he builds boats. I am expected to help him and have spent many years learning the craft so I can support him with his work. He makes boats sometimes for his own use but mostly to sell. This is how he earns money for our family to live, and his skills have come down through the generations of our family before us.

Sometimes my father travels in his boats and helps merchants with their trade. Our harbour is a very interesting place for there are people here who come from other lands. Their skin is different in colour to ours and they do not speak our language. Usually their boats are more primitive than ours. But they are still welcome to step upon our shores as long as they do not cause trouble. A few of these seamen who have been here many times can indeed speak some words of our language. These foreign traders need people amongst them who can make themselves understood. I like to talk to these people, the friendly ones at least, and learn about their travels.

Once, my father went to visit another land to the east. He described to us how the vegetation differed from our own and how that land was flat. I was quite fascinated, but I feel I love my own land better than I think I would any other.

Besides my father, I also live together with my mother and my sister. When I was younger, we also had our two grandparents with us, and we needed to look after them because they were very old. But they have since died, and now it is just the four of us.

My mother has had a disability with her hip. Many years ago, she had a fall, and so now, she can only walk with the aid of a stick. This happened when we were quite young. Consequently, my sister has had to take on many duties around the home that otherwise would have been for my mother to do. It has meant that I have felt more obliged as well, to make sure that I helped my father sufficiently.

My parents have been very kind to us and I love and respect them very much. We have had a rather sheltered upbringing and our education has taken place at home. When I was little, my grandfather helped quite a lot with this. However, we do not mix so much with people outside the family and have tended to keep ourselves to ourselves.

The other member of my family is my sister. Her name is Sheena and she is two years older than me. Besides her work around the home, my sister is very interested in healing. She spends much of her spare time at the local Healing Temple. Sheena must have some abilities because she has been accepted to train and learn some of those healing practices from the temple. She seems very content to learn all she can about healing.

Sometimes, she shows me some of the techniques she has been learning. I find this very interesting. I think, that if I did not have to help my father with the boats, I would like to follow the path of healing too. I can feel energies with my hands, and I sense an aliveness from the Earth Spirit very strongly in certain places. Sheena has shown me how to channel healing energy to help my mother. When I have tried this, I have managed to take away the pain from my mothers hip for a considerable length of time.

My sister and I are close, and we depend upon each other a lot.

The Earth sanctuary

When I have spare time, I like to go to the woodlands and hills away from the densely populated town where I don't feel very comfortable. These woodlands and hills extend towards the mountains that are further inland. Here I feel more free and at home with the energies.

On the top of a hill behind the town there is a cleared circle of land. This is the Earth sanctuary where I go. It is my favourite place to be. Sheena showed it to me. Sometimes we come here together. I have received blessings here.

It is one of the times when I am visiting the Earth sanctuary. I hardly notice that anyone else is here. It is very quiet and still. There is a particular stone where I like to sit, near the centre of the clearing. I go there now. The warm dense presence of the trees around the clearing helps me to feel very safe. Closing my eyes, I start to meditate. There is a great sense of familiarity in doing this. Then, slowly, I start to sense the presence of someone from Spirit with me. I feel energy like hands upon my shoulders and a great feeling of peace passes through me. When I finally feel this energy lifting, I sense this presence of light and I can only describe it like a blessing, as a form of Spiritual energy that is wishing me well and protecting me. This experience gives me the feeling as if God is with me, not only the Spirit of the Earth, but God, who is the creator of all things. I feel this within me.

I try to save my visits to the Earth sanctuary for special occasions. But it is a place of solace for me whenever I need inner nourishment.

I am surprised and disappointed that not more people appear to come here, even though it is very beautiful. I am sure that my sister loves it as much as me, although we do not speak of our personal experiences. Often though, when we have come, we have met hardly anyone else in the vicinity. With Sheena, we tend to come and leave in silence. It makes us feel much more bonded together.

When I think about it, I wonder about the beliefs of other people. I understand that in former times, all the houses used to have small sanctuaries built within them. From writings I have studied, I believe that this is so. However, in our modern society, this does not seem to be the case. There are many houses, I know, where there is no sacred space for Spiritual practices, at all. This makes me question what people can believe to give meaning to their life?

In our house, we have a little room which we use as a sanctuary. Our house, of course, has been passed down through the generations. Together, we go there and pray together and be with the flame. This helps us feel peace with each other, although I know I gain much more peace from the Earth sanctuary.

Fíre

It is later now. I am 21 years old and I have been spending time with my sister at the Temple. We have come back home and I am staring at a smouldering mound of ashes. Our house has been burnt. I think that my mother and father have been killed. The stone rubble is all that remains. A few people are watching nearby but no one is doing anything to help. My sister and I are standing together motionless. I can hardly believe my eyes. A few hours ago I was chatting with my parents, but now I am sure that they are dead. How could something like this happen to them? They were such good people. They didn't deserve this.

My thoughts are racing inside. Was this an accident, or was this intended as an act of violence and murder? I can hardly imagine my father having enemies, but I know there were people with whom he had disagreements. My mother and father were careful about the home. They were not people who would create this kind of accident. The workshop is burnt as well. The only fire in the house was the flame in the sanctuary or the stove in the kitchen. However, both these sources of fire were very well contained and protected. It couldn't have been an accident. With my inner senses I know that the fire was deliberately lit. As I look across at my sister, I feel that she knows this too.

My mind is in turmoil. I could try to trace those people who killed my parents because someone must know about it. However, I do not want to let bitterness take over me. I think I need to accept that this was something that was meant. Or, if it was not meant, then it was something that I can do nothing about. So I must let it go. If people want to do that to others, and kill, then I feel that in the end, they will cause their own undoing and there is little I can do about it. If I start trying to hurt others because they hurt me or someone close to me, it would only cause bitterness and hatred to well up in myself, and I do not want that.

As I turn to face my sister, she buries herself in my arms, sobbing. I cannot stop my own tears from coming down either. Eventually we turn to go. We have to go to the Earth sanctuary. There is nowhere else.

In the clearing I sit close by to my sister. Today we need to be linked. Silently I ask for help to know what we can do. We have lost our home, and our parents. It feels like the whole early fabric of our life has been destroyed.

I find it very hard to settle today, but slowly the energy of peace starts to seep through me. Today, I need much healing and much help. In time I begin to sense the light and the presence of my parent's energy. I feel them with me so close. They seem to be telling me they are well and OK. I cannot stop the sobs from erupting from within my chest. But gradually the thoughts seem to come for us to go to the Temple. I feel much quieter as I begin to accept this idea. We would be welcome there. Afterwards when we talk about it, we both agree. This is where we will go.

The Temple

I have been living and working in the Temple for a few years now. We were welcomed as we expected, especially when the healers discovered that I had abilities in that direction. I have enjoyed the training I have received and it wasn't long before I was working directly with people coming here for help. The area of healing where I have most aptitude seems to be with healing the traumas of the mind. Often now, when people come here with problems of this sort, then I am the one called to help.

The Temple often seems to be crowded with people. Many, many people come here. It is the only Temple to service our town. In fact, I feel that we do not have enough healers to cope with the demand. We try our best, but sometimes we find ourselves becoming very tired.

I find that I enjoy very much helping other people with healing. It gives me much more pleasure than working with the boats. Also, I like to listen to peoples stories and the problems they tell. This way I am learning more and more about our society and the way that people treat each other. Some of what I have learnt has disturbed me greatly. I wish I could do more to help.

People come here when they are ill, when they have suffered injuries, and when they feel stress from trying to work out their personal problems. However, people also come to us when they feel they have been wronged by someone else's actions.

The Temple is like a haven or refuge for them. They do not go to the council administration or to the military who have charge of security in our town - they come to us. I feel that people do not trust the government or the military establishment. They do not feel that these institutions would really help them. We are often asked to intervene on someone's behalf. However, we cannot apprehend anyone who has committed crimes. All we can really do is to help people find peace in their hearts, if they are willing to forgive. Usually, this is the most help that these people are able to receive.

The military are central to the government of our town and all the cities around us. They are supposedly the protectors of the peace within the town itself and also guarding against groups or factions who may want to cause trouble to the town from beyond its boundaries. They have quite a large presence without it being obviously imposing. However, I have realised that there is much corruption from within that institution. Many of the personnel from within the military use their influence to fill their pockets and make themselves richer by taking bribes and abusing their position.

When people come here suffering distress and complaining about the wrongs committed against them, it is often the military and the government whom they blame. They feel they are being made to do things which they don't want and it is making them feel ill inside.

There have been many instances where people have told of being forced to pay money to others, so that their houses and livelihoods would not suffer. People are being threatened. They feel they have to form allegiances with members of the authorities to protect their own lives. This situation is breeding more and more mistrust within our society.

I have learnt that there have been numerous cases of houses being burnt down without apparent cause. Ours was not an isolated event. Each time, nothing seems to be done about it and life goes on as if nothing happened.

This makes me ponder if the military had a hand in the death of my parents. I wonder if they had been threatened too?

Within the town there are civilian administrations governing education, building work, and other functions. But all these bodies seem ultimately to be linked to the military and even subservient to them. This makes me question how much our Healing Temple may also be influenced by the military government?

My role within the Temple is still a very junior one. Basically, I do what I am instructed to do by the senior healers. However, we do have to accept guidance about the way we pursue the healing. For instance, it is emphasised that we must not criticise the military in any way through our actions. Sometimes there are restrictions about who we may heal and in what way. Our leaders tend not to give reasons or communicate much about these situations.

I understand that the military do not want us to exceed our authority. They want us involved in healing people and nothing more. I am sure that the military are aware that people come to us with their problems, many of them complaining about the treatment they receive from the authorities. They know that the Temple is like a refuge where people feel safe. What the military do not want is for the Temple to become a fermenting ground for any form of challenge to their authority. I can appreciate how much pressure is placed upon our head healers to ensure that this is so.

Most of the time, I concentrate my attention upon learning more of the techniques of healing and practicing my skills upon people. My sister feels similarly to me about the wider situation. Sometimes we talk of these things together, but we do not know what we can do.

On occasions I still walk by the harbour near the boats and I hear the singing of the waves and feel the warm friendliness of the stones and the Earth beneath my feet. I sense that things are not as they used to be. There is not so much joy and well being that bubbles up any more. I feel it is the oppression of the people that makes it so. This is sad, and I wish it could be different.

A Proposition

It is later. The head healer has called for me to attend a meeting. There is an important man who wishes to speak with me. This man has authority over our Temple and many other Temples in the surrounding area. He is like an overseer of the various Temple's activities. I have not met this man before, and I wonder what he could want from me.

When I enter the room, I am aware of two military officers standing on either side of the doorway. The Administrator is seated behind a table at the far end of the room. There is nowhere for me to sit. As I approach him, I notice his pale skin. When he looks up, I see cold staring eyes. It feels as though he is sucking energy out of me. I feel very small and afraid and I do not like this man at all.

Trying to protect my energy field, I find it is difficult. This man is deliberately trying to make me feel uneasy. He expects people to be deferential to him. I sense his determination to make me do what he says, to submit to his will. Now that I am here with him, there is no escape. I feel very nervous and uncomfortable, hoping I will be strong enough.

When he speaks to me, his voice is so quiet I almost have to strain to hear him. However, in the rest of the room there is silence, so I am bound to listen.

He tells me that his colleagues have been watching me for some time. They have been impressed by my healing abilities and feel that I have considerable potential. Somehow, this makes me feel more anxious than contented.

He is aware of my background and the fire that destroyed my home and killed my parents. He offers his sympathies - but I don't feel it. As he continues, he suggests whether I may like a spacious home to live in, somewhere to share with my sister and be comfortable. It would mean moving to the city, he tells me, but I could have all the facilities that I need.

All I would have to do is to help him with his project. To be involved in this project, I would be working with many other scientists and healers. We would be working together to gather the Earth energies, using crystals.

The aim of the project is to bring wealth and power to the people of the northern region. He tells me that it is a worthy endeavour and that working upon this could bring me great status within the community.

As I listen to him, I am not impressed. In fact, I feel appalled. To work for this man is the last thing that I would want to do in my life.

In the pause that follows, he stares at me and I see the threat in his eyes. I feel that this project is not a good thing. He has not said anything about how it would help other people, or how it would help the Earth energy. Nothing he has said indicates that any form of love is involved with this. I feel very suspicious of him. Trying to gather my courage from within, I say to him that I am not interested. He reacts sharply and I sense his anger. Immediately though, he tries to disguise it, and he continues in his steady, quiet voice. The manner of his speaking is hypnotic and I have to battle to resist him.

He gives me an ultimatum. Unless I agree to help and to work upon this project at least part time, then I will not be able to work in this Temple or any other. There would be no place for me. When I still do not respond, he suggests that I may even be arrested if I do not co-operate.

This man makes me feel afraid. I feel shocked and startled. Fumbling to try to find something sensible to say, I ask him for some time to think about it. He replies that he can give me a few days until the time of his next visit. But then he expects me to be packed and ready to leave with him.

Inside, I feel deeply upset. I am going to talk with my sister. This is outrageous and I am sure she will support me. I could never work for this so called project. But neither could I work any more in this Temple, however much the Administrator may threaten me. This meeting has made me aware of the kind of infiltration going on with our work in the Temple. It is intolerable. In fact, the whole town seems to be seething with corruption. I don't feel I can live here anymore. We'll have to go.

Escape From the Town

My sister and I have come to the Earth sanctuary. This is our refuge. It is the only place in the area that feels safe to me now. We need to seek guidance for our next steps.

We have brought with us a woman, younger than me. She has also lost her family in tragic circumstances. We have been trying to help her. Like us, she has been developing to be a dedicated healer and I felt I could confide in her about my troubles. Immediately she wanted to come with us, and somehow this felt right.

We sit together within the clearing and gradually I become quieter inside. It is only us who are here. I feel the familiar sense of Spirit hands and energy moving through my body. Then the lightness comes. Today I feel myself joining with the energy of my sister and our friend, a joining together so we feel united. I feel an energy of encouragement, for me to be true and not give in, that I must withstand the tests that come to me. I feel that I am being shown a way forward, that there is much work which I need to do, and somehow I have to try and help our society, and help the balance of energies to be returned, if I can. These thoughts come strongly into my mind. I feel myself merging with my companions to form a common aim. What we are shown is for us to go to the mountains.

As we talk afterwards, we all feel that it would be dangerous, especially for me, to stay in the town any longer. We feel that if we were in the town we would be very likely to meet the same fate as my parents in one form or another. When I reflect about that Administrator, it would not surprise me if he is involved in criminal activities, beyond his supposed responsibilities. We have to leave today. In front of us the mountains seem vast and unending. We do not know for what we are looking or in what direction we need to go. We will have to listen inside and trust that we are protected and attune together for our path.

It is later now. We are in the mountains, and we have come to a sanctuary. It is a very beautiful and a powerful place. As soon as we approached it, I felt that we were arriving where we needed to be. The sanctuary itself is hidden from view by trees, and apart from the energy of it which attracted us, we were not aware of it until we were almost upon it.

The people here have welcomed us. We are talking with the man who is the leader of the sanctuary. His name is Shastar. He is a very kind and caring man. We have shared with him our story and he seems very concerned. Initially, I feel he was testing us to be sure that he could trust us. But now, he is confiding in us, sharing more with us about how he sees the situation.

Shastar is very disturbed by what is happening, not only in our town, but in all the cities and towns across the region. He sees it as part of a pattern which is extending in different degrees throughout the whole land.

Here in the sanctuary, they have to be very careful to protect themselves psychically from possible attack. They have to be discriminating about whom they allow to enter the sanctuary. Many sanctuaries have been violated, especially the ones in the cities and towns. Usually, these sanctuaries are stripped of their crystals. Then the healers are taken, the crystals used to summon up energy from the Earth to make weapons. The military are involved in this, and they seem to be wanting to develop these weapons to generate power.

However, the Earth energy does not want to be used like this. The healers here are aware that the network of energy across the land is becoming dangerously imbalanced. As part of the overall Healing sanctuary, there is a cavern devoted to Earth healing. This is a place of great power, with crystalline structures that tap directly into the Earth's energy grid.

The healers work tirelessly to try to channel energies into the Earth, to try to nourish and replace what is being lost. They are trying to co-ordinate their efforts with other mountain sanctuaries throughout the land.

Shastar is grateful that we have come. He feels there is a great deal for us to learn, but also for us to contribute. He needs our help. They have been feeling that they were losing the struggle. There is a fear of what may happen if the energies become too far out of balance. They fear what the Earth may do, how she may react. Even though sanctuaries are trying to link together and help, it is difficult, because some have been taken and violated, and so the strength is not there as it could be.

I understand that there is conflict between different factions in the land. Around further to the big cities on the east coast, there is fighting. It appears that there are groups of military who are wanting to assert a domination of their culture across the land. They are feeding their power to be able to assert their own interests. What we are also told is that the scientists who are involved in creating these weapons are so fascinated by the power that they are creating, that they are losing sight of the potential damage that could be done. They are really captivated by this power, and so this is like a thirst in them. Their weapons suck energy from the Earth. Then, as they experience this power, they become aware of the potential of how this power could create more power. But in the end, it can only lead to destruction, and we have to find a way to stop this.

Part 2

Life in the Sanctuary

We have been living and working here now for some years. It has been a very positive experience for me and I have learnt much.

If I can describe the sanctuary a little, it is mainly situated underground, within caves. There is some natural lighting coming through sky light from gaps at the top of the caves. It is quite a complex of different structures. Most of the healing work is done from within the caverns. However, there are also buildings, mainly wooden, that are outside the inner chambers. These are mainly for accommodation purposes and have expanded in number of late. There is an intense atmosphere of peace and dedication as the healers go about their work. It is mostly quiet, apart from one chamber which is used for sound healing, but this does not disturb anyone.

Our young female friend has settled in well. She has developed a great fondness for crystals and has been working with others who can teach her about these. I hardly see her anymore these days.

With my sister though, it is different. We have many shared interests and we both spend much time talking with each other, especially about the situation in the land.

However, the person with whom I have been spending most time is Shastar. He and I have become close friends. I have been surprised how much he values my judgment and opinion. He is somewhat older than me, but not by so much. He was still young when he had to begin to assume leadership of the sanctuary, but he is very well respected. Shastar tends to put the needs of others before his own, and there is much love in his heart. I am delighted that he has taken such a personal interest in my development.

I feel very much love for Shastar. He is very wise, having a very soft and calming voice, which contrasts with the anxiety that I sometimes feel when I think about the situation in the land. His influence helps to bring a serenity to the sanctuary that is very necessary. When Shastar speaks to me, it helps me to become more measured in my outlook. I know that my first tendency is to be impulsive - I want to get out and do something. Shastar though, is helping me to learn to think more before I act. He is able to caution me and help me to be aware of different procedures and contingencies that are necessary to plan before taking action.

One of my main trainings here has been to practice communication using crystals. I have been given a wonderful smooth black obsidian stone. It is a beautiful shining stone that I can hold in my hand. I sense that it is very ancient, and it feels somehow familiar. This stone has become very precious to me.

Using it, I have been learning to communicate and see through distances. Shastar gave it to me. He said that it was waiting for me. It had been here in the sanctuary without anyone using it for a long time. But as soon as he knew I was coming, he was aware that it was for me.

Shastar also has a stone. His stone is more translucent and is purple in colour, crystalline. Together with Shastar, I have been practicing to be able to communicate and see. With him, I find it quite easy for us to find each other's wavelength and frequency. He, of course, has a lot of experience. But I feel that the ease of communication between us is also to do with our closeness. Using our stones, we can communicate thoughts, feelings and words, without actively speaking to each other.

Gradually, Shastar has been training me to learn to pick up impressions of what is happening beyond our sanctuary in various situations throughout the land. He has been able to monitor what I perceive, help me focus it, and confirm its accuracy. I have become very proficient at doing this. More and more I have been given the responsibility for communication with other sanctuaries to co-ordinate our activities.

There are more people here now than there were when we arrived. It seems that many of the healers who have been working around the Temples in the towns and cities of the north, have been persecuted for non-cooperation with the authorities, in a similar way to what happened to me. People who refuse to join in with the projects of the authorities are suffering threats, torture and sometimes death. I notice that there has been a trickle of people finding their way up to this sanctuary because they have been called to come here.

Within the sanctuary, there are people continually working to provide a psychic shield for the sanctuary, so that those who may wish to know about the sanctuary for acquisitive reasons, will not detect it. At the same time though, others are using crystal communicators to actually invite healers and people of good heart, who are wanting to escape the troubles, to come here. So those two things are happening at once.

And I learn now that we were actually called to come here, my sister and I. It was not an accident. We were directed. And I could almost feel it when we came up the mountains, that we knew where we were going. We all did, and we had to follow that calling.

With all the various activities from within the sanctuary centred upon coping with the situation of crisis in the land, not so much attention has been given towards helping the sick and distressed. This has been given lesser priority because of the need of the land. Unfortunately we have had to put this second.

One of the most important places in the sanctuary is the Earth Healing cavern. Here people meditate and attune to the energies of the Earth, to channel healing, love and power from the creator being of the Universe, to nurture the Earth Spirit. In the centre of this cavern, there is a very large crystal sphere, as big as me. This sphere is very ancient and has been placed here long ago. It is gently held onto the floor of the cavern, with links through the stones that support it, to Earth structures that go deep beneath our land. The crystal sphere feels what the Earth mother feels. Our healing goes right to the heart of that aspect of the Earth Spirit that looks after our land.

We have groups of healers constantly being rotated to channel energy through the crystal sphere. This has to be done carefully because of the power involved and is done through physical touch of the sphere itself with two or four people engaged in that. Others sitting further away sometimes support the efforts with meditation and inner visualisation. My sister and I have been pleased to learn how we can join in this, and take our turn.

What distresses us is that the crystal sphere is shaking slightly. In former times it was completely still. The shaking is an indication of the disturbances that are taking place through the imbalances of Earth energy. In the time that we have been here, the shaking has grown stronger, and this is not a good sign for the health of our land.

The Northern Cities

It has been quite an education for me to learn about the activities of the northern cities. As we look from the front of the sanctuary, it is not so distant over the horizon to the coastline where these cities are situated. I understand now, that the military authorities of the various cities have apparently formed an alliance together. The little town where I grew up, is within their jurisdiction.

Shastar has suggested to me that I would be surprised, if I went to one of these cities, just how many people are living there. From my insulated upbringing, I have had no idea about the population structures around our land. But, from what he tells me, there are literally millions of people living in the vicinity of these cities. And he tells me that these places have become bad and corrupt, particularly within the ruling classes. Much of the energy drain from the Earth has been going there.

For a long time, Shastar has been studying the nature of the disturbances emanating from these cities. He has been using his stone, but also gaining information from people who have fled from these places and come to us. He tells me that psychically, the ruling class from there are working together to create an empire

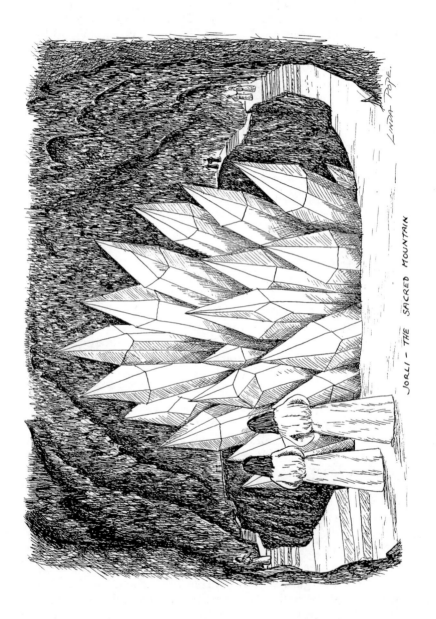

JORLI — THE SACRED MOUNTAIN

LINDA POPE.

of power. The healers and scientists are practicing psychic techniques to draw energy to them, for their own sense of power. Shastar has suggested that the leaders of the cities want to establish themselves as a centre of power within the land, and even beyond that. Spiritual energy and power are being extracted from within the Earth for their own use, so they can feel more powerful, feeling that sense of surging force which the Earth can bring, and also to make their position psychically more prominent so they can have power over others.

Practically, we do not know exactly all the details of how they are doing this, and for what purpose. However, we are aware that many important people in these places have had edifices of themselves constructed. A hierarchy has been established in the society where people are being brought in from other areas of the land, as slaves. People are being made to honour these leaders as great ones. This is quite contrary though to what we have been taught within the tradition of our land. We feel it is wrong.

Shastar and I have been focusing our awareness, using our stones, trying to discover what it is in these cities causing the most damage. Our attention returns continually to the activities of the Healing Temples and the corruption that has set in there.

These Temples have been there for millennia. But they are no longer being used for their rightful purpose. They should be centres of Healing and places of worship for people to connect with the Earth Spirit, both for their own nourishment, and to honour the Earth Spirit as well. However, the Temples have been taken over by corrupt priests, and they are using oracles to manipulate the population.

The Temples serve as places of gatherings for the people. When people come together for meetings by the Temple, they are made to feel that they are being blessed. But this seems to be an illusion. The oracles are people who go into trance and are channelling information to feed to the population. However, we can see that what is being channelled is not Truth as it should be, but corrupt lies designed to serve the interests of these priests. We cannot tell exactly what is being said. We would need to go

239

there to know that. But somehow, the people unwittingly seem to be being led to contribute to the drain that is taking place.

The people are no longer serving the Earth and the Earth Spirit, but they are serving the leaders of these cities, who only want power for their own gain. These oracles are going through an elaborate pretence with what they do. I can tell as I look at it, that there is no love in what is being channelled. Therefore, I know it is not from Spirit. With these priests standing behind the oracles, the oracles are being controlled, and fed what to say. We feel they may be punished if they do not say things correctly. Therefore, these oracles are little more than slaves for these priests.

I feel very concerned for the ordinary people of these cities. It seems that they have become poor, and have little scope for self-expression. I can understand that the promise that their community could become rich and at the centre of the world, may be quite alluring to them.

But they don't have an avenue anymore to connect with the Earth Spirit, except within themselves. I am sure that many of them probably don't even remember about the love of the Earth Spirit. And even if they do remember, they are being intimidated so they cannot be open about this anymore. The energy from these Temples does not make people happy anymore or enrich them. I sense that they are hungry, hungry in their souls. All that the ruling class appears to want is material wealth, material well being and power over others. This is very empty. We can perceive energetically, how the power is being drawn to these leaders, and it is these priests who are orchestrating this.

I feel a strong desire growing in me, that I wish to help those people if it is at all possible.

Plans

For the whole time I have been living at the Sanctuary, I have been aware that the only effective way that we are going to be able to help the land with regards to the disturbances that have been created, is to be able to change what is happening at the source of those disturbances. It has felt immensely frustrating to me that we have not been able to do anything about this.

However, now we may have our chance. Because of the trickle of refugee healers fleeing from the cities and towns of the north, Shastar has reached the stage where he has sufficient healers to cover all the basic functions of the sanctuary plus some left over.

With these surplus healers, Shastar is proposing that we engage in a mission and project of our own to try and liberate the people of these cities from their oppressors, and start to re-balance the energies at the same time. It is an audacious plan which could be highly dangerous. However, we feel we have to try something and everyone is supportive of the idea.

I have volunteered to be one of those engaged in the mission. My sister wants to come with me. We have been placed in charge of a group going to one of the cities. There are two more groups going to other cities.

The first stage of the project will be for us to set up a base for ourselves within the city from which we can build up a network and plan our operation. There are one or two contacts from within the city that may help us make our start. However, we'll have to be very careful and secretive, for we know that the military in these cities are ruthless and would not hesitate to torture or kill anyone whom they consider are getting in their way.

We will stay in contact with the sanctuary through our stones, and try to use this connection to increase the light and love energy in the cities as well. It will not be easy. But I know in my heart, that if people do not begin to intervene by some form of constructive actions soon, the problems of our land will only increase.

Preparations in the City

It is a horrible place to live in these cities. The streets are so narrow. There are many, many people crowded here in their stone buildings. The streets smell. People here are obviously poor, and unhappy. It is really quite terrible. But we've found a house, a house where we meet, and where my sister and I can live.

And there are people willing to work with us. We have already been here some months, but now there are about a dozen of us, meeting regularly. We need quite a few more people yet, but the ones we have can be our foundation.

When we are in the house together, we meditate. We attune with the Earth Spirit. Usually, I place my communicator stone in the middle of our circle. Using that, we can link with the sanctuary in the mountains and with Shastar. Generally, it is just after sunset when we meditate, so that this can be coordinated. We try to link with the sphere from the Earth Healing cavern, so that this can help us channel positive energy, and help to draw back the energies that have built up here negatively. In addition, we try to channel positive and loving energies to the population here. We feel we must be having some success. Otherwise, we would not be attracting more people to join us.

However, these meditations take a big effort. There is such an overwhelming energy of fear and oppression hanging over this city, that it is very difficult to break through. Quite often I feel exhausted after our sessions. However, if our numbers keep growing, and if enough people start to engage in these practices, then surely that could be of help.

Now that we have a core group of supporters we are able to engage more fully in the second stage of our plan. We are interested to study the activities of the Healing Temples and the oracles which are so much influencing the people. My sister and I are working separately on this.

The Temple where I go is the main one in the centre of the city. This, I visit quite regularly. I have seen that there are three young women used as oracles. They are rotated. Behind them is the priest who controls them. He stays more in the background, and the oracles are used to attract the people's attention.

There is a common ritual which is conducted daily. As the people gather, the priest draws them in, summoning them to come close and listen. He suggests the profound truths which the oracles want to spread and he goes around placing his hands on different peoples head, as if in blessing. However, this is just a gesture, as far as I can see. What he really wants is compliance.

The priest is a rather tall, thin man. His robes are elaborate and designed to give him authority. He expects people to bow down to him as he approaches and I've noticed how satisfied he looks then. The stare of his eyes is cold and feels dangerous to me. Most people will not look at him. The oracles say more or less exactly what I had thought. The gist of it is that the people need to direct their energies to the leaders of their cities, so these leaders can bring great power and wealth to all of them.

In the next stage of the ritual, they all do chants together. The chants are like prayers where the people are directed to draw energy from deep within themselves, and from the Earth itself, to the leaders of the cities. I have become aware that there are giant crystals hidden behind the stage. These crystals lap up the energies from the people. They are like leeches, drawing the power. During this practice, I need to be very strong and centred so that my own energy is not drawn away. The people seem so drained and lifeless after this is done, I don't know why they keep coming back for more, except they are instructed to do so. The priest exerts his power at these moments to insist that the people return for the next service, and when it is over the people walk away as if they are defeated.

This priest and his colleagues are feeding themselves with power, energetically, from the people as well as the Earth. So it is not just materially where the people have become poorer, but on other levels as well.

Today as I look at the priest, he catches my eye, but I am determined not to look away. The expression in his face though, is little more than contempt, and he soon turns his attention to other matters. I feel almost a hatred for him at this moment.

It is later now and we have gathered all the people that we need. I must admit that I feel rather nervous at this point because what happens next will be so crucial. We try to meditate together and ask for guidance. All that occurs is that we feel love enveloping us and wanting us to go out from us further into the city.

Tomorrow, we plan to make our moves. There are five Temples in the city. We have a group to go to each one. I will take my group with me to the large Temple in the centre of the city. My sister will lead a group to one of the other Temples. We have made our arrangements as best we can. Tonight we need to rest so we will be ready.

Uprising

The people are gathering by the Temple for the daily ritual, and I am in the crowd. There are a dozen of us here today, spread out amongst the people. We are wearing simple clothes, as we always do on these occasions, so that hopefully, we will not attract notice. We have become aware that there is only a very small military presence for the various Temple activities. No one has tended to challenge the authority of the priest, and so, he has felt quite secure.

In some ways, this is quite comforting, and it gives us more scope and freedom to issue our challenge today. However, if people have become so placid that they just accept and submit to everything that this priest does, what chances do I have to be able to help rouse the population so they will behave differently?

The oracle is speaking. She is seated, her head slightly tilted back, as if in trance. Her voice is quite loud, monotone and almost expressionless. Clearly, she has been well trained to be able to project her voice so well.

She is speaking as usual about the greatness of the empire that is being built and how important it is to give homage to the leaders of the city. I have to choose my moment, the best moment to do this.....

Suddenly, I am standing up. 'It is lies.' I am standing.' It is all lies.' I strive to be heard over her voice. Its only these priests and leaders wanting power for themselves. I try to say how they are destroying the land, urging the people to join us and oppose this. My friends are standing up too, issuing their own challenge, echoing the sentiments expressed by me.

It is all happening very quickly. The crowd is stirring. They do not know what to do. The oracle has opened her eyes and returned to normal consciousness. She looks pale and shaken.

The priest is striding forward to the front of the stage. In his hand he has a sword. Certainly, he is very angry. "Seize them", he commands to his military friends. The crowd begin to disperse. I keep shouting as long as I can. I hope that I have moved the people enough. I hope they can find their own courage to assert their rights. I shout, 'See what kind of people they are. See what they do with their swords.'

The military are coming. They are hacking through the crowd to get to us. People fall down injured. The priest is trying to wade through the crowd himself. So we have to get out of here. I have to move fast.

But we have planned this carefully. Our escape route is well marked. The people do not attempt to stop me. I rush along the alley and through the building where I can go, through another building and into the clear. Two of my friends are with me. There is a group of soldiers in the street in front of us. We slow right down and walk very casually around them. Then we continue so we can return to our base. We have done it!

A tragic loss

It takes us a while to assemble at our base, and there is plenty of nervous excited chatter. I am anxious to learn about the other groups. Each of the leaders of these groups has a communicator stone. I am trying to get through to them.

Something does not feel right. I feel increasingly disturbed. I am not able to get through to my sister. It feels wrong. I hope she is OK. She does not respond to my signal.

One of my sister's group has just arrived. He is almost hysterical. My sister is dead. They had to leave her there. What?....

I cannot comprehend this. I have to sit down. How can this be? My sister and I - we were always going to be together....

It is later now. I have tried to come to terms with my grief. One of my friends, Shoola, has tried to comfort me. He has been a great support to me. There has been much sadness in our group. Everyone knew how much my sister meant to me. We all admired her so much for her courage and tenacity and her caring love.

Apparently, my sister was very brave. She got up just as I had done, and she continued to yell defiance to the authorities even after the military were coming. And she didn't leave herself enough time. How could she do this to herself? She didn't leave herself enough time to get away. And soon some military were upon her, they stabbed her. They did not care that other people were around. They just stabbed her. And she died where she had been speaking. She just sank to the ground, and didn't have a chance.

The people were horrified. However, then, the oracle started talking about subversives, about people not being true believers. They tried to con the crowd again, into accepting that. But they were stirred, the crowd. My sister's words had their impact. They saw that she was dead as a consequence of what she said. The people scattered. They did not stay any longer.

Now though, I am questioning everything. I feel rather shattered inside. I know there always was a risk of death or injuries, but I never really had thought that it would happen, especially to my sister. I had somehow assumed, because what we wanted to do was good that we would be protected and that no harm would come to us. That belief has proved to be mistaken. I don't know how much I wish to continue with our project if people are going to die. That wasn't what we intended.

Shoola has been talking with me. He is urging me to not give up. My sister was speaking up for the land. The land needs our help. Now that we have started, we have to continue. The group are looking to me for my leadership.

With a heavy heart, I finally agree to allow our plans to unfold further. I cannot prevent though, doubts from gnawing away inside of me.

Meeting With the Enemy

It is some months later. We have been continuing in our efforts with mixed results.

Numbers have dwindled at the Temple meetings. People do not feel obliged to go anymore. Sometimes we attend and yell our defiance, but it is getting harder each time. The military presence has grown much larger, and more reactionary. A few of our group have been injured and taken. There has been nothing we could do.

As a group, we have become very close and committed, particularly with our meditations and Spiritual practices. However, for anyone doing what we are doing it is becoming increasingly difficult. The military will not allow any form of Spiritual worship or practices besides what is conducted officially at the oracle Temples. Therefore, people are not able to be open with their wish for an alternative to that organised by the priests. We have noticed that some of the statues erected to honour the city leaders have been damaged - so people are reacting. Certainly, because the numbers have become so small at the Temple services, the amount of energy being drained off has collapsed as well. This is encouraging to us. We are aware though, that there have been other methods of extracting the Earth energy, which the authorities in the city have been exploiting.

But I have been disappointed by people's lack of fight. To all appearances, life has mainly gone on as if nothing happened. People seem too afraid to stand up for their rights.

What is frustrating is that all the healers, all the people interested in a more Spiritual way of life, are being forced underground. They are being forced to carry on their activities in secret. We have to encourage this to grow, because it is only through engaging in Spiritual activity that we can counter the poverty and counter the transfer of power. However, I don't know anymore if we can succeed.

The military have been raiding houses looking for healers and subversives. Anyone under suspicion has been arrested and their house burnt down. There have been reports of torture and mutilation. People are being offered money for information about what we are doing. So people are losing trust. The numbers at our meetings have also begun to decrease. The people with us are feeling less and less safe. I sometimes wonder if the only thing we have succeeded in doing is to arouse the anger of the military.

One day, I feel that this confrontation has gone on for long enough. I can only think of one option. We must seek a meeting with the authorities, offering to suspend our public activities if they agree to listen to our thoughts about the situation. I feel there is little chance, really, that they will be receptive to us. But, if there is any chance at all, I feel we need to take it. I talk with Shoola about it and he agrees.

We have arranged for this meeting to take place. I recognise that for them, they would consider it advantageous to meet with us, because what we have done has been very disruptive. However, I do not trust them. In my negotiations with them, I have insisted on no military presence, that everyone attending this meeting be unarmed and that the meeting be held at a location determined by us. I am quite surprised that they have agreed to all these demands.

We have arranged a building to meet in where we have organised possible escape routes should we need them. The meeting is to be held in a room around a table to seat six of them and six of us. I hope I have done enough to protect us. Some of the group will be scattered around the streets and alleys nearby to hopefully warn us in case of trouble.

The meeting is about to start. I have checked with my stone. It is highly dangerous. There are military about very close, but I do not know exactly where they are. I feel though, that having gone this far, I cannot turn back now.

Two of their negotiating team are familiar to me. There is of course, the priest from the main Temple in the city. When he sees me, his eyes light up with a viciousness that he can hardly restrain. Their chief spokesman is the Administrator who spoke to me before I left the temple in the town of my birth. I still sense a coldness about him that brings a fear to my heart.

For a while, they let us talk. I try to explain about the imbalance of the energy, the threat to the land, and consequences of their actions, also in terms of the happiness and well being of their own population. Shoola backs me up, but it feels like talking to a brick wall. I suggest that if they do not stop what they are doing, then it may cause the destruction of the whole land.

They won't listen. I sense that they are too intoxicated with their own need to acquire power for themselves. The Administrator motions me to stop. He wants a turn now.

The Administrator dismisses any arguments and asks me again would I like to join with him: He tells us that there is no future in what we are doing, so that if we do not stop our activities with immediate effect, then we will be totally crushed, and there will be orders for us to be all killed. With a cold smile, he says that the military have been very lenient in their approach to this, so far. However, if any more objections are raised at the temple meetings, they have orders to be totally ruthless, and if any of us were found or captured, then that person would be tortured and killed brutally in public as an example to others.

He is trying to make us afraid. I cannot agree to what he says. There is an uncomfortable silence around the table. Slowly, the Administrator raises his arm. He is giving a signal. One of their negotiators goes to the door. I know he will call the military. They will arrest us.

I try to warn the others. We have to get out of here. The priest is on his feet. He is trying to grab members of our group. Meanwhile, the Administrator has edged away. He does not take part in physical battles. I try to help the others, but I know it is more important for us to break free. We have to run.

I escape through the side door. Some of my companions are with me. We are being pursued. We have to go so fast. Down corridors, through doorways, we have to keep going. It is desperate. We have some of our people to help us. A door is closed, a barrier put up. It gives us more time. Eventually, I can stop. The military are filling the streets, but we've got through the worst. I can pause for a few moments.

Swiftly, I reach for my stone. As I slow my breathing down and concentrate I can asses the situation. Two of us have been captured. One of them is Shoola. As I see more deeply, I perceive that they're being treated roughly and with violence. I know that the Administrator's threat will be carried out with them.

My body starts to shake with shock. The last thing I hear before I have to turn away from the stone, is the sound of Shoola's screams.

Part 3
Prison

I feel I have no choice. Whenever I think of Shoola and Keipic, I feel agony inside, and I cannot stop thinking about them. I don't sleep. I must take responsibility. It was my idea to call for that meeting. Therefore, it was my initiative that led to their capture. I know what I have to do.

We will have to abandon our project. I feel that it is not right anymore. When activities become like fighting, with people dying and being hurt, then the love goes out of what we do. Our whole endeavour becomes clouded by bitterness and despair.

The power structures in the city are still very much in place. People are afraid to oppose the military. If anything is going to change what is happening here, and help the land, then there will have to be another way. I feel that we have done all we can. My friends support me. They also feel defeated.

I just pray that something can be done. As I look into my stone, I sense the danger and the tension at the moment, not only in these cities, but across the land. Things are not going well. It feels as though action is needed, and urgently, before it is too late.

Even when I communicate with Shastar, his energy does not seem as calm as it did before. He is anxious for me to be careful, encouraging me not to sacrifice myself. However, it is too late. I am passing on my communicator stone to one of my friends so that it may be returned safely to the sanctuary in the mountains.

I am going to offer myself up in exchange for Shoola and Keipic being returned unharmed. In my heart, I would rather die myself than have them die, or suffer any more. I don't know if the authorities will accept my proposal.

I have sent a message guaranteeing that if Shoola and Keipic are released and they do not kill or torture me, then we will stop all our disruptive activity immediately. I have argued in my message that if they do not fulfill these conditions, then we have laid preparations to cause even more disruption than before. This is bluff of course, but I had to give them a reason to release my friends. I know that they may well kill me, and there is nothing anyone can do about it. To that, I feel resigned. I'll just have to go ahead with this in any case.

When I think of Shoola, I think of all the love, support and care he gave to me when my sister, Sheena died. I owe him a lot for that.

It is morning time now. I am standing in the square outside the Temple. There are few people about. I notice some birds flying overhead. Inside, I feel a strange sense of peace and stillness, even though my stomach is knotted with fear. I call out to them that I am here, and they can take me now. The priest appears and he has soldiers with him. They come and get me, jostling, pushing, grabbing and pulling me into the building. The priest grabs my hair and spits at me. They are all very rough and rude. I try very much to control my temper so I will not react to them.

The priest is very angry with me. He slaps my face and tells me that I am a fool. He taunts me that if I think my message has been received as I want it to be, then I am mistaken. They beat me more until my body feels numb and I can hardly feel the pain. I try not to resist and just let them do it. The priest tells me that he'll let my companions go, but they have been so much tortured that they'll be of no use to anyone any more. He says that I can expect the same for myself, or even worse. This man seems to relish trying to make me afraid. He cannot reach me though. I have tried to withdraw my consciousness as much as I can. My passiveness angers him even more.

They have put chains around me and I have been taken downstairs to somewhere very dark, some kind of cell. It is a small room in total darkness. This is where I have been left. I feel very small and very lonely. The priest has said to me that this is where I'll die. He has not given any hope to me.

I wonder about my friends, but I do not know anything about them. I hope that they were not as badly mutilated as the priest made out. I hope they were released.

Now, I only have my meditation practices to try to sustain myself from within. I don't know how long I can continue that. They have left me a small amount of water to drink, but that is all. Probably, they want to draw out my suffering for as long as they can. I want to try to seek inner guidance, acceptance and peace. I do not wish to blame anyone for what has happened to me, but I want to live if I can.

It is much later. I have become very sensitive to sounds. Occasionally there have been footsteps, a bowl of water left through a gate at the bottom of the door. Perhaps they monitor me a little. But no one has visited. Mostly, all I hear is my own breathing and heart beat, and that's all.

The room smells, and I have become very weak. My body has become wasted and it is a huge effort for me to move. My limbs ache and most of the time I slouch crouched in a corner. I can hardly concentrate any more to focus my awareness within. I feel that soon it will be all over for me. My body feels close to collapse. I feel cold and shivery.

Someone is coming, and they have brought food. The door is left slightly ajar and there is light beyond. It is agony for my eyes. I cannot look. My body can only take a little food. I eat slowly and gradually and drink in between. I'm given time. I can hardly think anymore what they want.

A soldier comes to take me somewhere else. By now my eyes have adjusted to the light. I cannot walk. He calls for a colleague. They have to carry me more or less to the room where they want me to go. I am pushed into a chair.

There are a group of men in here. The priest and Administrator are two of them. Soon I am being questioned by the Administrator. He has that same soft, cold voice. I can hardly make out what he is saying, but he is talking about the Healing sanctuary in the mountains. He wants to know where it is located, how many people are there, how it is protected. I will not tell him. I make out that I do not understand.

The priest comes over and slaps me. He threatens me that if I do not co-operate with them, then I will go back to my cell and die. My body shivers and shakes uncontrollably. I do not want to die in such a suffering way. I do not know if I can resist any more, but I cannot betray my friends.

He pulls my hair and hurts me. The priest punches me in the ribs. I feel bleeding inside. I'm sure the bone is broken. I try not to move to cough or splutter. I cannot take much more, but I still don't want to die. He knows he cannot make me talk. I won't say anything. I can hardly focus anymore on what they are doing.

I'm being moved. They are dragging me upstairs, out of the Temple confines and opening up the door. I am being dumped outside, left in a crumpled heap. Why would they do that? My breathing is shallow and rasping. It is night time. I hope someone will help me. My body aches so much. I can hardly move. They are letting me go, and I do not understand.

Release

The ground is cold underneath me. I'm hardly wearing anything. I feel so weak. There is a woman bending over me, an older woman. She was here before and went away. I have little strength to acknowledge her.

She has something warm for me to drink. I try to let it pass down my throat without spilling it all. She has to pour it for me. I feel grateful though. She wants to help me. The woman has a cloth, with some form of ointment. She's rubbing it gently over my wounds, onto the aching parts of my body. It feels soothing where she has touched me. The blood supply is stimulated and it is making me feel more conscious again.

Now she's trying to move me. She's trying to get me to lean against her, to stand up. I know I cannot weigh very much now, but it is so difficult. She tries to rub some more of the ointment in. However, my body just wants to collapse. I can't go very far at all. She tries to carry me, but I am rather big for her. I feel myself becoming dizzy. I may be losing consciousness.....

Waking up, I find I am in a room, the old woman by my side. She has me lying in a bed and is telling me she got friends to help bring me here. Who is this woman? She is kind to me. I never want to go through anything like that again. I still feel exhausted and faint. My body is in pain. She gives me a few sips of a broth to drink. My body needs that. I feel warmer inside and reassured. I close my eyes again.

There is someone with the old woman now. She says I've been sleeping for a long time. This man introduces himself as a healer. He says he wants to help me.

I feel the warmth from his hands. Waves of peace and energy flow over me as he works upon the various parts of my body. He tells me I need much rest and recuperation. I know he is right. He informs me that he'll come to attend to me on a daily basis until I'm well again.

I am able to sit up now. My body is slowly regaining strength. The old woman and the man are with me. They have been very kind to me.

Somehow, I feel puzzled by the events of my release from prison. I try to express my concern to them that I may be being watched by the military because of who I am. The old woman tries to reassure me that she saw no sign of any observers when I was brought here. She says her friends are few in number, but she can trust them. The healer tells me about his work, how careful he has to be working independently of the authorities. He has to work in a very confidential manner and he always checks his contacts before committing himself to any course of treatment with anyone. In reply to my concerns, he says that he senses we are safe and I should not worry. Although they say and do all the right things, something does not feel at ease in me. I do not trust them.

The healer asks me what I have been doing, how I come to be in the situation where I have needed his help. To this, I tell him my story. He sympathises about the corruption of the authorities and suggests that he would like to get away himself. When I ask about the activities of the Temples, he tells me that they have virtually stopped operating and the services they offer have become quite minimal.

When I look out of the window, I notice how the season has changed. I must have been in that prison for months. The time just passed.

I am now strong enough to stand and I move around. There is still some tenderness around my ribs from the blow I received from the priest but I know that soon I will be well enough to make my next steps. The healer has been making tremendous efforts, I feel, to become my friend. He has been asking me about my plans, whether he could come with me if I plan to leave the city. I still do not trust him.

One night I am thinking about this. I wonder if I have been set up so that the authorities can find information about the Healing sanctuary in the mountains. I don't want to betray my friends. This healer has been very kind to me, but if he is really meant to find a life beyond this city, then he can do so without me. The risks are too great. I cannot compromise my integrity. In this situation I am better off acting on my own.

I have decided to make my escape. In recent days, the healer has been staying and sleeping in the house with us. It is as though, as I have become stronger he has wanted to keep his eye on me. This has made me more suspicious. I have given him a date when we could leave together, to pacify him. But I will not keep that.

It is night time and I have left the house. I do not know where in the city I have been staying, but I basically know the direction in which I need to go - and that is up.

I thread around different streets and alleys to create diversions in case there are people trying to trace me. However, there is no sign of anyone behind me. I sense that I am safe. Still, I need frequent rests to conserve my energy. At last I feel I am going home. The further I am able to get away from the centre of that city, the more relaxed I feel.

Finally, I have come to the familiar hills around the entrance to the mountain sanctuary. It has been a long journey. Entering into the sanctuary, I see Shastar. He looks older, but when he sees me, his joy is unconfined. I virtually collapse into his arms. Several of my friends are there too. They are so surprised and delighted to see me. Shastar thought I must be dead.

I have met with Shoola and Keipic. Somehow my friends managed to get them here. They both received terrible injuries with permanent burn marks on their skin. Shoola has had his leg amputated below the knee. His foot was so mangled by the torturing that even the psychic surgeons from the sanctuary here could not save it. God knows what he had to endure.

Somehow though, Shoola is smiling and very pleased to see me. He has obviously had a lot of healing. However, I am amazed at his powers of acceptance. Even with his disability, he has dedicated himself to continue with his healing work.

It was the priest of course, that did it, or others who did it under his control. Such a cruel man, I feel a lot of pity for my friends. I feel such a sadness in my heart that our actions could lead to so much suffering. It is really very sad.

The whole project to disrupt the Temples in the cities, to activate the people and their sense of right and wrong, has been abandoned now. As we study the sphere in the Earth cavern, the shaking has further increased and energy is still being drained in that direction. Our plan did not work.

At least, I can stay for a while in the sanctuary here. The energies are so peaceful and vitalising, especially after that city. I can work here.

I need time to recover and reassess my purpose in all this.

The Sacred Mountain

It is some years later. I feel now that I have fully recovered from the efforts of my ordeal in the city. I have been resting, regaining my strength and doing healing work around the sanctuary. It has given me much happiness to use my communicator stone again, to be in contact with other Healing sanctuaries, and to monitor the general situation in the land.

Shastar is in agreement with me that the energy imbalance has continued to worsen. Sometimes when I have been in the Earth cavern, I have sensed a deep rumbling from below me. It has felt as though mother Earth is deeply unhappy and stirring from within. This has made me feel very frightened.

From my stone and from other sources, there have been reports of fighting among the different factions to the east of the continent, and this is causing concern. The soldiers there are using crystal power, and drawing energy from the Earth, using crystals, to fight and destroy buildings and communities. This of course, is making the whole system even more unstable. Shastar and I sometimes feel quite desperate. However, there is some hope in a message we've just received.

We have had a request for some help from the Elders of the Sacred mountain. Now I've had to ask Shastar about this and he has tried to explain to me.

He has told me that there are five major power points, places of enormous power in the land. These power points are the main regulators of the Earth energy system throughout the land. They are like outposts through which the Earth energy can express itself. All these power points exist in the mountain areas, and the knowledge of them has always been concealed from ordinary people so they would not fall prey to corruption. Perhaps the strongest and most powerful of these five places is the one known as the Sacred mountain.

Usually only a small number of healers live and work there. These are people, carefully selected, and with the utmost integrity and complete dedication to serve the interests of the land and the Earth energy. The fact that the Elders of the Sacred mountain have called for help is not a good sign. Shastar feels they would only do that as a last resort. They must feel they have no other means of coping with the instability of the land.

These Elders have called for as many healers as possible to come and convene within the Sacred mountain. The message is being conveyed to as many places as possible. The Elders are terming it a situation of real emergency. They are saying that help may be needed for a considerable duration.

I want to go. Not only am I curious to see this Sacred mountain, if there is a chance for me to help the land, I want to do it.

Shastar has decided to reduce the staffing levels at the sanctuary to a minimum so as many healers as possible can attend the request. He of course, will stay. I am going with my two good friends Nikei and Voolmar. They are two healers with whom I have worked very closely since returning from the city. I am sorry, that due to his disability, Shoola cannot be with us, but there will be many others.

It is later. We have been journeying for some days, further inland and to the south. The way has been hard, but we have managed. My stone has served as a navigational instrument. Just now, we have had our first glimpse of the sacred mountain. It is a crystalline mountain, and there are no trees that grow upon it To climb it would be very difficult, because its faces are so sheer. However, there is an internal entrance near its base, and that is the route we must take.

Before we proceed though we need to stop. The energy field of the Sacred mountain is extremely strong. Even being this close has made me feel quite disorientated. We need time to adjust. The Elders advised us to take this last stage very slowly.

It is later. We have finally made it to our destination. Now we are within the Sacred mountain and it is an awe inspiring sight.

We are standing in this vast cavern, hundreds of us huddled together in a circle. In the centre of the cavern is a huge crystal cluster, with crystals unbelievably large, much larger than any I have ever seen. Beside the crystals the people look very tiny. We are able to link right around the crystal base, but we are aware that the roots of these crystals go much deeper down. It is a natural cavern, created by the Earth Mother. I feel very small and humble to be here.

The Elders of the sanctuary community want to welcome us, and speak more of their intentions. They have a ceremony in mind that they wish to perform with us at the beginning of our work together.

There is an immense feeling in the cavern, peaceful and very quiet, but with a majesty as well. When the Elder speaks, the resonance of his voice reaches each one of us very clearly. We will be working with sound and visualisation.

We are told that the energy alignments of the land have shifted so far out of balance that drastic action is needed to restore it to its rightful order. What is being proposed is a practice to withhold energy from those places where the worst abuses are happening, stopping the energy from flowing along those particular meridians, and then allow the energy for the rest of the land to flow more easily, to recover its natural dynamism and feel its vitality again.

The places where the energy is to be withheld are the areas of the northern cities, the cities to the east and a settlement to the far south of the land. Immediately I wonder what will happen to those places where the energy is withheld? The thought is given that once their power is removed, these people will not be able to abuse the system any longer. This answer does not satisfy me.

I cannot question these Elders though. I must respect their wishes and do all I can to help them in their time of need. They are servants of the Earth, and I feel it is a privilege to be asked to work with them

The ceremony begins. One of the Elders leads us with prayers, asking the Earth Mother for forgiveness for the abuses of her children, all of us, on this land. The Elder asks on our behalf for the Earth mother to help stop these abuses.

We are guided to attune to the Spirit of the Earth through the crystal in our midst. As I am being led, I feel myself going very deep in meditation. Then we attune together, being guided through the many aspects of adjustment for the energy patterns across the land. In my thoughts, I feel that I become one with everyone else here. Our thoughts have merged and unified upon a single intention. We can feel and sense that our actions are having their effect. By the time we complete it, I can feel that the Earth has become quieter beneath us. The Elders are gaining the results they seek. When we complete the ceremony with a prayer of thanks, I feel a mixture of exhilaration and exhaustion. The power of doing this with so many is tremendous.

The Elders have informed us that our work will need to be sustained continuously over a long period of time. A shift rotation system is being applied so that all can have sufficient rest. There will be different methods of energy work and healing needed to consolidate what we have started. The Elders expect that the happiness of the land will be ample reward for all our labours.

When I am resting I feel very confused. I am not so sure. My thoughts keep turning to those people in the cities. What will happen to the people there when the love of the Earth energy cannot reach them anymore? What will happen to the land around those cities? How will the military and those in authority react when they cannot tap that source of power they so greedily want? Whatever improvements the rest of the land may enjoy, for these people, it may make them even more hungry for power. I wish this may not be so, but inside I feel much disquiet.

I just hope the Elders of the Sacred mountain know what they are doing, and that they have considered all the consequences of our actions.

Part 4

Death of a Friend

I have been many months now working within the Sacred mountain with the others. We have built close bonds of co-operation through our endeavours. The Earth energies have settled appreciatively, and the Elders are pleased. Somehow though, I have become increasingly restless. I feel that I am not in the right place. My thoughts keep turning to Shastar and our beloved mountain sanctuary. I feel anxious about whether Shastar has left himself enough protection. I communicate with him through my stone and he tries to reassure me, but I am not convinced.

When I am sensing with my stone around the northern cities, I feel desolation, anger and confusion. This is not right, somehow. What is happening there?

I am making a decision to leave the Sacred mountain. I want to go immediately and return to Shastar. Clearly, I feel I need to be there to help him. My friends Nikei and Voolmar will come with me. They share my concerns. Others will have to fill our places on the rota. However, in my mind I know where I need to be.

We are travelling along the mountain paths with still some distance needing to be covered, when suddenly I feel a need to stop. Hastily, I reach to take my stone out of its protective cloth. Nikei and Voolmar look on concerned. We all know that something is wrong.

I can hardly pick up Shastar....I sense danger around the sanctuary....It is being attacked.....I feel the presence of the military. There are so many of them....I sense the priest.....They are breaking down the barriers.....I sense violence, and deaths.......

I look across at the others. We must hurry. We must get there quickly and help if we can. But we are already too late. Why didn't I return earlier?

It is later now. We have gone as fast as we could, but we are having to rest. Our bodies are not fit enough to go on indefinitely.

I am using the opportunity to sense with my stone. As I concentrate, I try to reach Shastar. He's not there. He's not at the sanctuary. For a moment I panic. I hope he is not dead. I remember what happened with my sister. However, I do not give up. I search more widely, pleading with him to respond. There is a signal that is very weak. I wonder if I am imagining it, but it could be him. If we follow this signal, then we may find him. I don't want him to be dead.

I notice that I am more concerned for Shastar than I am for the actual sanctuary. Shastar has been like a father to me, and he has been such an important figure in my life.

As I turn my attention to the sanctuary, I sense a sadness and a deadness. It doesn't feel as though the sanctuary belongs to the healers anymore. The military have taken over. The sanctuary has gone, and can no longer be my home.

We keep on walking, and we come to a little wooden hut on the other side of the mountain from where the sanctuary is located. This is a hut used by travellers, as a resting place. We know he is there. My heart is pounding as I go and open the door.

I see Shastar lying in a bed at the far end of the hut. There are two other healers with him. One of them is Shoola, who then comes hobbling over to me as fast as he can. He embraces me with joy. I am so glad to see him.

Gently, Shoola motions us over to the bed. We sit beside Shastar. He is very pale and weak looking. I fear the worst. When I touch his hand, he opens his eyes and looks up at me. 'I wanted you to come', he says to me.

Shoola busies himself to make hot drinks for us and then proceeds to tell us the story of what happened to them.

They had been studying the conditions in the cities quite a lot, with their stones, and had been very worried. Their whole society, the fabric of the cities, was breaking down. There was chaos. The vegetation was dying. People fell sick. Food was not growing. People were becoming very upset and unhappy. The discipline of daily activities within the cities was not working. Some of these people were very angry and they wanted to lash out for what had happened to them.

The attack, when it came, was fairly much without warning. There were military, but also scientists and healers. They seemed utterly determined to break through, and find some energy sources to replace what they had been denied.

Shastar and a few of the others tried to hold them off by using psychic shields, but they had the will and means to break these down. These people, the soldiers and others, were brutal. They killed and slashed the healers in the sanctuary without mercy. It was like all their pent up rage found its outlet against the healers who were there. Most of them didn't have a chance. Some managed to escape through the lower entrance.

Shoola says he was fortunate to be near there when the soldiers came. But they had little time to retrieve what was valuable. The screams and agonies of some of the healers were horrible to hear.

Shastar, in typical fashion, tried to protect and look after others before himself. He left his own escape too late. Shoola thinks it was that priest who stabbed him in the stomach. Two of the other healers then sacrificed themselves so that Shastar could be helped away.

I look down at Shastar and feel so much love for him. Shastar really wanted to see me before he died. He tells me to go peacefully, and thanks me for my friendship. He says that he fears for the safety of the land.

He is urging me to try and preserve the secrets and Spiritual gifts of our land, whatever happens.....

264

I want to try and give him healing, make him stronger, but he says it is too late for that. His time to die has come.

Slowly, I feel the life energy withdrawing from his hand. Shastar closes his eyes, his breathing becomes slower until it stops, and there is peace in the room. I can sense that Shastar's soul is leaving, and I try to pray to wish him well. There is a beautiful feeling in the room, even though at the same time, I feel incredibly sad and desolate. Shastar was my best friend. He taught me such a lot.

The others want to go on, because they have a place where we can be. However, I want to be with the body of Shastar. I need time to mourn the death of my friend. I want to give him a simple burial and honour his passing. I want to reflect about the sanctuary, my time with him, all the good experiences we have shared, and how I feel now about his loss. My heart feels heavy and I cannot help the sobs from convulsing me. Once again, it is Shoola by my side to comfort me. I am glad at least to still have him.

Sometimes I think of the priest who killed Shastar and who afflicted my life with so much misery, while I was living in the city, and my emotions swirl with a mixture of feelings. One part of me feels extremely bitter at his cruelty and his callousness, wanting domination over others and power. But another part of me wishes he would change, and that he and his colleagues would just see what they are doing to our precious land. As I sit besides Shastar's burial place I feel a need to pray for the priest and that is what I do.

It is very hard for me to leave Shastar, but I am aware it is only his body that remains. I do not know how much more loss and suffering I will have to endure, but I feel I have to go on, and I want to respect the wishes Shastar expressed to me.

The True Oracle

I have had to let go completely of the sanctuary where I lived with Shastar. Briefly I tried to imagine if it may be possible in some way to retake it, but it would be hopeless. In any case, I do not wish to engage in a form of fighting such as these people have been doing. Whatever they want from that sanctuary I can't stop them now.

Although he is the slowest, because of his disability, Shoola is the one most urging us on. The others have gone on to another sanctuary further up in the mountains. This sanctuary is virtually unknown to me. It does not receive visitors, apart from invited healers. Shastar has never spoken of it before. Apparently, their work is taken up solely with Earth healing and distant healing, for people and the land. They have welcomed us to come because of our need, and this must be quite an extraordinary step for them.

Now we have arrived at this sanctuary, and it is a marvellous place. Much of it is deep underground. There are crystal formations, not as big as with the Sacred mountain, but I can feel the power. However, the strongest feeling that this place generates, is a deep peace. The people who live here are a very silent and meditative people. We are expected to respect this atmosphere in the way we are here too. When I look at the people here, I notice that their faces are almost expressionless. There is very little emotion or animation that seems to express itself through them. Rather, they carry within them a deep sense of calm. Their energies are directed to accomplish their work, and we have been invited to join them.

Their spokesperson has told us details of their work, our accommodation and some general welcome. He says that they all sympathise with our plight. They are all very concerned about the state of the land, and they hope that our presence will help them to add more power to the work they are doing. It is a very simple life we will live here. Somehow, this suits me. One of my favourite places is where they attend to the healing of the Earth.

There is a giant crystal formation where they sometimes conduct ceremonies, or allow mediation practices to channel healing to the Earth. This place feels very beautiful and loving.

The most interesting facet of the sanctuary is the presence of the oracles. Three of them live here and one of them, a young woman, offers herself in service to channel directly from the Earth Spirit. These are so different from the oracles in the city. These are true oracles. I know that their channelling is genuine. As well as channelling from the Earth Spirit, the people here also channel from other sources, beyond our plane. I do not fully understand it, but I am very interested to learn.

When the oracle channels from the Earth Spirit, the healers here gather to listen. What she says is communicated to selected sanctuaries across the land. The information which is imparted is precious, and the people here know that what comes through is true. I feel a great sense of awe when I listen to her.

It is one of those channelling sessions. I am gathered with the other healers in the special chamber. We are all here to listen. There is a stone structure upon which she lies. This has been carved to be narrower near its base and then curved outwards to look like an oval shaped table. In this has been carved a body shape so that when the oracle prepares herself, she is lying within the stone. A cloth is draped over the stone for the ceremony and the oracle lies on this.

The stone is a conductor stone with roots that go deep into the earth. I think that it is made of fluorite. As we wait, there are prayers and a low humming to help guide her into trance. We can feel her going deeper and almost merging into the stone with her energy. Concurrent with this we can sense a very rich vibration of energy rising upwards to meet her. Then when she speaks, her voice is different to normal, deeper, but the resonance of it flows easily to us.

The channelling begins with some specific guidance about methods of Earth healing and adjustments that are needing to be made within the sanctuary.

But then as the theme of the channelling becomes broader and more general, the oracle speaks that the Earth is reaching the end of its tolerance of what it can countenance from the activities of

267

people upon this land. The interference is growing and people across the land are not respecting the natural forces of the Earth energy sufficiently. The stability of the meridians of energy are being pushed and pulled to such an extent that the stability of the fabric of the land and its energy are being disrupted. Although efforts have been made within the Sacred mountain to direct the energy into its more natural channels, there are those now, in various parts of the land, striving to pull the energy out of alignment again. The tension is growing, and however much love and healing we pour into the Earth, it may not be enough to rectify the damage. The Earth Spirit tells us that the crisis is worsening and soon there may be no return. We must stop the disturbances, if we can, or soon it will be too late.

At the end of the channelling session there is a very sombre atmosphere in the cavern. I wonder what I can do. There is an impulse in me wanting to struggle with the people causing the disturbances, maybe even to fight them. But I know that is not the way. All I can do is to accept the oracles words and do what I can here.

Retuan to the Sacaed Mountain

It is some years later. I have continued to link with other people and places throughout the land by using my communicator stone. There appears to have been a backlash against what the healers in the Sacred mountain have been doing. Not only has our sanctuary been taken over by the military, and Shastar killed, but several other mountain sanctuaries have also been threatened. Now the Sacred mountain, itself, is in danger.

It seems that when the various cities had their source of Earth energy cut off, the scientists and military in these places tried to discover the reason for this block. They felt that there must be a strong power source of energy operating to be able to stop their supply. And of course, they have wanted this power for their own use.

So there are now scientists and military from the east that have been able to find the skills to be able to locate the general area from which their energy sources have been challenged. Their attention is now directed towards the Sacred mountain. Their soldiers are wanting to advance on the mountain and capture it, and they have started to make progress towards that goal.

Healers from the Sacred mountain are having to be used to erect psychic shields to prevent their exact location from being known. However, this is detracting from the other important work which those healers are still trying to do. Their enemies are making efforts to counteract these shields. So, a battle is proceeding on a psychic level.

However, the main problem has been that with extra healers living within the Sacred mountain, they have had insufficient provisions from there to be able to feed them all. The healers have had to arrange regular supply routes from nearby villages for there to be enough food for everyone. Now this has come to be very vulnerable to possible attack.

In the meanwhile, one of my friends, who is still in the Sacred mountain has requested my help in the situation, and I feel inclined that I want to go. I have been talking with my friends Voolmar and Nikei and they want to accompany me. We feel drawn to help with the maintenance of the supply lines. If we could add our experience to help build up stores and a secure supply route then this may help to stabilise the situation. We realise that the integrity of the Sacred mountain is vitally important.

When I try to tune into the military from this area I sense that they are very determined and are laying plans for a protracted siege. It feels like a noose that they want to tighten around the mountain more and more. Without help, the outlook for those in the mountain could be bleak.

It is later now. Nikei, Voolmar and I have been helping with others to organise a provision route into the Sacred mountain.

They have enough water through springs that bubble up into the mountain itself, so it is just food that they need.

There was already a food supply line in operation. We have had to strengthen that, so that the healers within the mountain could build up their stores in case the situation eventually became more critical. With this, we feel we have been successful.

As the months are passing our work is becoming more tense and dangerous. Soldiers are patrolling the local villages and people are being threatened and bribed for information. We have to be very careful with our contacts so that there could be no betrayal. So far we have been fortunate and the military have found no evidence of who is involved in the supply line. However, the number of soldiers is increasing and the people helping us are becoming afraid. The soldiers are even more brutal with people who they feel are not open. It is not the sort of circumstances that I like.

Now it is evening time and I am approaching the village from which we get our main supplies. Something is wrong. I can feel it. As I get nearer I can hear screams and shouts. There is a strong smell of smoke. The village is burning. The soldiers are burning the village. They are killing people. Voolmar and Nikei are with me. I hang my head in despair. We have to hide. I hear horrible noises of suffering, and know I can do nothing about it.

It feels that everything I do to try and help the land fails. Nothing I have done in my life has helped the situation. Everything dear to me, anyone who wants to try and help, is being defeated. I'm beginning to feel that there is no hope. Without this village, there are no supplies for the Sacred mountain. Without the supplies, I don't know how the people will manage inside the mountain. The soldiers will win. The stores may help them for a while, but what then?

I do not know what else I can do here. Inside, I feel that I want to return to the Sanctuary of the Oracle. I do not feel that it is my place to be in the Sacred mountain now. The guidance I sense is more for me to return from where I have come.

Nikei and Voolmar feel similarly. We have become very close now through all our shared experiences.

Together though, we feel very sad. We are distressed about what has happened. We feel a foreboding around the Sacred mountain, that it may fall into the hands of the soldiers. If this happened, then I feel it would be the end.

Sometimes we are experiencing strange weather. On occasions there are storms which are unusual in our country.

I keep having visions of the sea. When I look inwardly I see visions of the sea, and it is in upheaval and the sky is black. I do not understand this. Through my stone, when I gaze at the sea there are images of ugly storms, huge waves and surging torrents of chaos and violence. I cannot understand what that could be. It frightens me.

We must return to the Sanctuary of the Oracle. We do not want to be here any longer.

Prophesy of Doom

At last we have arrived at the Sanctuary of the Oracle. It took us a considerable time to manage the journey. My legs do not move as swiftly anymore as they did in my youth. However, it is a relief to be here, to be with my other friends again.

Today is an important gathering for all the healers. There are even some who have come from other sanctuaries. We have been warned that there is to be an important transmission from the Earth Spirit today. I sense that it is not something pleasant that I will want to hear. Instead of the usual peace and calm, I feel a lot of nervous apprehension. We are gathered close and huddled together.

As the oracle lies on her stone, the healers hum as she goes into trance. I feel a strange mixture of intense love and sadness, rising with energy from within the Earth. When eventually the oracle speaks, the message is short, and completely shocking. The Earth Spirit tells us that the land will be destroyed. There is no hope anymore. Adjustments will be made. A new start must be found. But the people have wrecked this land through selfish designs, and now must bear the consequences.

The channelling ends abruptly, and suddenly the oracle raises her body. She has been startled as much as the rest of us. In my heart, I feel a great heaviness and a sadness. I can hardly believe what I have heard. A large part of me does not want to believe it. How could the whole land be lost? There is a stunned silence among our group, with one or two people quietly sobbing.

The oracle lies back, there is more she needs to channel. There is still some time for the land. However, once the Sacred mountain falls, the end will shortly follow. She says that the Sacred mountain will fall and there is nothing we can do about it. The forces of determination to take that mountain and use its power are overwhelming.

We need to make plans and preparations towards leaving the land. There is much that needs to be preserved, so that the new places of civilisation can have the best of the knowledge that we have gained, so all is not lost.

It is later now. The oracle has informed us of some options for our migrations. The main ones would be for us to either travel to lands west or east of our land. I sense in myself that I will be going more in the direction east. The oracle has channelled that reaching this land, we will need to cover much distance passing through dense vegetation until finally coming to a place where there is a great river. The river is a centre of power from which a new civilisation may arise. People are already living there. People are arriving there from different origins, attracted by the energy of the river.

Although I know my time will be fully occupied with tasks connected with the planned migrations, I feel reluctance in me to proceed. My knowledge of boats will be needed. We will have to be very careful and precise in what we do. Visiting harbours in the

272

towns to the north, we will not want to arouse suspicions about our intentions.

However, the thought of what is going to happen to our land, is almost unbearable to me. I have not wanted to live my life for this.

Part 5

The Oracle Speaks For the Last Time

It has been a hard struggle, these last years, living in a kind of limbo, gathering resources in readiness to leave our land. I still don't want to do it; I don't want this precious land to be destroyed. However, there are forces much greater than mine at work, and it makes me feel very small. I feel no enthusiasm to go to a new land, but I do want to serve and help preserve some legacy from what we have here. I could have given up long ago, but I refuse to do that. There must be some fruit for my labours even if I cannot see what they are. At least I still have friends with me. I still feel a great love of people. It feels good to work together and do what we know we must.

My body is quite old now. I feel my body must be about 60 years old. My bones are quite stiff but my mind remains very alert.

We are gathered in the cavern where the channelling takes place from the Earth Spirit. My friends are with me - Shoola, Nikei, Voolmar and many others. We are all close. Everyone has come today because we know it will be the last time that the oracle will speak to us.

The news has been passed on about the Sacred mountain. Although they were able to hold off the invaders for a long time, much longer that I thought would be possible, I have seen in my stone that the mountain has fallen. The soldiers are now in that mountain, and controlling the crystal at the heart of the mountain. They are wanting to use it, of course, to increase their own power.

The atmosphere in the cavern is a mixture of almost grim resignation and nervous elation. Some of the younger ones here feel a sense of excited anticipation with the adventure of going to another land. Their time has almost come.

For me though, I feel only loss, because I love the land here where I have lived my life - so much. I love the mountains, I love the energies, I love the seas, the country and the Earth here. It breathes with me. I feel part of it and I just do not know that I could feel a sense of home anywhere else as much as I feel it here.

The oracle is now preparing herself and, besides the faint humming of sound, we are otherwise silent in expectation. Now the energies rise up and the oracle starts to speak. The Earth Spirit is telling us that it is with sadness that our efforts are no longer required on this land. The time has come for the upheavals to begin. For us to survive, we need to make urgent preparations and leave. It is a matter of days, not weeks before the Earth movements will engulf the land and it will be no more. She is thanking us for our efforts, the work we have tried to do. She regrets that more did not join with us to possibly avert this tragedy. She assures us there will be other lands, there will be other places. There will be other civilisations. She says that the Earth Spirit is resilient. The Earth Spirit in the end needs to look after herself. We, the children of the Earth, need to learn respect. And if we do not, then we bear the consequences.

As these last words die away, I try to absorb what has been said to us. It is another ending that again pushes us forward.

Last Goodbyes

We have made our last preparations to leave. It is a long distance from the sanctuary to the seaside. Shoola is quite old like me, and making progress with him is very difficult. We have a device that has been constructed to help carry him down the mountains because he cannot walk very fast. At least he is still alive and able to be with me, as are Nikei and Voolmar. These long-standing companions are particularly precious to me. With them I can share the joys of earlier times when perhaps things were not quite as they are today.

I am grateful that I have not lost everyone important to me. I am also glad that I still have some strength, and so I am able to walk down the mountains unaided. However, the younger ones do need to be a little patient with me at times.

There is one place I have to visit before we leave. This is very, very important for me. I want to go to the Earth sanctuary where I went many times as a young adult when I still lived in my hometown. I have to go there to say farewell. It is very, very shocking for me to feel that I need to do this. But this place, I still remember, was the most significant and nourishing refuge for me when I was young. I still feel that it was the place that helped me most then, when I really needed it.

I am now approaching the Earth sanctuary. I have come here alone, feeling that I did not want anyone here to support me. I had to do this by myself, even though my friends wanted to be here with me. This is my place, not theirs. And I am sitting on the stone where I sat as a child. It is still here. And I feel such sadness looking around at the trees, the familiar trees, and clearing. This place, I've loved so dearly and I still feel the peace that exists here. I can hardly believe or fathom that soon it will be no more.

As I sit on the stone, I close my eyes in the way I did when I was a child. I ask for help. I ask for guidance and I feel the energy. I feel those hands again upon me. And it is a great comfort just to know that I am not alone, that I am being supported even now, by the guardians of this place. And I feel the sense of light, I feel the blessing. It is almost incomprehensible for me to believe that I won't be able to come here again. I just say 'thank you' inside. I say 'thank you' with all my heart and then know I have to leave. Walking slowly away from the sanctuary, going beyond the clearing to the trees heading down the hill, I know that however much I may wish it, I cannot turn back. I have to go forward now, away from this place that I love, away from this home, and every home that I have ever known, to a new land.

It is later and I am with my companions again. Our preparations are advanced and we are standing by the harbour. Our plans are for us to leave in various boats in small groups, from different ports. It is with poignancy that my group is going to leave from the harbour where I was born. My familiarity with the town has been important, as has been my knowledge of boats. I suppose that most of the people I may have known in childhood have long since gone, but the place is still familiar and much as it was then.

We have had to carefully consider the type of boat which we would use, because we know that the disturbances that destroy the land are certain to affect the sea. So we have chosen a small merchant vessel. It is made of white wood, which is very strong. In appearance, it is sturdy and solid rather than fast and sleek. We know that we need stability much more than we need speed. The boat is broad in its beam with a deep draft. Underneath, there is a long keel, which we hope will prevent it from sinking. It is a boat designed for the roughest waters, and we know that it will be tested. The boat has sails and oars but we don't know how much we will be able to use them once the disturbances are in motion. There are twelve of us travelling together and we will be able to store our provisions below deck. I sense that it may take considerable endurance for us to survive this journey.

It is now the point of our leaving. I am with my friends, Shoola, Nikei and Voolmar. Together we are boarding the boat now. For some moments, I pause, and look around. People are occupying themselves in the harbour and the town much as always. There are no indications that people are aware in anyway of what is to come. This makes me feel helpless, because I want to tell them.

I see a child by the harbour-side throwing stones into the water. I would like to shout at him and take him with us, protect him. But I know I can't. I can't do anything now for these people. So even if we survive, somewhere in my heart, I know that they are doomed. This gives me a heavy feeling in my heart and I can hardly bear to turn away from them, but I know I must. I must get into the boat now, and go with my companions. I am sure that they feel just like me. I cannot help it, but once on board, we find ourselves sobbing together in the boat.

276

It would probably be strange if others saw us like this. However, we feel such a bond, such a love for our land. It is ever so sad to have to leave. We have with us scrolls, maps, stones and many other important articles. I have with me of course my communicator stone. There is no chance that I would leave that behind.

We have equipment with us which we hope will be helpful in the new land, to carry on our knowledge. We have tried to pool this among different members of our sanctuary. By splitting into many small boats, we hope that at least some of these valuables will get through to safety. We know there are many other sanctuaries upon the land, aware of the situation, like us. Surely, they are acting similarly to ourselves, and may be going to other places. So there is a migration, and some of our people will survive. However, when I think of the number of people who are leaving, and the number of people who are staying, who will be victims of this tragedy, I am just aware of the size of the catastrophe which is upon us.

There is one other of our boats leaving from the harbour. We can see this boat further along the quayside. There are friends of ours from the oracle sanctuary who will travel in it. In fact, the oracle herself is within that boat. I hope that they will have a safe journey, as ourselves.

As a last act before our departure, we say our blessings, and we unite in asking for guidance and help to protect ourselves during this transition. We ask the Earth Spirit to be with us to guide us, that we may respect her always. We do this simple ritual together in a circle, holding hands. Then we know we have to move.

The Journey

We have just slipped the ropes to release our last ties to the land. It is a very strange feeling. The sky is a very odd colour of grey, mixed with other colours. It is late afternoon and the purples and reds around the horizon make for a light that would normally come much later in the evening. We sense that there is a huge storm gathering around the land behind us. I keep looking at it, as we get further away.

Some part of me wonders if it can really be true what the oracle said, if it could really be the case that this land is going to be destroyed. It is quite a test for my faith. However, deep inside, I know that it is true. We are not doing this for nothing. This is the time now when the destruction of our land is imminent. We must make good speed to be well clear before the changes happen. But how could such a place of beauty, such a place of goodness, energy and love, how could such a place like this, turn in such a way, so that people end up destroying it. I do not know the answers to this. I just know that inside myself, I feel incredibly sad. It feels such a waste, such a dreadful, dreadful waste.

It is later, and we have made as much progress as we could, but I sense the changes have begun. I fear the land may have begun to be destroyed. The sea is choppy. I'm sure the sea will become even more unsettled soon. There is a darkness in the sky. It is daytime, but the sky is dark. I have been looking through my stone. I know, I know it is happening. I can sense the explosions. For our own sakes, I feel we have to go further, we have to go further away, to somehow protect ourselves. It is going to be violent. It is going to be very, very, very violent, and I do not know if we can survive.

In my stone I sense the screams, the bewilderment, the horror. The people, the towns and cities, the structures are collapsing. I feel there is nothing anyone can do. It is so horrific. I am transfixed by what I see in my stone. I have to know what is happening to those people, to the land, even though it is ending.

Nikei has her arm around me. She is such a source of comfort to me. She can tell in my face what I am seeing and the tears are coming down from her eyes as well.

The waters, the waves are getting higher and higher. We have to protect ourselves. We have to make sure that our boat will not sink. But we have planned for this. We have a special covering to place over the top of the boat, to prevent water from coming in. It is made of a form of toughened cloth and we place this cloth over

278

our boat now and climb below deck. This way, we are more or less sealed in, with some spaces for air. So this is where we'll have to stay at the mercy of the waters to be tossed round. We cannot do anything else now. It may be days, it may be many days before the waters settle. I know it will be a test for us personally, and a test for the durability of our boat. We only hope that the cloth and the wooden construction of the boat will be strong enough to withstand the onslaught of the waves.

Now we are in the midst of the storm. Our boat is being driven forward. Inside I feel tense and anxious and I cannot relax. I am close together with Nikei and Voolmar.

There has been a loss, a tragic loss. Shoola, he has died. His heart has given up. So now I've lost him as well. He couldn't cope anymore. Within himself, he felt broken and could not go any further. We've had to lay his body in a corner and leave him there.

But now the boat; it is turning; it is being shaken. It is horrifically pounded as we go up and down. I just hope we can manage to hang on until it settles. The sea is remorseless. It goes on and on. I find it impossible to sleep, even though we are all exhausted by it. The boat heaves and then drops and there is scarcely any break. We only have each other to hang upon. I try to pray, to ask for guidance and support, but it doesn't change it. This must be the most horrific experience I have ever had. It is so frightening. At times I just cannot believe that our boat will be able to continue going when the seas are like this. The sounds of the waves pounding against us are almost deafening at times.

Now it is later, days later. The storm has finally passed. I have been sleeping. I think we all have been sleeping. It is quiet. We are starting to rouse ourselves. The waters have finally settled. We all need to adjust ourselves as the covers are taken away. It is like a miracle to still be alive. That covering has saved our lives. We had to protect ourselves in our quarters with much padding so we would not injure ourselves.

It takes me a long time to be able to move my body normally again. There are aches and pains everywhere. I need healing

JORLI — THE LEAVING

ointments. However, once I'm on deck, I feel astonished. It is so calm, and there is sunshine.

The sea gives the appearance as though nothing happened. It is difficult to tell how long we had to endure the storm. There may have been slight modulations of light and dark through the cloth but it was difficult to tell night from day. It felt though like a long time. I really wondered if it would ever end.

When I gaze into my stone, I turn my attention towards our former land. I have to know what remains. But I see only ocean, calm seas, and it looks as if there was never anything there. Now we are trying to get our bearings for our location. One of our companions has climbed high onto the prows. She has seen land. We are near to land.

It is strange with the night sky, the orientation we usually use, from the stars, seems somehow to have changed. The new land is not quite where it should be, according to our calculations. We feel the Earth has moved.

The New Land

It feels different. The vegetation is rich. I find it very strange to feel solid ground beneath my feet. It takes me a while to adjust. I feel the energy, of course. However, with this, I feel disappointed. The energy here is not nearly as intense as it was in our land. Somehow, I'm beginning to realise what we've lost.

I feel that we have lost something very precious. My inner intuition tells me that there may be nowhere on the Earth at this time, where the energies are as strong and powerful, as in the land where we lived, the land that is no more. We've lost so much. I feel that collectively, people may not be able to regain that again, maybe for a long, long, long time. It feels like a tragedy, not just for us, but for the whole human race.

We have little knowledge of the other boats. I have tried to use my stone to contact them, and I do sense that some of them have reached land, but not near us. However, I also feel that some of the boats have been lost. I sense for the boat from our harbour with the oracle in it, but I cannot raise any contact with it. I feel that it must have gone down.

Anyway, we know the next stage of our journey. We have to cross this land till we eventually find the big river. My stone can serve as a navigational instrument. I hope that we can make it.

Now it is later. We have been travelling a long, long time and it has been very difficult for us. The vegetation is so thick and unyielding. Two of us have been killed on the journey, from animals that have attacked us. We did not bring weapons to protect us. It has been very hazardous. I've never seen animals like this, so fierce and big. Some are like cats.

We have met no people on our travels. There are knives and cutting instruments that we have had to use to force our way through the vegetation at times, to make progress. This has taken much longer, than ever I thought it would.

We have needed to gather food for ourselves to eat. This has proved to be a task. There has been much variety of food. However, because it is so unfamiliar to us, we have had to test which of the berries and nuts and plant life would be edible for us, and which were not. We do have sensitivity for this, and so we have needed to try out many of these possible foods for their qualities. In a way, this is helping us, because we are learning what foods in particular we may need to cultivate, once we have settled, in order to survive. But this has also taken time, and sapped my patience.

I notice that my own body feels very tired. This whole journey has been an ordeal. I feel determined to make it, but I feel I may nearly have had enough. I feel exhausted in my physical body, but even more exhausted in my soul.

It is later. The vegetation has become less dense. Our progress is now more rapid. I think we have arrived because I can see a river. It is a long and wide river. I can tell that it has a power. There is a power in the land around here, and the power is within the water of the river. I have noticed with my stone that there are other people here, settlers - some from our land, some from other places. We are not the first. I hope that we will be welcome.

My Death

We have now been settled in the new land for a short while. I feel my time has come. I am sitting by a tree close to the river. I am sitting by myself, and I feel the tall presence of a woman beside me. This is not a human presence, but Spirit. I feel that she is my guardian. It is the same Spiritual being who visited me at the Earth sanctuary in my homeland when I visited there. She was with me as well as the guardians of that place. I feel happy that she is here with me now. She is telling me that I need to come home now.

I am looking at the river and I feel a peace. I know there is much potential here for the growing of a civilisation. However, that is for future generations, and not for me. I reflect back upon my life and see how far I have travelled, and yet I feel so much a sense of loss. How much easier and more happy I would have been if things had turned out differently. By being true to myself though, I had to face that loss and I had to endure much suffering. It has been a very hard life, and I feel weary as if I have carried a heavy burden with me and now I want to let it go.

With this thought, I feel myself slowly rising upwards, going to somewhere very light. Gradually, I become aware that there are others waiting, here with me. I see here are my friends, my family, my mother, my father, my sister, Shoola, Shastar.....the people that I loved. They have come to welcome me. I thought that I had lost them all. I thought that I had lost everything. I feel so relieved but still feel sadness. I feel their love. They commend me for all that I did.

Slowly, my thoughts turn to all those souls whose bodies were killed when the land was destroyed. I wonder what became of them. I suppose they all had their path of learning just like me. As I think of this, I become aware of the presence of the soul who was the priest. He looks even more sad than I am, and it makes me want to comfort him. I feel a connection and a love.

I feel my guardian close and start to feel a strength of Spirit rising in me, making me feel taller and stronger, and more ready to face the challenges of what is to come. In that life, I learnt to love in adversity, to keep my heart open, even when everything seemed to go against me. It was a tremendous learning experience for me. But I feel that my own journey still has a long way to go yet, more lessons to learn, and I feel prompted to let the experience of that lifetime go behind me, and move forward.

Connections

When Denise read my account of Jorli for the first time, she found herself reacting particularly strongly to my sharing about Shastar's death and about the Sacred mountain. I had perceived Denise to be my young female companion who accompanied my sister and I to the mountain sanctuary when we were forced to flee from our home town by the harbour. I had little awareness of her presence after we reached the sanctuary. Denise felt that she had in typical style, devoted herself to working with crystals and Earth Healing once she settled in the sanctuary. Because of her interest, she had been called to work at the Sacred mountain before I as Jorli, went there. Then she returned to Shastar's sanctuary while we were still there. When the mountain sanctuary was attacked, Denise felt herself to be one of the healers whom Shastar tried to shield from the soldiers. Unfortunately, he was unable to protect her and she was killed.

On many occasions in Atlantis, Denise's soul had a tendency to seek refuge in the sanctuaries rather than engage in more normal human activity. She was afraid of being hurt by people, being drawn into troublesome situations. But the sanctuaries were not always the safe places she would wish them to be.

284

Working through her Atlantean past lives is helping Denise to address issues around her involvement with people in her present life. She has recognised a tendency in her present life to hide away from people, just as she did in Atlantis. This process for Denise has been complex with many layers of emotional reactions to particular situations that had become deeply engrained. As she is gradually releasing her fear of people and letting down her barriers to closeness with others, Denise is becoming a much happier person as a result.

I identified Lynne as the priest in Jorli's life. When she read in my account about the actions of the priest, Lynne felt very unhappy. She started shaking and she felt sick and nauseous. When she read the account for the second time, she realised that she had blocked out the memories of many of the incidents of the priest's actions from her first reading. Lynne felt the coldness of the priest and was very distressed by his seemingly total self-interest and lack of compassion. She could not feel his heart and he felt very remote from her.

The life of Jorli was very rich with human relationships for me. I have sensed many of the other main characters in the story as people whom I know today. Some have remained a mystery.

Linda, by the way, when she read the account felt a close involvement with what was going on, as if she had been watching closely from Spirit. She had a strange sense that she had been advised to take on a lifetime at this time because of its soul growth opportunities, but she had refused.

Lynne's Regressions as the Priest

About two months after I completed my regression sessions as Jorli, Linda showed Lynne a drawing she had done of boats leaving a harbour shortly before the destruction of Atlantis. Lynne did not want to look at that picture, and her body reacted immediately. All down her right side, she experienced a strong pain.

Over these days, Lynne had also been having problems with her teaching job. There were occasions she noticed, when she was reacting to her pupils by using excessive control in a manner that was not typical of her. From her experience, Lynne sensed through her abnormal behaviour that it was likely that memories of a past life were wanting to come forth. By listening within, her inner senses told her that it was the life of the priest whom Jorli had encountered.

Lynne had dreaded the thought that she would ever need to go through this past life because it was obviously very difficult. However, now her body and inner psyche were prompting her that the time had come when she needed to process it.

As we began through regression, our exploration of this life, Lynne experienced herself as a young boy, living in a very overcrowded city. Buildings were packed tightly together, and many people had not enough food to eat. There was a sense of general deprivation from which the population suffered. Lynne felt as this boy, that he had been left abandoned on the street. His mother had not been able to feed him anymore and had just left him. Through her body, Lynne could feel the fear, weakness and helplessness of this boy.

He was rescued and taken to the local Healing Temple where he could live with other children. However, this was a very austere place and he had to live under very strict conditions and obey the priests. At some stage when he grew older, there were riots in the City and families died in disputes over food. He wanted to help the people, but the priest supervising him beat him with a stick for expressing this view. Within the Temple, he was not allowed to question anything, and he would be punished if he acted differently from what was expected of him. The supervising priest told him that the people needed to be more firmly controlled and regulated so that these problems would not occur.

During this long and painful beating, the boy's heart closed, and became cold. He did not want anyone to control him again.

He grew up to become a priest himself and adopted the attitudes of the supervising priest who had beaten him. He was clever and could easily manipulate people. He became quite arrogant in the manner that he regarded other people as fools and he thought that his way was the right way. Soon he rose to a position where he was the leading priest in the Temple and a member of the ruling Council within the city.

His beliefs were that the people needed to become more orderly and be managed by the central authorities. Only when the people respected this and worked harder could the problems of the city be overcome. As the priest, he could do much to control the people through the activities of the Temple. His main means of doing this was by manipulating the oracles. When the oracles were relaxed, he could speak to their minds and give them the correct ideas and right guidance of what they needed to say to the people. The priest felt he knew better what the people needed than what the oracles would otherwise channel. Once his thoughts were deeply implanted, the oracles would repeat them in their own words during the Temple ceremonies without realising what had happened.

On one occasion, the priest came across a young woman who was resistant to his thoughts. She writhed about and seemed to be in pain as he tried to manipulate her. Then, when she channelled, her words spoke from another source than what he wanted her to say. It could be that she had the potential to be a true oracle. However, this resistance disturbed the priest greatly. Therefore, he arranged for her to be taken away and killed.

With the crystals in the Temple soaking up the energy from the people, the priest could feel this energy through his feet. He was sensitive to this energy and found that it would fill his body, making him feel strong and powerful. There was an addictive, compulsive quality about it, so that when he left the temple, it felt like something was missing. This energy made him feel invincible, as if he was capable of anything, and it fed his feeling and lust for power. The people were submissive and would do what he told them.

When it came to the disruptions caused by Jorli and his followers, this caused great anger to the priest because it interrupted the energy flow. He could not accept that other people could think differently to him and oppose him. His rage continued until Jorli was finally captured. The priest wanted Jorli to rescind in public his opposition to the central authorities and to say that he was wrong. Jorli refused to do it. The priest tried various forms of torture including sleep, food and water deprivation and beatings. His favourite weapon was a wooden club, made of a very hard wood. The priest could wield this expertly and was able to cause pain, bruising, agony and broken bones as he willed. The extent of this physical torture as Lynne experienced it went far beyond what I allowed myself to experience when I went through my regression experience as Jorli.

The priest was immensely frustrated that he could not control Jorli and bend him to his will. He desperately wanted to kill him and make him disappear, but the authorities of the council forbade him to do that. The authorities released Jorli as part of a carefully calculated plan. The priest was in charge of operations to secure outlying sanctuaries and direct power and energies from their crystals into the central grid for the city. Methodically he was succeeding with this task, but Jorli had information of hidden places he needed to know about.

When Jorli escaped from the healer and old woman and made his way back to the sanctuary in the mountains, he was tracked without his knowledge, all the way back to his home. The priest saved this knowledge so he would be able to use it later.

Once the Earth energy supply was cut off to a large extent from reaching the city, the priest's power diminished. He personally led the attack upon Jorli's sanctuary in an attempt to resurrect the energy flow to the city again. By using his wooden club and dagger, he accounted for several of the bewildered healers who were trying to resist the military presence. But this attempt to revitalise the city's energy supply failed. His dream of making the city into a showpiece of power and regulated activity was shattered.

As he got older, the priest maintained his position within the Temple. However, he felt very tired and weary. He did not feel that he could get enough sustenance and support from the energy any more. The situation deteriorated with less and less energy coming in through the crystals and the priest felt himself weakening with it. The life of the people got no better, rather worse, and they did not listen to him anymore. The words he spoke through the oracles were not respected.

The priest lived right up until the destruction of the land. As this event approached, he felt very old and tired and could sense that something was very bad. The first thing he noticed was that the energy had dropped to an even lower level. He felt fearful of what would happen. There was a feeling of dread and coldness. All around there seemed to be darkness. He was certain there was something wrong.

The priest could sense an eerie and strange atmosphere. The birds and animals seemed to know something, and they were all disappearing. Birds were flying away out to sea, and not only the sea birds that would normally fly there, but other birds too.

Then as he woke up one morning, there was a shaking in the ground, very gently at first, but not stopping, and growing in intensity. The people were becoming more and more disturbed. It was not like an Earthquake, which would end after some minutes. These rumblings kept on becoming more severe. Buildings were beginning to shake and people tried to work out where it was safer. They were leaving the buildings, trying to protect themselves.

As he watched all this, the priest felt tired. There was nowhere to go. He would stay in the Temple. Memories came to him of the past and days when he could feel the power. However, the disturbances increased. There was a terrible sound and noise that arose. It was unbelievable in its intensity. There was noise from the rumbling of the Earth beneath his feet, from fierce winds that whipped in all directions, and the sea that was churning and very upset. People were screaming and there was nowhere to hide.

People came pouring into the Temple hoping that this would be safe. But the priest knew that nowhere was safe. The noise that was rising higher was indescribable, really indescribable. Suddenly the Temple was torn apart. The priest felt himself thrown to the ground by these Earth movements. He could feel utter helplessness. There was nothing anyone could do. Within the noise people were screaming and children crying. He felt weak, so weak, and without control.

The priest could sense that the Earth was splitting beneath him. Then came the awareness of fire; of molten rock erupting and streaming towards him. He could not get away, for he was trapped by some rubble that had fallen upon him. His legs were trapped. The priest could feel the heat of this lava getting closer, knowing that soon it would engulf him. He was just starting to feel its burning on his body when, suddenly, he was floating and leaving. It was over.

Leaving that body, the priest felt very sad. He realised abilities that he had that could have been used to help people, but he had only been interested in himself, and he had been very cruel to others. More and more people were joining him in Spirit. It was overwhelming in its confusion and feelings, people bewildered and shocked, not knowing what they were doing.

From having lived as this priest, there was no comfort being with these people. Somehow, he felt responsible, that he had contributed to their deaths and the destruction of the land.

Lynne felt a very tight band of pain around her head and a shaking inside. This was very hard for her to bear. Lynne could feel the sense of failure and waste, feeling that it was her fault for what had happened. She wanted to curl up and try to be safe, much as that little boy had wanted to do when he was left abandoned on the street by his mother.

Lynne recognised a tendency in herself to blame herself excessively when things went wrong. She found it very difficult to be at fault.

290

As a conclusion to the sessions, Lynne found herself bathed in light. She was taken to a time in that life, where as a young man, he could have made a different choice.

Chapter 18

Commentary: The End of Atlantis

Paul: Can you say how the situation developed from Tarsha's time towards the eventual destruction of Atlantis?

Albani: *It is well known that the continent of Atlantis was very rich in Earth energy and crystal energy. It had a great wealth in these things and there were great masses of crystal and beds of crystal which gave the land its tremendous life and energy and vibrancy. This was well known to the people. And the people reacted to this in many different ways. Eventually, when you have a build up of a militaristic society, which started to happen in a very slow and gradual way, but of course, gained momentum, for one thing brings another, and people will start to behave aggressively to their neighbours, their neighbouring country or city or something like that, and when this happens they desire more power. It was realised that power could be gained from the Earth herself. But a lot of this knowledge was lost in the crystal war. However, the souls who were alive then were again alive later, back in bodies, and still existing on the Atlantean continent. Some were not there, but quite a lot were. The knowledge was deep within them. Gradually, over a long period of time, this knowledge began to surface again - just one or two people at first, and then that was passed on - and elaborated on, and anything grows in this manner. Eventually the people who desired power began to realise that one way of getting it was to harness this massive Earth energy that was all around them all the time. Each person desired more than the person next to them or the group or the country next to them. So began a form of corruption of this power.*

Opposite this was the vast network of healing sanctuaries, and healers who were very, very powerful also. They tended to shy away from this kind of greed and power. But they used their energies in a positive manner and they honoured the Earth and honoured the power that she gave them, and used that energy for healing others. So you had this development of a two level system, where the Earth energy was being used, one positive and one negative.

This went along for some considerable time, probably 2-3000 years, in quite a slow and gradual manner. And as with all things, it began to increase. Knowledge was beginning to spread. And the population was getting larger. There was more competition for space, for the power over the people, for there were more people to control. And there was this combination of factors that led to the rise in the use of negative sides of the energy that contributed to its eventual downfall.

Around Tarsha's time, the military were beginning to gain power. There were quite a few pockets where they were powerful indeed, but others where they were not. However, this gradually changed. Eventually, the aggression of these people subjugated the more passive. The healers and the groups that were with them and the people who sympathised with the correct use of the energy tended to go to the mountains, well away from the cities where this negative energy was pulling down everything around them. They went away from the physical aggression and the physical population. It was much too crowded and difficult there to practise what they needed to practise. There were many points over the whole of the continent that were energy points, that were protected by the healers. These were well known amongst that fraternity. In general, people who needed help, would still go to the mountains, to the sanctuaries, to gain that help they needed, for illness, for solace, for many different reasons. But finally, I am now talking after Tarsha's time, and heading towards the final years, the aggressor became stronger, and the others weaker, for they did not know how to fight. They did not wish to fight, and the power and energy, albeit negative that the others generated in various forms, gave them even more energy that fed upon itself, and essentially became like a monster out of control - leading the people, leading the leaders, leading the soldiers. And they were almost under a compulsion to be greedy, and take more and more of this energy, and convert it to their own usage. And this essentially is what caused the eventual break up of the continent.

Paul: Can you tell about the main pockets where the corruption occurred?

Albani: *In the end times, the bulk of the population was where Jorli lived in the north and along the eastern seaboard. The west remained relatively low in population although there were some fairly large communities on the north west coast as well. But they were not anything like as big as those along the north and the northeastern coast.*

There was one point right in the centre, which developed in the last thousand years or so. That was a very central point. And this was a very large city that was built purely to harness the power of the Earth. This was built by the people who understood these things - the priests and people like that - people who thought they could handle this energy. The main development in weaponry came from the eastern cities and this one central place. This was possibly where the most scientific knowledge was based, rather than the knowledge around the temples and the priests. There were many experienced scientists, particularly, in this central city. It was built especially for them, to work there, and to harness this very powerful energy. And they were developing weapons that were very bad indeed. A lot of them never came to fruition, for although they had the energy and understood it, they did not understand it quite well enough to be able to control it. They could harness it, yes, but in a very erratic manner. And they realised, and they were fighting very hard, to make that final step, to have a controllable energy - totally controllable, with which they could destroy people whom they thought were their enemies. But it tended to backlash a little, and was very unstable, and they could not, and never did manage to control that instability. So, although, yes, weapons did exist, very terrible weapons, they were rarely used, for they could harm the operators as much as the people they were trying to aim at or destroy.

The central city was called Sandoris. It was built on the earthquake line which destroyed the city of Thrumbis in Elayna's time, and was a very powerful point because there was a criss cross

294

of energy lines there, very, very powerful Earth lines. This, for the scientific establishment, was very attractive, and they gravitated towards there. They had a central point within this city. It was built in a circular manner, with everything radiating out in concentric circles, the streets, the houses, and the buildings.

Right in the centre was this energy point, and it was immensely powerful. They augmented this with crystal, and their own methods for summoning power.

The corruption was not just in this central city, but in other places too. This came about for the same reason, that certain men and women wanted power over others. In whatever way they did it, the ultimate idea, the pattern of what they did was much the same, the desire of one person to control another.

There were very powerful people, rich people who could buy what they wanted. They could buy power. They could buy military. They could buy and bribe anyone they wished to have power over others. And they saw the gaining of power almost like leeching other people's energy. It fed into them and made them stronger. This happened in all the places of corruption, to a slightly lesser or greater extent, depending on the individual situation. Of course, where you get one powerful man feeling using power to control others, you always get another one feeling he can do it better, and will perhaps go and kill that first man and take his power. Therefore the corruption will spread. They will bend the rules. They will destroy their enemies by whatever means they can, in order to get this energy.

For, it has an addictive quality. Within the healing sanctuaries, and anyone who does healing even now, knows it is a nice feeling, to feel that energy flowing through your body. It gives you what you would normally term these days as a 'high'. It makes you feel good. Imagine that multiplied many, many times. It is the most wonderful feeling for the human frame to feel, and once it is experienced, it is much enjoyed. But the healers understood that this power was given them for a very good reason, and they could use this. They could control it, for the energy through Spirit and from the Earth, was used for its intended purpose, and therefore *allowed itself to be controlled and channelled. The healers were very strong people. But they had the characteristics and understanding, and were humble enough to realise that it was not their power. They were simply using it. And they understood this well. Therefore, it was used to the right ends. The energy is felt by everyone in much the same way. Someone with a darker character will think `I like this, and I want more of it. I can use this to control and manipulate. I can use this personal power and energy to gain money, to gain position, to gain standing. I can use it to control others and have them do what I want.' Of course it can be used this way, but it is wrong! Through this it becomes like a monster. The more power they have, the more they desire, and they are channelling it through themselves into the wrong places. The negativity comes back to them, and they counteract this with more power. For now they have learnt to do this, and the whole thing begins a downward spiral, whereas with the healing energy, that is an uplifting spiral and a beautiful thing - which helps a person. With the negative side of it, it ultimately can destroy the person doing it, or make them into a very evil character indeed.*

Paul: What were the events in the last years that led to the destruction?

Albani: *At some point, someone realised that there were great beds of crystals within the mountains. Within your account of Jorli, you rightfully referred to one as the Sacred mountain. These had power, incredible power. The ones who wished to control, desired this very much, and set their will in motion to acquire it. At the same time the scientists and others in the central city were also working on this. They had crystals they could use, large ones. And they were on a very, very sensitive Earth point. Initially their intentions were simply scientific research and to learn about these things, but corruption entered there also, and the negative energy started to feed into that giant crystal which was on the Earth point. This in itself could be countered by the Earth to some degree. But once the others started falling, the large power centres within the mountains themselves, then it became more and more difficult for the Earth to maintain energy that was good for the land and somewhere deep inside, it was decided that this must stop. The Earth decided to disrupt this energy field completely, and destroy the land that was causing it. As you rightly found in*

your Jorli past life regression, the oracles of the time knew this.
They spoke of it. They predicted it for some years before the actual
destruction. For they could feel the Earth, they could sense her
thoughts, and they knew.

She tried to warn the people. She tried to warn them to stop what
they were doing. But, by then, it was far too late. They would not
listen. They were mad for the power. They were all taken. Then it
was simply a very short time, before the energy coursing through
these very giant beds of crystal was very negative and bad indeed.
That was when the Earth destroyed the connections and destroyed
the land.

The actual destruction started at that central point, for that was
the point that was most easy to break apart.

In a very similar manner to what happened in the crystal war, the
crystal beds in a way, to use a modern term, went into a critical
state. The Earth pumped so much energy through, as much energy
as she could - and this was completely uncontrollable. This began
to split the Earth apart. It began to split the crystal bed and that
in itself created a vibration along the weakening lines of the Earth,
the earthquake belt, the fault line. And it began to move. But not
only that, the energy caused a form of implosion. And that again
created a large vortex, a vortex of energy - almost like a vacuum, as
something which would suck energy in. This, joining with the
movements of the fault lines, was so intense that nothing could
survive it. The whole plate containing the continent began to shake
itself apart. Parts of it were being pulled in one direction and parts
of it were being sucked inside and others were moving in yet
another direction. This was very deliberate. This was done so that
the mass of the rock, mountains and the mass of everything that
contained this continent would shake apart, and fall inwards.

It split lengthways as well as horizontally, roughly. This took some
time. The whole destruction took about three weeks. But in that
time, the Earth movements were the most violent, imaginable. The
Earth was moving at a tremendous rate. It was shaking, it was
trembling. Mountains were falling. The land was being torn apart,
and falling in on itself. When these fault lines opened under the

sea, the sea came in. The water, as you can imagine, for this was an ocean we are talking about, vast amounts of water, flooded in through these fault lines and shaking land and simply destroyed it. Not only were the mountains falling, but also the ocean levels were rising. It was complete destruction. This caused a huge shock wave around the Earth.

No part of the Earth escaped the shock and the tremor of it, although some were fairly minor because they were a long was away. But it was a massive, massive effect upon the Earth's surface. The sea took a long time to settle down. There were tidal waves, and various other things associated with that. There were high winds, hurricane force winds, that were all created by that massive movement and falling of the land.

Climatic change did not necessarily take place at that point. It has occurred at other times. The main thing that affected the water levels was the fact that there was a large hole where the land used to be, and the water had to fill that space. Therefore, around the world in general, the water levels dropped slightly.

Paul: What was the outcome for the world's civilisation when the Atlantean continent went down?

Albani: *The Atlantean population was completely destroyed. Relatively few survived, as well you know - the ones who had fled in advance and listened to the warnings. But from a population of many, many millions, it was only a very small handful. The physical effect upon the lands bordering around what you now call the Atlantic, although it was not quite the same then, they suffered tidal waves, very high seas, and very strong gales, winds. There was a certain amount of atmospheric dust created. Therefore there was a darkening similar to what you get with a volcanic eruption. But this was relatively small. It happened in the way the wind took the debris from the destruction. That tended to be northwards - it tended to come north - for the bulk of the continent was north of the equator. There was relatively little effect upon the actual population of the world, apart from those in the coastal areas that had to suffer the effects of the tidal waves and gales. There was some atmospheric disturbance, like freak storms, major storms - something like that. The people who did not know of the existence* *of Atlantis would have just put it down to some other force of nature. It caused some degree of electrical storms also, but that was relatively isolated, and only in certain areas.*

Paul: You have mentioned about uranium upon Atlantis?
Albani: *There was a high density of uranium upon Atlantis and this increased the explosive effect of the destruction. But we are talking about natural things here rather than man-made. And therefore the Earth can control this, and control the effects of this very strong substance. It was rich with uranium, particularly in the north. Yes, it did add to the destructive element involved.*

Paul: What was the legacy left behind by the destruction of Atlantis?
Albani: *The ones who escaped from Atlantis were mainly the more educated, and shall we say, more sensible people who had listened to the Earth energy. Therefore, they were sensitive to this. But they were very, very low in numbers. Where they went, they started other foundations of civilisations. Some of these are well known. Some of them have never been found or known about. The one, which is most well known, is the ancient Egyptian civilisation. But we are talking now of a period again of several thousand years. Over that time the knowledge gets corrupted, it gets changed, and becomes in some ways inaccurate, for other things creep in. Although, the essence of the knowledge was contained for some time, eventually, it began to get lost. This happened in most of the places where the Atlanteans landed.*

They went northwards to the northern continents. They went to what is now the northern American continent and founded cities and civilisations there, which are little known about. A lot of knowledge was passed down. A lot of the written knowledge was lost. It was passed down in oral tradition after that. But this becomes bent with time - it becomes exaggerated with time, altered. It is the nature of humans to do this. However a lot of this knowledge was quite true to the original. This is where you often find a lot of the old legendary things come from. They are coming from real knowledge from the past. Now you are beginning, at the start of the new millennium, to discover a lot of what you thought - I mean you in the general sense - as legend, fanciful stories, complete fantasy, are actually based on fact. It is based on real memory, and reality - but a reality very, very different to your current one.

The Atlanteans themselves were very, very sensitive people. The continent was so alive, so vibrant. The people there were equally like that. They could sense those energies, quite normally. They had what now you refer to as psychic ability. It was considered pretty normal. Anyone who couldn't sense these things were regarded as a little odd or strange, as opposed to the reverse of what is happening now. Again this sensitivity has been handed down, through some people, through some genetic lines. But it is very much weakened from what it was. For I do not think the Earth has produced another land quite so rich as Atlantis. I think, the Earth probably realises that people are not mature enough to control these vast powers.

People are not mature enough to understand them and use them for good. Therefore, the opportunity has never been presented again. For even now, could you imagine, with today's technology and knowledge - and look at what you see around you. You see greed. You see corruption. You see angry people. You see the desire to take over land from others. Aggression, war, destruction...With the power Atlantis held, that would lead to another very large problem. People have still not matured. People are foolish animals. They do not have the knowledge or the capacity to handle the vast power that would give them. They would still become corrupt and evil.

There are some who would not of course. There are some who would handle this beautifully and bring about great gains for others. There are still the healers. There are still the academics who understand. But on the whole, especially the people who favour the military, which is still very strong, very strong in some places. You have only to look at recent developments within your world history, and imagine what would happen if they had the power and energy that was available in the Atlantean continent. They would destroy themselves and everyone else.

300

Paul: What about the positive side of the Atlantean culture?
Albani: *The beautiful side of Atlantean life was the incredible strength of the healing ability of people there. Those who trained as healers, were very, very different to the people you have in your medical profession now. They had skills. They had abilities that were all encompassing, and very, very complete. They had abilities that you can only dream about now. That is the positive side of this. If people could harness that, and not the other side, then there could be great benefit.*

The people who are learning healing, like yourselves, are learning a tiny, tiny part of what the Atlanteans had. You have only got to access some of these healing lives that you have been doing and you realise what abilities these people had, and almost took for granted. They learnt like any other profession, all these skills and technical abilities which you consider quite magical and amazing. It was just part of their everyday work. They could heal the mind. They could heal the soul. They could heal the physical body, in ways which modern medical science can only dream about. It is possible, hopefully, with a great deal of learning and training, to find these skills again, and to harness these abilities. Of course nowadays, when someone comes out with things like this, they are considered strange - a quack, one may say, or even a fraud. People do not believe. A lot of people do not even believe that healing energy exists, so it is a very difficult thing to push forward. It would be wonderful if those abilities that the Atlantean healers had could be harnessed again. That would make a very beautiful contribution to your world. That side should also be emphasised, for there were many good people in Atlantis as well. They seemed to be overwhelmed by the negativity and the darker side. But they did exist and it is certainly worthwhile remembering that.

Postscript

During my regression sessions to Jorli, I was unaware of this central city of Sandoris. Whether Jorli was unaware of its existence, or whether his knowledge regarding this city, just didn't come to my consciousness during the regression, I am not sure. I know that Jorli's focus of attention was very much connected to the northern part of the continent. The Sacred mountain was inland in this region. The central city of Sandoris must have been a vast distance further away.

Chapter 19
Soul Connections

One of the most fascinating and transforming aspects of writing this book has been the discovery of the breadth and depth of the soul connections that exist between, Linda, Denise, Lynne and myself. At the beginning of my research into Atlantean past lives, I had no idea that these existed. More and more, for all of us the awareness of this has grown and it has changed our lives.

In general, I feel it is very likely that for at least most of us, we travel through our unfolding journey as souls in a group, so we are not alone and we can help each other learn. There may be a group of us that start our incarnations together and the connection will always remain strong. Then there may be the possibility, through love, of establishing bonds with other souls, so that they may also, accompany us on our soul journey, leading to an expansion of consciousness.

Through my regression experiences with clients I have come to believe that it is possible for souls to incarnate on many other worlds besides Earth, and so the potential for gaining soul experience from physical incarnation is vast. But I feel there is a beginning and there may be also the moment when lessons have been sufficiently learnt so that physical incarnation is no longer necessary. With Denise, Linda and Lynne, I feel that they are my soul friends and that we have been together since our beginning as souls. We have not always incarnated together, but very often I feel we have chosen to do so. Each of us has taken on particular characteristics and individual pathways of learning, but as souls we have tried to support each other with this. During various physical incarnations, it seems that at times one or more of us have made big mistakes, but the mutual dedication to each other has remained.

On Atlantis, the four of us were incarnated together many, many times. The relationship patterns we shared varied tremendously, and there were also periods of Atlantis history where we did not incarnate together. I know for instance, that there was a period of some thousands of years where in the early stages of Atlantis' history, I left Atlantis altogether and had lives elsewhere. I largely did not share these lives with our group of four. There was another shorter period after my Commander Arune life where I did much the same thing. However, for the remaining time of Atlantis' history, when I was living lives there, I was very closely bonded to the other three members of the group. We know that all these lives exist as a shared memory within our minds, and so nowadays, it does not take much for the memory from a particular past life of one of us to trigger very easily experiences from that same lifetime of another member of the group.

However, just because we are very close as soul friends, it does not mean that we have always got on very well together in physical incarnation. Often as souls, we would deliberately place ourselves in very challenging relationships with another member of the group to help each of us to learn how to cope with a particular situation. Because of the very close soul bond that we all share, then when we met with one of the other members of the soul group during our physical incarnations, this would tend to make a big impact upon us. Therefore, this would help us focus upon what we needed to do.

Unfortunately, as souls, we have not always coped very well with the lessons we have needed to learn. Consequently, often the people we have hurt and maimed and tortured and killed most have tended to be members of our own soul group. This then has sometimes caused problems for us in our relationship with each other.

During her incarnations on Atlantis, Linda went through a very difficult patch, where she stopped learning her lessons and kept making similar mistakes through one life after another. Here, the pivotal life was Sofira. In subsequent lives, the members of the group gathered during Linda's lives to try to help her change. During Tarsha's life, I as commander Arune, Denise as a child,

Lynne as a mother, all appeared in Tarsha's life as potential victims but also with the potential that we could help Tarsha to open her heart to live with compassion rather than hate and anger. We did not quite manage.

From the Sofira incarnation my relationship with Linda's soul was disturbed, as was the relationship between Lynne and Linda. In subsequent lives there were many triangular situations where I tended to favour Lynne over Linda because of a deeply felt abhorrence I continued to carry related to the Sofira episodes. These lives often ended destructively and added to the problems.

In recent months the three of us have been working hard to clear the disturbances relating to these lives and our relationship together, so now things are much easier and more loving between us as a result.

It is remarkable how in spite of all the hurt and cruelty the four of us have imparted upon each other in past lives, now in our present lives as we have met again, there is a genuine closeness between us, and a love to be together. We feel that in our present life we have met to work together and to combine our energies in a positive way for healing and helping others.

We have found as we have all become more aware of the bond that exists between us, that we have felt ourselves naturally drawn together, attracted to want to spend more time with each other. The depth of contact that exists has meant that we have been as catalysts for each other to continue to learn more deeply about ourselves and release deeply held patterns.

With our present life relationships, because of the very close soul bond the four of us feel with each other, some of the other important relationships we have had with people, have not seemed as significant anymore. This has created problems we have had to overcome, and big tests for all of us. Inevitably, there has been some shifting in our relationship patterns as a result.

Although I have been emphasising the closeness of the four of us, I have been aware that really, the four of us are but part of a much larger soul group and we have been like a little unit within that. I feel also that there are other souls with whom I have shared many lives in Atlantis and with them, there is a deep and loving bond, just as with Linda, Denise and Lynne. This I feel, is an individual process too. There are souls with whom I have had a very close contact but who have not been so close to either Linda, Denise and Lynne - and they have their own orbit of close soul friends as well. So it is a more complex pattern and more multidimensional than it first appears to be. There have been people I know now who I sense were present in many of the lifetimes mentioned in this book. However, I have not mentioned their names for privacy reasons.

In the end, I feel that the soul patterns of how we wish to travel through our various physical incarnations is up to us, and what we want to create. We have a lot of choice and can be more on our own or more with others. I do feel that love is one of the key cornerstones of what is necessary for our soul to learn, and that means learning to link with others in peace.

For me, it gives me a lot of joy and satisfaction to know that I belong within a soul `family'. I know that for me, Linda, Denise and Lynne are part of that family with me, but not all!

Chapter 20
Other Lives

In choosing the lifetimes regressions we have for inclusion in this book, we have had to be extremely selective. Because we have wanted to convey pictures and understanding of the main historical junctions of Atlantis' history, we have had to choose lifetimes that were relevant to this. In addition, because we have also been writing from the perspective of how these regression experiences can be pertinent to inner personal growth, this has been another criterion, which we have had to take into account.

However, in making our decisions there have been many, many regression experiences from this fascinating continent and our connections to it, which we have had to leave out.

There have been numerous healing lives, detailing some of the intricate healing practices of Atlantis. Some of these lives have been quite adventurous. There is one where Linda was an oracle channelling the Earth Spirit. In a further experience, Linda lived as an astrologer in Atlantis. There are lives connecting with people's relationships to the plant and animal kingdoms and many about the use of crystal power. There are some interesting psychological lives, connected with soul growth and also some quite diabolical lives where things went wrong. From the golden age there are several inspirational lives from a time when Atlantean society functioned really well. There is one life where I was a pirate and another where I was a fanatical priest. Linda and I have both had lives living in the central city of Sandoris. And there have been many more.

Altogether, there is easily enough material for a second volume, which we could write about Atlantis. If the interest is there, then we will do it.

Chapter 21

Conclusions

From our regression and with Albani's channelling, I have speculated that there may have been hundreds of millions of people living on Atlantis at the time of its destruction. That is a lot of souls. Even if some of them have moved on, I imagine that many of those souls are incarnated on Earth today.

The accounts that we have presented in this book represent the shared memory of four of us, Linda, Denise, Lynne and myself plus a few others - whose inner responses have collaborated our findings. We have used the teachings of Albani, Linda's spiritual guide to gain a wider perspective and found this to be helpful.

We cannot be certain that what we have presented represents a `true' history of Atlantis but we have tried to be as honest as we could. When we have found inconsistencies, we have been quite ruthless between us to try to get at the truth even if that could be emotionally very difficult.

We have had to approach our learning about Atlantis and our relationship to it, step by step. It has been a dual process of learning about the continent itself and the life of its people and at the same time, learning about ourselves. It is not something that we have been able to do in a detached way. At times, it has felt that our research involved every fibre of our nervous system. The result has changed each one of us involved considerably from when we started. In the way that this exploration has led to massive personal growth for all of us, I feel confident similar results could be attained for others who are willing to undergo these explorations too.

We imagine that memories may be triggered for some readers of this book and we are willing to offer our support if possible.

Also we welcome feedback and further thoughts regarding our findings - so the knowledge of this subject can be shared and increased.

However, we caution anyone undergoing Atlantis' past life explorations, that this may not be easy. We have called this book `Atlantis - the dark continent' for good reasons, in that nearly everyone, I feel, who has lived lives on Atlantis is bound to have had lives rather on the dark side, and these experiences are difficult to allow. We recommend anyone seeking to do this work to gain the support of a trained and experienced therapist to help you.

There still feels to be much that is unknown to me about Atlantis, both on a personal level, and about the place itself. It seems so vast and mysterious. There is an aura of awesome power and energy about it. So many legends have sprung from thoughts of Atlantis. Yet, it may be comforting if there are soul memories and Spiritual records of what took place on Atlantis, so all is not lost. Perhaps there is a reason for these memories to come to the surface again today. If we can learn from them, then we may not make the same individual and collective mistakes again.

Healing Journeys by Paul Williamson

Paul Williamson is a Past Life Therapist, Hypnotherapist and Healer. Here, he tells about his own unfolding spiritual path and what he has discovered about past lives, healing the inner child, channelling, spiritual healing and earth healing. Using numerous case studies, Paul shares his approaches to therapy and methods of healing that have helped people from their inner experiences to find peace and well-being. Within these stories, Paul charts some fascinating possibilities about the nature of our inner reality. From this, Paul affirms the relevance and importance of honouring the inner spiritual dimension of our being, so that if we can find peace within, then this could help us find greater meaning in our external lives, and help us to create a happier, healthier society too. Told simply and from the heart, this book shares many touching human and spiritual experiences that will interest seekers everywhere. These experiences can be truly called "Healing Journeys". ISBN 186163 100 6   £11.95

Physician, Heal Thyself by Mary Russell in Collaboration with Lisa Sand MD

"Physician Heal Thyself" consists of inspired and channelled writings covering all aspects of physical, mental, emotional and spiritual health. The book takes a practical approach to maintaining well-being, focus, direction and creativity in a difficult world. As such, it is of interest to open-minded health professionals and their patients as well as those looking for a deeper understanding of life on planet Earth. The book deals with such areas as the difficulties of being a 'sensitive', the art of psychic protection and the importance of 'spiritual hygiene'; it examines the kind of situation frequently encountered by the old soul, the traps into which such a one may fall and how to avoid them; it shows how past life traumas can affect the well-being of the current incarnation and how these may be resolved; and it highlights the false assumptions behind difficult or failed relationships, marriages and partnerships. "The book also considers the wider context of our lives. It explains the present situation of the world and the energies involved, positive and negative, and sets out how to understand, avoid, or even derive benefit from negative energies and situations. ISBN 1 86163 124 3   £10.95.

The Healing Book Chris Thomas & Diane Baker

"The exercises are well described and arranged in a good order of development, clearly relevant case examples..a good basic book written in plain English by two clearly competent healers keen on sharing their knowledge" Touchstone (OBOD)

A book for those who wish to heal, with simple, easily followed exercises which can begin to unlock the healing potential inherent in all of us. Nobody needs to feel left out of these abilities. We are all healers, all we need to do is to stop telling ourselves that we are not. Whatever level of experience you have of healing, this book explains in simple uncomplicated language that does not use mysticism or any form of ritual, how to understand the "Chakras" and the way in which our daily lives influence them, to relate medical conditions to the chakras and to learn methods which will bring the chakras back into balance. These methods apply equally to humans and to animals. If you do not have any experience of giving healing, but would like to learn, this book can set you on that path. If you already work as a healer, and would like to explore your greater potential, this book is also for you. The authors have a combined experience of over twenty five years of providing healing and have taught many people to unlock their own healing potential. This book is not only about learning to heal from the beginning, but also explores some of the energy manipulation techniques used by the authors in their daily practise as "Psychic Surgeons". ISBN 186163 053 0   £8.95

FREE DETAILED CATALOGUE

Capall Bann is owned and run by people actively involved in many of the areas in which we publish. A detailed illustrated catalogue is available on request, SAE or International Postal Coupon appreciated. **Titles can be ordered direct from Capall Bann, post free in the UK** (cheque or PO with order) or from good bookshops and specialist outlets.

Do contact us for details on the latest releases at: **Capall Bann Publishing, Freshfields, Chieveley, Berks, RG20 8TF.** Titles include:

A Breath Behind Time, Terri Hector
Angels and Goddesses - Celtic Christianity & Paganism, M. Howard
Arthur - The Legend Unveiled, C Johnson & E Lung
Astrology The Inner Eye - A Guide in Everyday Language, E Smith
Auguries and Omens - The Magical Lore of Birds, Yvonne Aburrow
Asyniur - Womens Mysteries in the Northern Tradition, S McGrath
Beginnings - Geomancy, Builder's Rites & Electional Astrology in the
        European Tradition, Nigel Pennick
Between Earth and Sky, Julia Day
Book of the Veil , Peter Paddon
Caer Sidhe - Celtic Astrology and Astronomy, Vol 1, Michael Bayley
Caer Sidhe - Celtic Astrology and Astronomy, Vol 2 M Bayley
Call of the Horned Piper, Nigel Jackson
Cat's Company, Ann Walker
Celtic Faery Shamanism, Catrin James
Celtic Faery Shamanism - The Wisdom of the Otherworld, Catrin James
Celtic Lore & Druidic Ritual, Rhiannon Ryall
Celtic Sacrifice - Pre Christian Ritual & Religion, Marion Pearce
Celtic Saints and the Glastonbury Zodiac, Mary Caine
Circle and the Square, Jack Gale
Compleat Vampyre - The Vampyre Shaman, Nigel Jackson
Creating Form From the Mist - The Wisdom of Women in Celtic Myth and
        Culture, Lynne Sinclair-Wood
Crystal Clear - A Guide to Quartz Crystal, Jennifer Dent
Crystal Doorways, Simon & Sue Lilly
Crossing the Borderlines - Guising, Masking & Ritual Animal Disguise in the
        European Tradition, Nigel Pennick
Dragons of the West, Nigel Pennick
Earth Dance - A Year of Pagan Rituals, Jan Brodie
Earth Harmony - Places of Power, Holiness & Healing, Nigel Pennick
Earth Magic, Margaret McArthur

Eildon Tree (The) Romany Language & Lore, Michael Hoadley
Enchanted Forest - The Magical Lore of Trees, Yvonne Aburrow
Eternal Priestess, Sage Weston
Eternally Yours Faithfully, Roy Radford & Evelyn Gregory
Everything You Always Wanted To Know About Your Body, But So Far
    Nobody's Been Able To Tell You, Chris Thomas & D Baker
Face of the Deep - Healing Body & Soul, Penny Allen
Fairies in the Irish Tradition, Molly Gowen
Familiars - Animal Powers of Britain, Anna Franklin
Fool's First Steps, (The) Chris Thomas
Forest Paths - Tree Divination, Brian Harrison, Ill. S. Rouse
From Past to Future Life, Dr Roger Webber
Gardening For Wildlife Ron Wilson
God Year, The, Nigel Pennick & Helen Field
Goddess on the Cross, Dr George Young
Goddess Year, The, Nigel Pennick & Helen Field
Goddesses, Guardians & Groves, Jack Gale
Handbook For Pagan Healers, Liz Joan
Handbook of Fairies, Ronan Coghlan
Healing Book, The, Chris Thomas and Diane Baker
Healing Homes, Jennifer Dent
Healing Journeys, Paul Williamson
Healing Stones, Sue Philips
Herb Craft - Shamanic & Ritual Use of Herbs, Lavender & Franklin
Hidden Heritage - Exploring Ancient Essex, Terry Johnson
Hub of the Wheel, Skytoucher
In Search of Herne the Hunter, Eric Fitch
Inner Celtia, Alan Richardson & David Annwn
Inner Mysteries of the Goths, Nigel Pennick
Inner Space Workbook - Develop Thru Tarot, C Summers & J Vayne
Intuitive Journey, Ann Walker Isis - African Queen, Akkadia Ford
Journey Home, The, Chris Thomas
Kecks, Keddles & Kesh - Celtic Lang & The Cog Almanac, Bayley
Language of the Psycards, Berenice
Legend of Robin Hood, The, Richard Rutherford-Moore
Lid Off the Cauldron, Patricia Crowther
Light From the Shadows - Modern Traditional Witchcraft, Gwyn
Living Tarot, Ann Walker
Lore of the Sacred Horse, Marion Davies
Lost Lands & Sunken Cities (2nd ed.), Nigel Pennick
Magic of Herbs - A Complete Home Herbal, Rhiannon Ryall
Magical Guardians - Exploring the Spirit and Nature of Trees, Philip Heselton
Magical History of the Horse, Janet Farrar & Virginia Russell
Magical Lore of Animals, Yvonne Aburrow
Magical Lore of Cats, Marion Davies
Magical Lore of Herbs, Marion Davies
Magick Without Peers, Ariadne Rainbird & David Rankine

312

Masks of Misrule - Horned God & His Cult in Europe, Nigel Jackson
Medicine For The Coming Age, Lisa Sand MD
Medium Rare - Reminiscences of a Clairvoyant, Muriel Renard
Menopausal Woman on the Run, Jaki da Costa
Mind Massage - 60 Creative Visualisations, Marlene Maundrill
Mirrors of Magic - Evoking the Spirit of the Dewponds, P Heselton
Moon Mysteries, Jan Brodie
Mysteries of the Runes, Michael Howard
Mystic Life of Animals, Ann Walker
New Celtic Oracle The, Nigel Pennick & Nigel Jackson
Oracle of Geomancy, Nigel Pennick
Pagan Feasts - Seasonal Food for the 8 Festivals, Franklin & Phillips
Patchwork of Magic - Living in a Pagan World, Julia Day
Pathworking - A Practical Book of Guided Meditations, Pete Jennings
Personal Power, Anna Franklin
Pickingill Papers - The Origins of Gardnerian Wicca, Bill Liddell
Pillars of Tubal Cain, Nigel Jackson
Places of Pilgrimage and Healing, Adrian Cooper
Practical Divining, Richard Foord
Practical Meditation, Steve Hounsome
Practical Spirituality, Steve Hounsome
Psychic Self Defence - Real Solutions, Jan Brodie
Real Fairies, David Tame
Reality - How It Works & Why It Mostly Doesn't, Rik Dent
Romany Tapestry, Michael Houghton
Runic Astrology, Nigel Pennick
Sacred Animals, Gordon MacLellan
Sacred Celtic Animals, Marion Davies, Ill. Simon Rouse
Sacred Dorset - On the Path of the Dragon, Peter Knight
Sacred Grove - The Mysteries of the Forest, Yvonne Aburrow
Sacred Geometry, Nigel Pennick
Sacred Nature, Ancient Wisdom & Modern Meanings, A Cooper
Sacred Ring - Pagan Origins of British Folk Festivals, M. Howard
Season of Sorcery - On Becoming a Wisewoman, Poppy Palin
Seasonal Magic - Diary of a Village Witch, Paddy Slade
Secret Places of the Goddess, Philip Heselton
Secret Signs & Sigils, Nigel Pennick
Self Enlightenment, Mayan O'Brien
Spirits of the Air, Jaq D Hawkins
Spirits of the Earth, Jaq D Hawkins
Spirits of the Earth, Jaq D Hawkins
Stony Gaze, Investigating Celtic Heads John Billingsley
Stumbling Through the Undergrowth , Mark Kirwan-Heyhoe
Subterranean Kingdom, The, revised 2nd ed, Nigel Pennick
Symbols of Ancient Gods, Rhiannon Ryall
Talking to the Earth, Gordon MacLellan
Taming the Wolf - Full Moon Meditations, Steve Hounsome

Teachings of the Wisewomen, Rhiannon Ryall
The Other Kingdoms Speak, Helena Hawley
Tree: Essence of Healing, Simon & Sue Lilly
Tree: Essence, Spirit & Teacher, Simon & Sue Lilly
Through the Veil, Peter Paddon
Torch and the Spear, Patrick Regan
Understanding Chaos Magic, Jaq D Hawkins
Vortex - The End of History, Mary Russell
Warp and Weft - In Search of the I-Ching, William de Fancourt
Warriors at the Edge of Time, Jan Fry
Water Witches, Tony Steele
Way of the Magus, Michael Howard
Weaving a Web of Magic, Rhiannon Ryall
West Country Wicca, Rhiannon Ryall
Wildwitch - The Craft of the Natural Psychic, Poppy Palin
Wildwood King , Philip Kane
Witches of Oz, Matthew & Julia Philips
Wondrous Land - The Faery Faith of Ireland by Dr Kay Mullin
Working With the Merlin, Geoff Hughes
Your Talking Pet, Ann Walker

FREE detailed catalogue and FREE 'Inspiration' magazine

Contact: Capall Bann Publishing, Freshfields, Chieveley, Berks, RG20 8TF
Website: www.capallbann.co.uk